FORTUNES OF WAR

The Somme

GENERAL SIR ANTHONY FARRAR-HOCKLEY
GBE, KCB, DSO, MC BLitt

CERBERUS

First published by BT Batsford, in 1964

PUBLISHED IN THE UNITED KINGDOM BY;

Cerberus Publishing Limited

22A Osprey Court

Hawkfield Business Park

Bristol

BS14 0BB

UK

e-mail: cerberusbooks@aol.com

www..cerberus-publishing.com

British Library Cataloguing in Publication Data.
A catalogue record for this book is available from the British Library.

ISBN 1 84145 043 X

PRINTED AND BOUND IN ENGLAND.

Contents

Preface

The Somme covers several major battles fought in the region of the river between 1 July and 19 November 1916. Each interspersed by a series of trench actions of dreadful intensity and loss. In this book it is clearly impossible for me to describe every action of every day, and thus some readers may discover that I have omitted reference to part of the battlefield, where the effort was no less worthy, no less gallant than others to which I have given space. I mean no disrespect by these omissions. Similarly, I have made reference to the Royal Flying Corps only in certain contexts. This does not imply any disregard of their work, or of their potential, which was sometimes unrealised.

In telling the story of the battles, I have made use of three main sources with perhaps a fourth subsidiary of information: published and unpublished accounts (a bibliography of the principal reference books is given on page 222), personal discussion with survivors; a study of the battlefield – I have walked the ground of every action described. As a subsidiary advantage – its perhaps disputable as such – I have been shot at in battle.

In laying out the material, it has seemed best to maintain certain principles. Firstly, I have tried not to insist that individuals thought or acted in a certain way on the balance of probabilities – 'Haig must have thought...,' Rawlinson must have decided...' In recounting dialogue I have checked in every case the words used to the best of memory. In all cases I have avoided describing the manner of delivery – '...snapped Falkenhayn', '...Joffre remarked bitterly.' It is surely better to let words speak for themselves. Where I hold a personal opinion concerning an individual or action, I have plainly said 'in my view...', or 'It is my opinion...'

With regard to military appointments, I have used the modern term where this connotes more nearly the responsibility. Thus, Kiggell's post at General Headquarters is referred to as Chief of Staff, though the established ride at the time was Chief of the General Staff. In describing the battlefield, I have done so left to right, the system now used, instead of right to left as employed in the Great War. It is both more natural to study in this way, and easier to follow the order of events in this particular case. In desccribing the German chief field headquarters, I have neither used the full title of *Oberste Heeresleitung* nor its abbreviated form OHL. I have used the English translation and called it the Supreme Command. It may be of value mention that I have employed the British military terms 'unit' for Cavalry regiments, infantry battalions, artillery batteries and similar bodies, and formation when speaking of a group customarily organised under one command such as brigade, division, corps or larger force.

Though formal acknowledgements are made elsewhere, it is perhaps appropriate to note here those from whom I have recieved personal kindnesses. The librarians and staffs of six libraries have extended exceptional help and advice, and have borne patiently the long absence of books. I refer to Mr D W King, OBE, FLA, of the War Office; Miss R E B Coombs, of the Imperial War Museum; Lieutenant-Colonel E H Whitfield, MC, formerly of the Joint Services Staff College, Latimer; Lieutenant-Colonel Walter Young, MBE, of the Staff College, Camberley; Lieutenant-Colonel Alan Shepperd of the Royal Military Academy, Sandhurst; and Lieutenant-Colonel L H Yates, OBE, of the Prince Consort's, Aldershot. The librarian and staff of the photographic library, Imperial War Museum, have also helped in every way possible. In this context, the assistance of my son, Dair, in investigating and sorting, photographs was most valuable. Overseas, I must acknowledge with warm thanks the kindness of the Commandant of the École Supérieure Militaire Inter–Armes, St. Cyr, for permitting me to search through his library and museum at Coëtquidan; and Dr A A Schmalz, Archivassessor, Militararchiv of the Federal German Bundesarchiv. I am in the debt of Major G Haltorffg, assistant military attaché at the Federal German Embassy in London who explained certain passages of his country's history to me, and to Mrs E B Jewkes and Mrs B Crossman for the time and trouble they have taken in making translations of books and papers for me.

Brigadier Peter Young, DSO, MC, MA, Reader in Military History at the Royal Military Academy, Sandhurst, provided me with unpublished papers for which I am most grateful, as indeed for the many discussions with him and his staff which have provoked thought and ideas about the Somme battles. I am indebted to Major–General R A Bramwell Davies CB, DSO, Colonel, the Royal Highland Fusiliers, for granting permission to see private papers of the Highland Light Infantry and the Royal Scots Fusiliers; and to Brigadier Charles Dunbar, MBE, for finding and preparing those for my use. I acknowledge the ready help of the curators and staffs of almost every museum of the British infantry taking part in the Somme actions. Major John North and Mr Morley Kennerley were both kind enough to offer me papers relating to the battle which were enlightening. In considering the higher direction of the late Mr C T Atkinson, Fellow of Exeter College, Oxford; Captain B H Liddell Hart; and General Sir Clement Armitage, KCB, CMG, DSO, whose first-hand knowledge of staff and regimental conditions of the time is unrivalled. In gatherings of the British Legion I have found many opportunities to glean new facts or corroborate old accounts. In particular, it was good of Major-General B K Young, CBE, MC, chainnan of the Aldershot Branch, and Mr Paddy Smythe, the energetic and enterprising secretary – himself a Coldstream Guardsman on the Somme – to provide me with so many opportunities to meet veterans of the battle. Lastly, I must thank my wife, As so often in the past, she has given many hours to researching, typing, correcting, fetching and carrying in the most helpful manner Without her, little would have been done.

PART I

THE MEN AND THE HOUR

FALKENHAYN

'On the evening of the 14th September, 1914, in Luxemburg, Lieut-General von Falkenhayn, the Minister of War, was entrusted by His Majesty the Emperor and King with the post of Chief of the General Staff of the Army in the field, in the place of the invalided General von Moltke.'

In this long and solemn sentence Erich von Falkenhayn tells[1] us how he became the director of German operations[2] in the first first autumn of the Great War. He assumed his new post at a time of crisis. The Army's war plan[3] had failed in France almost in the moment of triumph. The German field armies in the west had thrown back the French attacks across the common frontier, whilst themselves developing, through Belgium, a huge turning movement. The unexpected appearance of four British divisions in the field on the French left Flank checked but did not prevent the German march south and west. For thirty days the plan prepared in Berlin with such care over so many years seemed to be unfolding with scarcely a fault. Only in the moment of *coup de grâce* were the Franco-British armies found to be

---

[1] Falkenhayn, *General Headquarters, 1914-16, and its Critical Decisions*, p.1 (Hutchinson, 1920).
[2] Although the Emperor was commander-in-chief of all armed forces, Falkenhayn had *de facto* command of the Army. He also remained Minister of War until January 1915.
[3] The Schlieffen Plan. See Ritter. *Schliefen Plan* (Wofff, 1958).

intact, the German manoeuvring forces in balance. The prospect of advance effaced, the pattern of deployment was unsuited to defence and the vast German war machine was necessarily thrown into reverse; a withdrawal began, limited in space but profound in purport. It was at that moment that Falkenhayn took charge.

Took Charge. He controlled, it is true, the whole apparatus of war-making: intelligence, operations, personnel and supply policy. In the west, that is, on the new line from Oiseto to the Alps – seven army commanders awaited his orders; and though they might at times protest against his instructions his insistance would ensure their obedience. In the east, against Russia, the movement of the lone German army there depended upon his approval. Yet his master was the Emperor of Germany and King of Prussia, Wilhelm II; and this capricious man might interfere as he saw fit at any moment, in any sphere. However, there is no evidence that Falkenhayn feared such intervention in September 1914. The dying Moltke had failed; William trusted Falkenhayn to put matters right.

This was more easily commanded than executed. How was he to reorientate German strategic policy when all planning, including economic planning, had reckoned on the total defeat of France in seventy days? Clearly, the battle line must be stabilised and the enemy's advance checked while the relative threat of each front – the western, in France; the eastern, in Russia – was reassessed. A redeployment of manpower would be necessary, a new effort in armaments essential. To these herculean tasks Falkenhayn applied his keen mind.

Along the battle line, local commanders mounted a series of minor counter-attacks; but they were too widely dispersed, too feebly pressed to regain more than a few tactical features. More important, the German battalions and batteries succeeded in holding the equally laboured attacks of the French and British. The fact was that both sides were temporarily spent. Shells were running short,[4] equipment was scarce or worn out, dead and wounded officers and NCO's had not been replaced, the men that remained from the early battles of manoeuvre needed a rest from the incessant marching and fighting. As each side sought to remedy these weaknesses a curios situation became apparent: the Channel Departments, through which the outer wheeling German armies had

---

[4] All the combatants had underestimated the expenditure of ammunition. For example by 20 September, 1914, France had fired over three-quarters of her total mobilisation stocks of shells.

passed were once more empty; a huge stretch of territory remained uncontested from the Oise, where the battle line reached its northernmost point, to the Channel coast, over 100 miles distant. The Germans now saw that they might yet pass round the French flank. The French supposed that they might yet march round the Germans.

With that organisational facility for which the Germans are justly famous, Falkenhayn began to assemble a force for this purpose by diverting formations in transit.[5] He hastened send them north of the Oise.

So, too, the French commander-in-chief, General Joffre, reshuffled his order of battle and packed troops northward by train. Piecemeal, French and German divisions – sometimes brigades – reached the flank, ready to march, only to find that the enemy had appeared simultaneously with a force of roughly equal numbers. There would be a clash, each side would dig in. Thus neither was able to achieve an outflanking movement; each had to be content with a gradual extension northward of the battle line along hastily made entrenchments or behind raised sandbag walls. In this fashion, the line reached at last to the sea: the French had held the Pas de Calais, the Belgians a fragment of territory west of the river Yser, the British had secured Channel ports to cover their lines to England, the Germans had gained the industrial complex, including the coalfields, of Belgium and northern France.

Meanwhile, Falkenhayn had had the opportunity to assess the threat on either front. The premise on which the German war plan had been founded was that a dual offensive – one east, one west – was beyond their means.[6] Notwithstanding the enormous potential of Russia, they had decided to strike first at France because the latter was expected to mobilise and deploy more swiftly. France crushed, the whole German field army would turn upon Russia. Now, in October, though expectations in France had not been realised, the Russians had been beaten in their first major encounter at Tannenberg and the onset of winter in the east reduced the likelihood of a Russian counter-offensive in 1914. A critical situation was unlikely to develop there for some time.

The same might not be said of the western front. The French Army remained resilient, the British were expanding their numbers in France. It

---

5 To which were added certain elements withdrawn from the line.

6 *Schlieffen Plan*, op.cit., p. 172, etc

seemed clear that all available reserves must be committed to the west in an attempt to break through the Allies' front and break up thereafter, their remaining battle formations.

In appreciating the area in which he should mount this attack, Falkenhayn was attracted to the Channel flank by the weight of his own forces in Flanders and the comparative disorganisation of the Allied defences there. He struck first at the Belgians and the French on the Yser and, shortly after, met the British in a major encounter immediately east of the ancient cloth city of Ypres. Through October into November the summer veterans and young reserves from the homeland snuggled to break through. At last the Belgians earned a respite by flooding their front. Around Ypres, the old professional British Army fought its final battle as an entity resisting into November every effort to breach its positions. At times, the issue was decided by the committal of a single company On 11 November Falkenhayn discontinued the bank. He saw no prospect of its success. Indeed, it is likely that this shrewd man discerned that the prospect of victory; as such, bad already passed beyond German attainment.

While the battles were being fought upon the Yser and the Flemish plain against Belgians, French and British, the German army in the east was pressing in upon the Russians. Hindenburg, nominal victor of Tannenberg with his chief-of-staff Ludendorff, advanced his force into Poland. Though temporarily checked here, be believed that the Tsar's armies were vulnerable to a crippling blow and he repeated an earlier demand for reinforcements. when Falkenhayn refused, Hindenburg attacked with his army[7] as it stood.

On 11 November, the day of the final attack at Ypres, he began to advance across the steppe. A sharp frost had hardened the ground but there was no sign of heavy snow. The Russians continued to oblige their enemy by broadcasting uncoded their orders by wireless. Their intelligence of German movements was correspondingly tardy. These factors, combined with the skill and method of the Germans, sped Hindenburg's armies'[8] forward and brought him to the edge of a spectacular victory in Poland. But a skilful stroke by the Grand Duke Nicholas[9] and a short run of luck

---

[7] Hindenburg became commander-in-chief of all German forces in the east on 1 November, 1914.

[8] *Ibid.*

[9] Commander-in-chief of Russan armies in the field.

in his favour permitted a Russian withdrawal. By the time reinforcements were available to Hindenburg from the western front, the bitter winter had set in. The Russians, suffering difficulties from lack of munitions and ordnance, were saved for a breathing space. The German commanders whom they had eluded were left to remark that Falkenhayn's retention of men in the west had availed nothing there; and denied victory in the east.

This claim was widely discussed and popularly supported in military circles in the German homeland. The Emperor, looking anxiously for victory wherever he might find it, began to show that partiality for Hindenburg and his chief-of-staff which was subsequently to influence the course of the war. When Falkenhayn again denied reinforcements to the east in the new year of 1915, William reversed the decision. Of the six corps husbanded as a general reserve for a spring offensive in the west, four were sent to Hindenburg. As if to underline the correctness of this decision, a winter battle was fought against the Grand Duke in Masuria, hard marching in the blizzards producing almost 100,000 prisoners and an advance of thirty miles. It was impossible for Falkenhayn to convince his sovereign that this success against Russia was, in relation to the war effort, wasted. As the year continued, the struggle between east and west was intensified. Falkenhayn's operational policy remained unchanged; his arguments in favour of a decisive campaign against France and Britain were strengthened by the naval supremacy of these two, and the expansion of the British imperial war effort. There were few arguments to attract him eastward. The spaciousness of European Russia alone defied, conquest. Austria-Hungary Germany's principal ally along the borders of south-eastern Russia, had proved incapable of sustained operations against the Tsar's armies. Turkey was too distant, lacked too much in expertise and equipment to be more than vexatious in the mountain passes of the Caucasus. But even if the former had been moderately sound, it is doubtful whether Falkenhayn would have been persuaded to change his views. A decisive victory in Russia – if attainable at all – would be expensive in time and effort It was the west with all its potential that threatened. The longer the Franco-British allies had to develop this threat, the greater their strength; the greater the danger to Germany, inferior in numbers and cut off from overseas supply.

Robbed of two-thirds of his reserve by Hindenburg in January, Falkenhayn withdrew three battalions from each division in France, reinforced these with men from regimental depots, and built-up by April a striking force of fourteen divisions. With a new weapon, poison gas, and a substantial increment of artillery ammunition obtained by industrial rationalisation, he was able once more to consider a spring offensive.

Just then, the position of Austria-Hungary became desperate. Wisely refraining from tackling the Germans the Grand Duke had opened his 1915 offensive against the weaker ally. At great cost in men he began to force his way through the Carpathian passes in February and it now seemed that the Austrians would be unable to contain him. Once the Russians readied the southern exits, the entire Hungarian plain would be open to them; and if the Austro-Hungarian forces were unable to hold the Russians in the Carpathian mountains, they were hardly likely to do so in this open country. A major defeat here would mean a separate peace between Vienna and Moscow. With this in view, Italy and the neutrals of eastern Europe would join the Allies *'courir au secours du vainqueur'*.

However reluctant he was to abandon an offensive in the west, Falkenhayn saw that circumstances demanded it. By mid-April Emperor and Cabinet were agreed; all aid must go to save Austria-Hungary. The whole of the reserve and certain other elements from France were transported east and south by rail against Russia. In this way the Western Allies gained that time for military expansion which Falkenhayn sought to deny them.

JOFFRE

Unlike Falkenhayn, General Joseph Jacques Césaire Joffre had been appointed the professional chief of his nation's Army – before the outbreak of the war. He thus bore the responsibility for the disastrous plan which led to France's defeat on her frontiers in August 1914, though it follows that he must be given credit for the subsequent withdrawal, intact, of his armies to the Marne and their actions upon it which forced the Germans back. At this point Joffre, the impassive, bourgeois, engineer officer, had to reshape strategy after initial failure on his own part while Falkenhayn, the former commanding officer of a guard regiment, the newly promoted senior member of the Great General Staff, had to begin anew from the failure of his predecessor. Falkenhayn was then fifty-three; Joffre, sixty-two.

Like Falkenhayn, Joffre never doubted that the issue of the war must, be decided on the western front. 'The best and largest portion of the German Army is on our soil, with its line of battle jutting out a mere five days' march from the heart of France. This situation made it clear to every Frenchman that our task consisted of defeating this enemy, and driving him out of our country. My views, on this matter, remained unchanged during the whole time I was directing operations. While far from denying that the other theatres had their interest and value, I consistently refused to attribute to them the importance with which some people sought to invest them...'[10]

When the line became fully extended and stabilised, Joffre had to face the fact that open warfare was past and a decisive manoeuvre out of the question until a major breaching operation had destroyed a wide portion of the enemy's defences. In order to make this breach and to exploit it he would require a substantial force. By now his reserve in men and munitions had dwindled dangerously; the numbers ready in depots fell far short of his needs. The principal source of any new striking force must come, therefore, from the men in the battle line. Where his men held positions of tactical superiority, thinning out would be possible; elsewhere, a strengthening of defence works would permit him to relieve high grade units by older men or those with a large proportion of recruits. There was, too, the prospect of handing over a greater sector of the line to the British, whose present responsibility was, man for man, much less than the French.[11] Like the majority of his brother officers Joffre regarded the British Expeditionary Force as a collection of amateurs, not without courage but largely without skill. 'Sir John French's forces had been considerably increased, and he now held a front of thirty miles with four army corps, whilst many of our corps occupied as much as ten and a half miles. I, therefore, instructed General Foch to request him to relieve the French Eighth Army, which was interposed between the British and the Belgians. The Field Marshal offered no objections to the principle involved, but the execution of the relief began only in January [1915].'[12]

[10] Joffre, *The Memoirs of Marshal Joffre*, Vol. II, p. 327 (Bles, 1932).

[11] This was to be a bone of contention between the two allies throughout the war. The comparison was hardly a fair one; the British held a series of sectors in which the enemy were constantly active and in greater strength than on many of the French.

[12] Joffre, *op. cit.*, p. 331.

Joffre was unwilling to wait upon the British. By December he was partially convinced by his operations staff that certain sectors of the German line were undermanned and vulnerable to a breaching operation. It is probable, too, that he wished on his own account to test his enemy's defences, having in mind an offensive in the spring. Two major and four minor attacks were mounted; all failed, some totally. Apart from losing a few minor villages, the German lines were never at any time placed in the slightest danger, and their reaction to this renewed activity was swift and effective. On all but one of the corps fronts they counter-attacked at once and retook much or all of the paltry prizes of the French. In addition, between Christmas 1914 and 14 January, 1915, they attacked locally in both in the Argonne and from the Aisne heights, restricting their activities to features of immediate tactical importance and calling off the battle as soon as these were won. 'It was evident', Joffre wrote subsequently, 'that we should have to make stupendous efforts if we were to succeed in uprooting the Germans from our soil.'[13]

For a little while, it was hoped that the popular support in Germany for the campaign against Russia would have the effect of drawing off forces in that direction. The Second Bureau[14] in Joffre's Headquarters searched for signs of withdrawal of divisions from the line. In January the Secret Service reported a flow of reinforcements in both directions – the Emperor's support for Hindenburg was taking effect simultaneously with Falkenhayn's redeployment – and this apparent abundance of manpower impressed Joffre that the hour was not suited for optimism, still less for delay. He had chosen for his principal attack that point between Rheims and Verdun where the lateral railway in German hands ran within five miles of the front. Even if the assault failed to open a breach for exploitation, surely the ardour of his soldiers would carry them forward to cut the railway line. Further to the south and east he ordered First Army to eliminate the enemy's bridgehead on the left bank of the Meuse at Saint Mihiel. He now urged through political channels that the British should contribute by relieving his Eighth Army in Flanders.[15]

The weather was seasonable – the air cold, the ground hard with frost; sleet and snowstorms were frequent. A German local attack disrupted the

---

[13] Joffre, *op. cit.,* p. 337.

[14] The Second Bureau of the General Staff dealt with Intelligence.

[15] Joffre to French Minister of War (letter), 15 January, 1915.

preparations of de Langle's Fourth Army in the Champagne. These unsettling events and a heavy fall of snow delayed the main attack until 16 February when, amidst the support of an immense bombardment by artillery the French infantry went forward. For more than a month; the fighting continued as the assault forces attempted to push forward up the bare slopes of the rolling hills. When it ended on 18 March, they had advanced on a front of twelve miles to a depth of about 800 yards. It had cost Joffre 240,000 men.

At Saint Mihiel, too, the attack was a failure.

The British now followed suit. Before the period of these disasters, plans had been completed for a joint enterprise round Arras, a movement forward which was lined strategically with the Champagne offensive. When it was clear, by the beginning of March, that all hope of a break-in by de Langle's Fourth Army must be abandoned, the French contribution was cancelled. Surprisingly, the British commander-in-chief, Sir John French, decided to persist in his own part to capture the Aubers Ridge with the aim of threatening Lille beyond.

Perhaps Sir John was aware that the French had little respect for the ability of his command to attack; he had certainly been told indirectly that his two armies[16] were not pulling their weight. Whatever the reason, however laudable his motives, the operation which was hazardous with French troops in parallel was scarcely feasible without them, not least because his theatre reserves of artillery ammunition were exhausted. Of course, Joffre made no demur: let the British take their turn. If this mood seems strange in an ally, the disappointments of the winter must not be forgotten. Sir Douglas Haig, commander of the British First Army, was charged with the operation and his plans have since been extolled as examples of prudence and clarity. On 10 March they were put to the test. Fourteen battalions of British infantry assaulted three of Germans. A rapid initial success was succeeded by a complete stalemate: the Germans held, the British went to ground. They had captured the village of Neuve Chapelle and taken 1600 prisoners. They had killed or wounded 12,000 of the enemy and lost about the same themselves. They had fired 100,000 rounds from their guns which they could not afford. The blame has been placed, correctly, on the commander-in-chief, Sir John French.

---

16 The BEF comprised two armies – First and Second – as from 26 December, 1914.

Unfortunately, the army commander, Haig, drew no conclusions from his own mistakes. His staff assured him that he – and thus they – had done all that could possibly have been done to ensure success. They – and he – had neither the honesty nor the imagination to see that they had failed the soldiers committed to battle on their plan by employing a system of control suited to the Crimea.

The Germans now attacked. Though deprived of his major reserve in the west, Falkenhayn was loath to abandon all offensive action in this theatre. The novel weapon of poison gas, tried tentatively against the Russians,[17] was available and he selected the Fourth Army in Flanders, under Duke Albrecht of Württemberg, to assault the enemy salient at Ypres once more. On a beautiful spring morning, 22 April, 1915, the Franco-British positions were shelled with high explosive and two hours before sunset the cylinders of chlorine gas were opened while the field artillery fell silent so as not to disturb the bluish-white clouds that drifted westward on a light evening breeze. The effect of the fumes was dynamic. Before dark a group of Zouaves in the line had broken completely and soon others who could still move were running back to escape asphyxiation. Many withdrew only to die in the clear air behind. In this confusion four miles of the line were completely unmanned and the advent of darkness alone saved the Allies from a German breakthrough. Fortunately for the defence, Duke Albrecht and his local commanders were unprepared for their success. Like Haig at Neuve Chapelle, they had failed to make provision for the rapid passing of information from front to rear, and their plan for the follow-up was too rigid to permit quick exploitation. North-east of Ypres the Canadians thinned out, forming an attenuated line as a temporary measure, and by next morning there was sufficient reorganisation to check the advancing German infantry. Duke Albrecht continued the battle to gain a few thousand yards until his reserves were spent.[18] By this time Falkenhayn had other problems on the western front; the French and British were again attacking in Artois.

The mishaps and disappointments of past battles had made Joffre more

[17] In January 1915. Either the cold prevented the Russians from being affected, or their habitual carelessness caused them to make no report of the incident.

[18] He had been warned earlier that there could be no question of sustaining a major offensive at this time. Indeed the attack was particularly designed to lest the offensive power of chlorine and its means of release.

cautious in the expression of his intentions and more modest in his expectations. When he approved the new plan for a joint attack north of Arras – in place of that scrapped immediately prior to Neuve Chapelle – he accepted its aim as being the capture of Vimy Ridge and certain other features to the north. He hoped inevitably for greater things:[19] perhaps this capture of ground would create a situation for a complete break-in to the enemy defences. Yet if it did not, neither troops, nor public or posterity would judge the operation too harshly. The stated aim was the capture of ground of tactical importance – Vimy Ridge offered a view across the entire plain of Douai – a task well within the potential of the forces he placed under command of his Tenth Army. Immediately to the north, between the Tenth Army's left flank and Neuve Chapelle, the British were to attack once more towards Lille.

On this front Field-Marshal Sir John French attacked on the morning of 9 May. The infantry assault was preceded by a bombardment of forty-six minutes, a brief time dictated solely by the quantity of shells available on the ground. Since few of these were high explosive, the Germans were not forced underground but remained in their trenches, sheltering from the shrapnel in bays with overhead protection. Thus, when the British guns lifted to permit their own infantry to close with the enemy, the latter were ready. They had moved the few paces from protection bay to fire step and were soon engaging the exposed attackers scrambling forward under the weight of seventy pounds of ammunition, weapons and equipment. The effort was totally wasted. Enraged and frustrated. Sir John sought release from his burden by complaining to *The Times* correspondent about his shortage of shells.[20]

On his southern flank the morning was rich in success. An enormous barrage – some 700,000 shells, mostly high explosive – had been fired in preparation. In two hours, the French XXXIII Corps advanced two and a quarter miles, breaking through the entire trench system of the enemy. Now was the moment for the launching of reserves through the breach. Those of the corps, six battalions, were five miles in rear; the army reserve, a division, almost eight miles. The most forward regimental commander reported his success at 11 am and, appreciating the run of the battle, the divisional commander asked for the corps reserve at about the same time.

[19] See Joffre, *op. cit.*, p. 349, para 5.
[20] See *The Times* of 14 May, 1915.

Yet the first three battalions did not appear until 4 pm, the remainder at 6. Though the army reserve was passed to XXXIII Corps at 1.30 on the afternoon of the battle, its first elements did not reach the corps rear boundary until 2.30 am on the following morning. Wisely, it had been decided that the reserves should be kept back in safety from enemy artillery fire during the early stages of the battle. But neither the senior commanders nor their staffs had apprehended that, if they wanted safety for their reserves, they must provide adequate communications to them to ensure their timely committal; and if these could not be provided over the distance, then the reserves were too far back and special measures should have been taken to provide them with a measure of covered accommodation forward.[21]

The inevitable result of all these delays was that the Germans sealed the breach. The prospective strategic success on the morning of 9 May had become, next day, a local tactical gain. Attack and counter continued into late June without effecting a notable change in the line.[22] In studying the reasons for failure Joffre appreciated that the problem was one of getting the reserves forward speedily into the breach and under the effective control of the sector commander concerned, yet seems to have made no significant effort to look for a better system of control.[23] In contrast, he and his chief of operations were struck forcibly again by the fact that a single sector of attack permitted the enemy to concentrate reserves in its defence. Since these reserves were not inexhaustible, they concluded, an offensive mounted in two widely separated sectors must surely find the enemy without means of reinforcement for one of them, particularly where the first attack was separated in time by, say two or three weeks, as well as in space from the second. But, immediately, the succession of losses made talk of a renewed offensive impracticable. For the time being it was agreed that the enemy must be worn down by widespread and recurrent 'nibbling'.

When operations came to an end in Artois in June, the Austro-German offensive against the Grand Duke Nicholas had been in progress for some six weeks. It had made remarkable progress, thanks to German direction and stiffening amongst the heterogeneous Austro-Hungarian forces. The

---

[21] For an example of German preparations to this end, see p. 34 concerning Stollen.

[22] The maximum French advance was 4500 yards. The British took three miles of the German front to a depth of half a mile in a second attack at Festubert on 18 May.

[23] See Note 8192, addressed to armies, 20 May, 1915.

Russians no longer threatened. In part surprised, in part exhausted by their winter effort in the Carpathian passes, lacking almost every form of warlike supply, they were in full retreat, leaving hordes of prisoners behind and, more important for this populous but ill-organised country, quantities of artillery.[24] Not unnaturally the Tsar's government began to call for a relief offensive on the western front.[25]

Even if he had the means to hand, Joffre would have found it difficult to mount a major offensive immediately. There had been agreement amongst the Allies at Calais in early July that attacks should be localised – '*bousculer la ligne, ne pas percer*', a continuance of the policy of '*la guerre de l'usure*', destruction by attrition.[26] He had already conceived a plan, however, to attack at two widely separated points – though not in time – and the crisis in the east permitted him to widen the scope of his project. While pressing strongly with his Tenth Army and the BEF in Artois, he would make his principal thrust in the Champagne, a decision that is difficult to understand in view of his partial success in the former and his total failure previously in the latter. Reluctantly, Sir John French agreed to attack with him once more amongst the grey mining villages and pitheads north of Arras.

September was to be the month. Joffre feared the onset of autumn weather as a series of postponements took them through the first three weeks. On the 22nd, the artillery bombardment began in the Champagne, continuing through two days of sunshine and white clouds. On the night 24/25 the rain came. Under grey skies the assault began at 9.15 am next morning with that power characteristic of French infantry. By the 27th they had captured the enemy first line on a front of nine miles, a success due partly to the close proximity of the divisional and corps reserves behind the leading elements. The second line lay, however, on a series of reverse slopes. In consequence, the attackers had to come over the crest to get at their enemy and this disadvantage was made the greater because the French guns in close support were unable to drop their shells over the high angles of the crest-line. Two or three times a day battalions would scramble from their slippery, broken trenches to the ridges above, where they would be shot down as they appeared in silhouette to the Germans. For ten more

[24] By December 1915 medium and heavy artillery of Russian origin in the Tsar's Army was reduced to eighty-four 105-mm, 389 120-mm 141 155-mm pieces.

[25] For example, see Joffre's *Personal File*, Vol. II, Book 3, Folio 8-A.

[26] See Hankey, *The Supreme Command, 1914-18*, Vol. I, p. 349 (Alien & Unwin, 1961).

days the offensive tottered on, ending at last with a vain charge by two cavalry divisions, launched in a desperate hope of advancing with such speed over the crests that the enemy would be unable to react with fire.

Horses now joined the litter of dead men on the wet chalk. Each side had lost about 150,000 casualties, a slight credit balance lying in the French favour with the capture of 25,000 prisoners and 150 guns. These prizes were given public prominence.

North of Arras, the British and French armies had little more success. Foch, the Army Group commander, showed scant consideration for his ally and made no effort to coordinate the attack. After a typically intense and prolonged barrage, his Tenth Army assaulted at 12.15 midday without achieving a quarter of the spectacular advances made in the same region in May. The British had assaulted at 6.45 am after a fractional artillery preparation, with a release of gas in the last hour as a weapon of surprise. The 47th (London) and 15th (Scottish) Divisions quickly overran the mining village of Loos, an area in which the Germans had not expected them,[27] and for a few hours here the enemy line was all but broken. For personal reasons, however, Sir John French had kept the principal reserve in his own hands sixteen miles in rear of the start line, and was not even in telephonic communication with the headquarters of First Army, responsible for the operation. He could not hope to trifle successfully with such professionals as the Germans in this way. When at last the three reserve divisions appeared, the salient exploited on the first day had been sealed off; the Scots, foremost victors of the advance, had been cut down. The one chance of attaining a major result in the entire offensive, north and south, had passed.

Thus ended the struggles on the western front in 1915 – at least, in so far as the men actively fighting were concerned.

At the headquarters of principal formations in rear, and in the national capitals, the allied commanders and politicians reached an honest but ugly conclusion: on balance, the year had been successful for the enemy. In Russia, Germany and Austria-Hungary were exploiting the advantages of a vast summer campaign which might well hasten to disaster the strained

---

[27] Because of the light artillery fire.

Russian war economy. In the Mediterranean, the Dardanelles had been evacuated, Serbia crushed, and the Italians, newly joined to the Allied powers, were already a burden upon the arsenals of Britain and France. On the western front, the German attack at Ypres had been held but the Germans had held the Allies in offensives of greater fury and magnitude.

The principle of the simultaneous double blow had not proved successful, even at a time when numbers of the enemy had been withdrawn to Russia. Where now? What hopes of victory in 1916 might be held out against this record of recurrent failure?

Joffre remained constant to his belief that military decision was to be found only on the western front. His appointment as Supreme Commander of French military forces throughout the world on 2 December gave him the opportunity to reduce the diffusion of soldiers to theatres overseas. He was, moreover, able to look forward to a simultaneous double blow at the enemy on a wider basis and with greater power than his own resources could offer. Russia, to be resuscitated during the winter, would strike in the east as France and Britain struck in the west in a gigantic spring offensive. Joffre and Sir John French were in accord on the principles of operation in the coming year.

Yet it was not Sir John who would put the British contribution into effect. In London, Haig's report on Loos, sent to Kitchener behind the back of his commander-in-chief, brought about the downfall of the brave but inept field marshal. And since Sir Ian Hamilton had become associated with failure at Gallipoli, there was no one else beside Haig – with the necessary seniority, prestige and confidence – to succeed to the chief command in France. Thus it was Haig who became Joffre's colleague on the western front.

HAIG

The date of the handover of the British command in France was Sunday, 19 December, 1915. Sir Douglas Haig assumed full responsibility at noon and signalled this fact to the War Office. At last he was master!

He was fifty-four years of age, a Cliftonian, a commoner of Brasenose, a prizewinner at Sandhurst,[28] a graduate of the Staff College. From his

---

[28] At that time it was possible to enter the Royal Military College, Sandhurst, as a university graduate, the lateness of age being inconsiderable in face of the long periods spent as a subaltern.

forty-first year, he rose rapidly in the Service, and the reason is not hard to find. In an era when cavalry officers were long on courage but short on brains, Haig had both. It is true that his acquaintance with battle, prior to 1914, was fleeting, as indeed was his experience of command in the field. His first close brush with the enemy was as a staff officer of Egyptian cavalry with Kitchener at Khartoum; his second as principal staff officer of French's cavalry division in South Africa. Later he commanded a small column successfully against the Boers. These opportunities demonstrated a cool head and proved that his reputation as a shrewd, practical, soldier in peace held good for war. On the veldt, in India or at home he mastered problems consistently, great and small, whether assisting Haldane to establish a staff organisation or training his regimental polo team. Though diffident with strange officers and agonisingly shy with soldiers he did not know, Douglas Haig earned not only the praise of Edward VII and his heir but the esteem of a wide circle amongst the officer corps. Talented, self-effacing, handsome, orthodox, he was the very model of a British major general.

In 1912 he was promoted to lieutenant-general, on appointment to the Aldershot Command – a post which became, on mobilisation in 1914, general officer commanding-in-chief I Army Corps.[29] On 4 August of that year he formed-up his two divisions at Aldershot, whilst his headquarters shook off the encumbrances of local administration, to take the field in the British Expeditionary Force under Sir John French.

They were both cavalrymen: French an Irishman, Haig a Scot, extrovert and introvert. Haig liked French, pitied him, perhaps – he had lent him money earlier – but thought nothing of his prudence or intelligence. Not unnaturally, he disliked the idea of going to war under such a man – a reaction which led him into an underhand correspondence with King George V, with Kitchener, the Secretary of State for War, and occasionally others. Since it was clear by the spring of 1915 that he was the most likely successor to French, he would have been less than human had this factor not influenced him to continue criticism consistently – sometimes with subordinates – even when this criticism was scarcely justified.

In observing Sir John's errors he tended to overlook his own: an act of panic at Landredes on the retreat from Mons; a tardy, over-cautious

---

[29] This was the only regular corps in being in peacetime. The remaining elements of the BEF, corps and army staffs, were formed piecemeal. Hence Aldershot was a coveted command.

advance to the Aisne, when speed was essential; the failure to organise his communications forward and, hence, promptly to commit his reserve at Aubers Ridge;[30] the inability to see for many months the overwhelming potential of the machine-gun. He was not above reproach, yet his diary contains no admission of his errors, no recognition of his fallibility. At Christmas 1915 he took command with every confidence that he had learned the business of modem soldiering from the success of his own judgements and the mistakes of others.

By this time the broad pattern of strategy for 1916 was being underwritten in some detail. The meeting of the Allied commanders at Chantilly, 6-8 December, 1915, which had agreed upon a simultaneous offensive on all three fronts[31] in the following year, had looked forward to March as the period in which these should open, in order to take advantage of the spring and summer weather. Almost at once, however, it had become clear that this was impracticable. The gigantic British reinforcements of men and guns would not be complete before May, while the Italians and Russians required even longer.

Apart from artillery[32] the latter needed, for example, more than a million rifles: 160,000 were needed urgently to equip men currently in the line without arms.

Joffre had tentatively selected, amongst others, a sector of thirty miles between the Somme and Lassigny for the offensive on the western front, for which he had charged General Foch, commander of the northern group of armies, to prepare plans. Seeking a realistic date to begin the operation he had chosen 1st July, though he had wisely warned Foch to have a plan for April in case the Russians were once more assailed in the spring. When Haig visited GQG[33] on 29 December, he was invited to commit the British Expeditionary Force to an offensive at the same time. He assented, aware that the War Committee of the Cabinet had approved participation, in principle, on the previous day.

Often, it is popularly represented that the British and French politicians gave their consent cynically or casually, careless of the loss of life that must follow their authorisation of another mass attack on the enemy battle line.

---

[30] At the battle of Neuve Chapelle.
[31] In Russia, Italy, France/Belgium.
[32] See p. 21, footnote 24.
[33] *Grand Quarters-Général*: the French General Headquarters.

It was not so. Not one man round the cabinet tables consented readily to the strategy; all shrank from blood-letting. But they were forced to face the hard fact that they must either consent to peace[34] with the Germans in possession of almost all Belgium, much of northern France and the whole modest Duchy of Luxembourg – territory it would be hard to prise loose from an unbeaten foe – or fight on. The latter course meant taking the

offensive, since they could not hope to win by defensive means. In London the Cabinet saw also the difficulty that they were running short of volunteers to fight. If an offensive was to be undertaken, it must succeed; the members of the Coalition Government[35] were agreed on that, even though they were at odds on how to find the men to fight in it.

Haig was not present at the Cabinet, but he was confident that the means were coming to hand towards victory. At Loos he had seen his First Army catch the enemy by surprise; the French had attracted the German local reserves while his own short barrage had led the enemy to remain under cover, believing there was more to come. Galling as it had been to see his opportunity lost through lack of reserves, the battle had shown that it was possible to break into and through the enemy defences. He was confident that he could do it again. But where?

Joffre wished him to extend the front of Foch's planned attack, the British Expeditionary Force to assault between the Somme and Arras.[36] Haig was already studying a more attractive prospect of a summer offensive in Flanders, where *inter alia* the Channel flank could be exploited by the Royal Navy, and he issued a first planning directive to General Plumer to this end on 14 January, 1916. But whatever the venue, Haig and Joffre were agreed that a necessary preliminary to the offensive would be a period of wearing down the enemy reserve – the *'bataille d'usure'* – an unpleasant task which the French clearly expected the British to take on, and the British commander-in-chief accepted with reservations.[37]

Through January and February the matter remained undecided, while the British Cabinet had second and third thoughts about an offensive in France

[34] The Germans first began to explore the prospect of an armistice at this time.

[35] Asquith's Liberal Government fell in May 1915, to be succeeded by a coalition of Liberals and Conservatives under his leadership.

[36] Letter from Joffre to Haig, 29 December, 1915.

[37] See Haig, *The Private Papers of Douglas Haig, 1914-1919*, ed. R Blake (Eyre & Spottiswoode), London, 1952, p. 135; Joffre, *op. cit*, p. 462; Joffre to Haig (letter), 23 January, 1916.

[38] See, for example, Robertson to Haig (letter), 13 January, 1916.

and wild, occasional hopes that there might be no offensive at all.[38] Joffre was now determined upon an offensive north and south of the Somme and expected the British to undertake the bulk of the northern assault. He proposed directly, moreover, that the BEF should carry out its wearing-down operations for three months before-hand in addition to taking-over the remainder of the front of Tenth Army (in the Arras sector). On 14 February Haig struck a bargain with him. The BEF should attack with the French on the Somme front proposed. They would mount wearing-down operations beforehand, but only ten to fifteen days prior to the main offensive. They would not relieve any more of the French front. Finally, he accepted Joffre's wish to encroach with French troops on the left or northern bank of the Somme river where, GQG explained, they needed 'elbow room for the manoeuvre' – an explanation of tactful deceit. The French feared a British failure on the northern bank would endanger their own operations towards Péronne. Whether this was prescience or prudence, we do not know.

'Today's was a most important conference', Haig wrote in his diary that night, 14 February, after his return from seeing Joffre at Chantilly. Indeed, the whole position of the British Army in the operations of this year (1916) depended on my not giving way on: (1) The nature and moment of carrying out the wearing out fight and (2) Not using up divisions to relieving the Tenth Army. By straightforward dealing I gained both these points. But I had an anxious and difficult struggle...[39]

He had more anxious and difficult struggles to come. The Germans were massing in secret at Verdun, where Falkenhayn's initiative was to change radically the concept of the Somme offensive.

VERDUN

In a sense Falkenhayn and Joffre shared common problems in the exercise of their responsibilities. Each believed that victory was to be found only on the western front; each was impeded in his pursuits by superiors and colleagues who looked for solutions in other theatres. Each had populous but ill-organised or equipped allies: Austria-Hungary and Turkey; Russia and Italy. Each feared that the other would discover a means of breaking through the line before himself. But here the identity ended. For France

[39] Haig, *op. cit.*, p. 129.

had Britain and her empire as ally – an empire widely based, rich in raw materials, possessing a vast industrial potential and a great navy.

From the first winter of the war Falkenhayn had feared that Britain's intervention might prove decisive in withholding victory from Germany. Though he had doubts about the sincerity of Britain's contribution in troops to the western front, he had none concerning her determination to persist until Germany lay defeated. In his appreciation of strategic policy for 1916[40] he again urged that the British Isles should be subjected to submarine blockade: a course again postponed by the German government for fear of bringing the United States into the war.[41] Given such assistance by the submarine fleet he believed that Britain might become agreeable to an armistice. In such case, he had little doubt of his ability to bring France to the same frame of mind: for months the intelligence service of the Great General Staff had been pouring money into the hands of dissidents and traitors in France to subvert public opinion. Whilst there were no real signs of widespread pacifist reaction in Paris or the provinces, French dead already approached a million.[42] A host of fresh casualties, such as might be forced upon the French Army by a new German offensive, must surely prove insupportable.

In considering such an offensive Falkenhayn was aware that he could not be prodigal in the expenditure of his own manpower. Already German officers and men had achieved what previously had been believed impossible: the prosecution of war on two major fronts simultaneously for a year and more.

The trenches were seriously short of experienced officers and NCO's. The time had passed when reserves of manpower at home permitted the raising of new formations. A striking force for a major offensive could be found only by concentrating theatre reserves and supplementing these by withdrawing troops committed to defence of the front and by combing out men from depots, schools and training regiments in the homeland. Even so Falkenhayn could not muster more than twenty-six divisions. For operations on the grand scale he would need a minimum of thirty, and he was by no means sure that this force would secure a decisive result. His

---

[40] Falkenhayn, *op. cit.*, pp. 209-218.

[41] The arguments for and against unrestricted submarine warfare are contained in *Official German Documents*, Vols. I and II (Carnegie Endowment for World Peace).

[42] Total French killed/dead and missing on the western front, up to 31 December 1915 was 1,001,271. See *Les Armées Françaises dans la Grande Guerre*, Tome III, pp. 588-602 (Paris: Imprimerie Nationale).

own experience during sixteen months of battle on the western front, and the examples provided by the vain assaults of the Allies, made a return to the conventional frontal attack an unattractive proposition. He was aware, too, that relief attacks by the Allies at other points of the line while his own operations were in progress might find the defence too weak to resist. There was clearly a requirement for a novel strategy.

As I have already insisted (Falkenhayn's memorandum concluded) the strain on France has almost reached breaking-point – though it is certainly borne with the most remarkable devotion. If we succeeded in opening the eyes of her people to the fact that in a military sense they have nothing more to hope for, that breaking-point would be reached and England's best sword knocked out of her hand. To achieve that object the uncertain method of a mass break-through, in any case beyond our means, is unnecessary. We can probably do enough for our purposes with limited resources. Within our reach behind the French sector of the Western front there are objectives for the retention of which the French General Staff would be compelled to throw in every man they have.

If they do so the forces of France will bleed to death – as there can be no question of a voluntary withdrawal – whether we reach our goal or not. If they do not do so, and we reach our objectives, the moral effect on France will be enormous. For an operation limited to a narrow front Germany will not be compelled to spend herself so completely that all other fronts are practically drained. She can face with confidence the relief attacks to be expected on those fronts, and indeed hope to have sufficient troops in hand to reply to them for counter-attacks. For she is perfectly free to accelerate or draw out her offensive, to intensify it or break it off from time to time, as suits her purpose.

The objectives of which I am speaking now are Belfort and Verdun. The considerations urged above apply to both, yet the preference must be given to Verdun. The French lines at that point are barely twelve miles distant from the German railway communications. Verdun is therefore the most powerful *point d'appui* for an attempt, with a relatively small expenditure of effort, to make the whole German front in France and Belgium untenable. The removal of the danger, as a secondary aim, would be so valuable on military grounds that, compared with it, the so

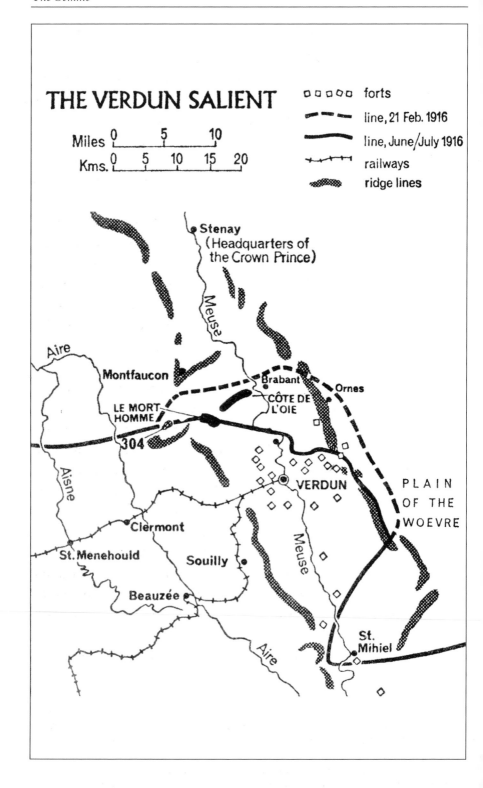

to speak 'incidental' political victory of the 'purification' of Alsace by an attack on Belfort is a small matter.

In post-war years there has been adverse criticism of Falkenhayn's reasoning and the strategy to which it led. Much of this has arisen from the wisdom of hindsight and some, perhaps, from prejudice. In terms of strategy he may have erred in selecting the western rather than the eastern front for his blow but, with the former chosen, his reasoning is difficult to fault. His arguments disposing of a mass frontal assault are irrefutable. His proposal for the slaughter of the French Army on a narrow front displays a gruesome imagination, yet it is hardly more macabre than the concept of the atomic bomb. It offered a means of engaging the enemy at maximum disadvantage to the foe with maximum advantage to himself – he had spent his whole military life learning to select such circumstances. In the matter of a sector he chose Verdun by appreciation, not by instinct.[43] Flanders was held largely by the British; and in any case the weather precluded operations there before April. The Arras sector had attractions[44] but the difficulty would be to confine operations continuously to a narrow front. The Somme and the Champagne were too open to offer any restriction of frontage from the outset. The Argonne was too densely wooded, the Woevre plain too wet to offer advantage to an attacker. If the French lost the region of Belfort, they would lose the only fragment of Alsace regained for France. Certainly France would battle for that. But the positions there did not particularly favour the type of battle Falkenhayn had in mind, and the railway consideration did not apply. Verdun had more to recommend it than he had stated. It had cerstainly acquired through the centuries a popular significance, it had the railway complex of Metz at hand. It was also close to the iron industry of Briey-Thionville from which the Germans manufactured many of their shells. The ground favoured the limitation of frontage. The approaches favoured secrecy. Verdun was not chosen carelessly.[45]

On his way back from making his proposal of policy to the Emperor,

---

[43] For the background to this choice, see *Der Weltkrieg, 1914 bis 1916*, Vol. X, pp. 20-25.

[44] Prince Rupprecht of Bavaria commanded this sector. He correctly indicated that, south of the city, his artillery could be positioned for the entire breaching and break-out battle without having to move. He envisaged a force of 24 divisions at least, in addition to his own command. See Crown Prince Rupprecht of Bavaria *Mein Kriegstagebuch*, Vol. I, p. 420 (Munich, 1929). The adversary would nave been principally British here.

[45] It is believed that the fact that the Crown Prince (of Germany) would command at Verdun influenced the Emperor in favour of the sector, but I can find no evidence to support this.

Falkenhayn was joined aboard the train by General Schmidt von Knobelsdorf, Chief of Staff to the Crown Prince, whose army faced Verdun. The plan was discussed between them, When it was passed to him, the Crown Prince, though full of enthusiasm for a project which was to be the principal German effort for the year, '...could not regard the future with an altogether serene confidence. I was disquieted by the constantly repeated expression used by the Chief of the General Staff [Falkenhayn] that the French Army must be 'bled white' at Verdun, and by a doubt whether the fortress could, after all, be taken by such means.'

Whether the Crown Prince saw Falkenhayn's memorandum for the Emperor or not – and it is conceivable that Falkenhayn showed it to von Knobelsdorf aboard the train – it is clear that the Crown Prince knew the aim of the forthcoming offensive, as his disquiet in the use of the term 'bled white' shows. There was no question, of course, of using such a term or at suggesting its fulfilment in the orders for battle; it would scarcely have commanded vigour and enterprise amongst troops in the assault. The Chief of the General Staff did not, in any case, issue a written directive, being concerned to secure the secret of the venture. The Crown Prince, necessarily more precise, ordered his army to capture the fortress of Verdun by 'precipitate methods', a term that should not have given Falkenhayn grounds for concern. Yet some apprehension must have existed in his mind, for throughout January and February he took the foolish step of meddling in tactics which were properly the concern of the army and corps commanders. His initial mistake was to meddle with the frontage of assault.

'The fortress of Verdun' refers to the fortified region protecting the city and its crossing over the river Meuse from an enemy approaching on the west, north or east. At the end of 1915 the French trench line lay in a rough semicircle through these three compass points about ten miles from Verdun city and some three to five miles in advance of the covering forts. They formed a rounded salient in the German line. Ideally, when it is planned to take out a salient, the neck is closed by assault, pinching out those forces remaining inside. This is the weakness of such a position. At Verdun, however, the neck was not altogether vulnerable, its lower side lying upon a steep and wooded ascent from the Woevre plain which favoured defence. On the upper side, to the north-west, an assault in isolation was impracticable; the course of the Meuse restricted the frontage even more than Falkenhayn would have wished, whilst an attacker would have been exposed from the outset to fire from high ground to the east of the river. All this was clear at Fifth Army headquarters. With nine assault divisions to hand – in addition to the divisions already comprising the army – and an enormous reinforcement of artillery, the force was sufficient to make a simultaneous assault from the north-west, on the left side of the river, and the north on the right or eastern side. Falkenhayn would not have this. He may have feared that his principle of an offensive on a narrow front was receiving too little consideration. Whatever the cause, he was adamant that the initial assault should be made on one side of the Meuse only,[46] and in view of the restricted frontage on the western bank, it was to be on the eastern. Such is the folly of capable executives who trust none but themselves.

On the other side of the line developments favoured a German success. The fortresses of Verdun had largely been stripped of their guns[47] to compensate for France's shortage of heavy ordnance, not only because of her losses in an expanding army but due to her generous assistance to Russia and Italy. That such an abatement of strength was accepted[48] is surprising unless the experiences of 1914 are called to mind. Numerous modern forts were reduced in the first month of the war by the giant 420-mm howitzers from the Skoda works in Austria-Hungary. At Liege, for example, the steel plate and concrete of the earthworks had been shattered. Though critics now mock Joffre's decision to remove the guns from their turrets at Verdun, they do so in the knowledge that Falkenhayn mounted a novel offensive there. Had there been no German attack in this restricted area – and there was not the slightest indication of one in 1915 – the post-war sages might have scorned the French commander-in-chief for leaving useful guns idle in an out-moded system when they were so short elsewhere.

The secret of Falkenhayn's intention remained secure into the new year of 1916, no hint of an impending offensive at Verdun reaching GQG before 10 January.[49] But some time before this – before Falkenhayn had

[46] For an explanation of this policy, see Falkenhayn, *op. cit.*, pp. 228-229.

[47] 4000 guns had been removed, of which 2300 were medium and heavy.

[48] An act of parliament was required constitutionally for such a measure. Doubtless due to the emergency, the removal was authorised by a decree negotiated by the Ministry of War.

[49] See Joffre, *op. cit.*, p. 440.

made his proposal to the Emperor – Joffre's attention had been drawn to the defences of the fortress region. Lieutenant-Colonel Driant, commanding a regiment[50] of Chasseurs in the foremost line beyond the forts, was far from satisfied with the state of the trenches and the defensive obstacles that should have lain in front of them.

Though mobilised, he was still a member of parliament and on, 22 August he wrote to the President of the Chamber of Deputies, complaining of lack of men to dig and barbed wire to make his own sector inviolable, the more so as he anticipated – wrongly and without foundation – a German offensive on the line Nancy-Verdun. In due course there were enquiries by the Army Commission and the Minister of War. General Gallieni wrote to Joffre on 16 December, mentioning that fears had been expressed in reports to Paris from 'various sources' concerning weakness in the fortified region.

The commander-in-chief's reply,[51] mordant and coldly respectful, challenged the minister's acceptance of reports that by-passed his headquarters. After expressing himself as being entirely satisfied with the defences at Verdun – apart from shortages of barbed wire there, as elsewhere, due to the failure of supply by the Ministry of War – he concluded, '...Soldiers who write these reports know that the Government take them up with their chiefs; the authority of the latter is diminished and the morale of all suffers from the discredit thus implied. I cannot admit the continuation of this state of affairs...'

This was 18 December, 1915. Falkenhayn had not returned from his Christmas visit to the Emperor; his proposal remained in draft. Joffre was quite right to demand the termination of backstairs reports to the authorities in Paris and was generally correct in saying that the defences of Verdun were adequate to withstand any local attack in the region, such as the Crown Prince might mount within his own resources. Certainly there were other sectors of the line which, on the probabilities of attack, needed defence stores more urgently. All this said, it is a pity that Joffre's mind was not more questing and that he permitted his staff to insulate him from the events of the battlefield. Otherwise, in the first fortnight of January, his reaction to events might have been swifter.

Despite the bad weather French observers noted in the early days of the

---

50 He had only two battalions under his command.
51 Personal letter to the Minister of War, 18 December, 1915 (see Joffre, *op. cit.*, pp. 438-440).

new year that church spires behind the enemy lines, useful as identification marks for controlling artillery fire, had been demolished. A few deserters spoke of tunnelling in progress, and some said, wildly, that extensive mines might be approaching under the forts. It is probable that the stories originated in the spacious dugouts – *Stollen* – under construction in the forward areas to shelter the assault battalions during the opening barrage. In the second and third weeks of January the commander at Verdun, an artillery general named Herr, received more definite indications of impending attack. He was a mild man and fearful in his responsibility. For months he had been requesting men and defence stores but had made little effort to drive his subordinates to work with their own resources or to seek materials locally from the damaged villages of the region. Reports now mentioned concentrations of troops immediately opposite and the deployment of fresh hospitals in rear. The weather and German fighter interdiction combined to deny close air reconnaissance of the enemy gun lines among the Woevre forests, but the pattern of artillery fire had changed: in addition to the regular harassing programme, there were clear signs that a number of guns were ranging on widespread targets for future action.

Though the staff at GQG sought to dissuade their chief that these reports portended trouble, Joffre sent his principal assistant,[52] General de Castelnau, to Verdun on 24 January to review defence preparations. His report to the commander-in-chief indicated a need for extensive action if they were to withstand the offensive clearly in preparation. Men were needed urgently as a labour force. The roads and railway[53] into the area were suitable only for the backwater that the region had become. While engineer plans were set in hand to improve these communications, including the Meuse crossings, a corps – two divisions – was earmarked for labour duties under General Herr's headquarters though, owing to the lack of urgency felt at GQG, some days passed before they were available. On 19 February Joffre himself came to Verdun.

The activities he had sanctioned were performed on borrowed time. As successive French headquarters came to realise from the interrogation

---

[52] General de Castelnau was appointed in December 1915 as chief staff officer to Joffre at the urging of the Government, who believed that he would exercise a benign influence upon the commander-in-chief. Castelnau was not Joffre's chief-of-staff (the 'major-general') but a special appointee, available to undertake special missions and to be Joffre's *confident*.

[53] The only usable railway to the region was the '*Meusien*' a narrow-gauge single track. See Pétain, *Verdun*, Ch. Ill (London, 1930).

reports of the deserters coming in between 5 and 18 February, a mighty offensive was poised; was, indeed, overdue from 13 February onwards, being delayed by the recurring storms of snow or sleet. The assault now awaited only a fine day.

On 20 February, the weather cleared.

At 4.30 in the morning of the 21st a single 380-mm shell hurtled across the battlefield into Verdun. Slowly, from this beginning, '...a hurricane of iron and steel' raged across the frostbound soil, the fire of 1,400 guns, howitzers and mortars. High explosive struck infantry trenches, dugouts and concrete strongpoints; field, medium and heavy artillery positions in the open and those left in the forts; roads, bridges, the railway and its goods yards. To ensure that the French battery positions were untenable, gas shells were spread amongst the explosives.

Falkenhayn expected that this monstrous blow would crush all organised opposition. There should be no need to launch infantry masses blindly into the forward defences; fighting patrols would come forward to investigate whether any vestige of resistance remained and, on the basis of their reports, the battalions of the three assault corps would break into the main position on the following day. Meanwhile the gunners' barrage would continue to prevent French reinforcement of their line by men or fire.

So much for theory.

The patrols of all three corps made their way forward individually after eight hours' bombardment of the French trenches, reaching these about ten minutes after the German guns had lifted to the second line. Though torn beyond all possibility of cohesive defence and seldom supported by their own guns, the French infantry maintained a dogged defiance along a front of 12,000 metres from the eastern bank of the Meuse on the left towards the edge of Ornes village on the right. For several hours on this darkening winter afternoon the close battle continued with machine-gun, rifle and grenade. The German flame-throwers, a ghastly novelty, proved to be effective in 'sterilising' trenches and dugouts. Eventually most patrol commanders found it possible either to crush the little groups of heroes resisting amongst the tumbled defences or to infiltrate between them to the rear. Here the second line of defence offered more coordinated opposition. At dusk, when the runners had departed with battle intelligence for the main infantry attack next day, the Germans had penetrated, at most, 1,000 metres on a front of 10,000. It is a significant fact that the right-hand corps, VII Reserve under the ardent von Zwehl, had not waited to bring forward its battalions until 22 February; they had followed close behind their patrols. Yet even the striking power of twelve battalions in his first echelon had not carried von Zwehl's corps through the French second line. When darkness fell the barrage resumed on the forward defenders, some German patrols continuing to probe throughout the night, aided by flares from the regimental '77 batteries.

On the 22nd all three corps assaulted together. Part of the French second line fell, its defenders once more shattered by the barrage. Colonel Driant, who had reported his fears to Pans, was killed – 'about ten yards from the trench a bullet hit him in the forehead and he fell without a word'. Six officers and 120 men survived of his 1,200 Chasseurs. Next day, the 23rd, the process of crushing fire and infantry follow-up was repeated, another narrow strip was taken; the prize enhanced by the forced evacuation of Brabant on the eastern river bank. The Crown Prince's soldiers had now closed up to the intermediate trench line in front of the forts.

The following three days were critical. On the 24th the losses amongst the two divisions on the narrow frontage of attack became insupportable. None of the battalions could muster more than a company of men; more than half the artillery had been destroyed and battery survivors had been taken prisoner with few exceptions. The German gunfire, unabated, forced gaps in the trench line here; as it had done in the foremost positions. The third division of the corps was broken up piecemeal to fill these gaps with single units; but they were North Africans, fighting in this confusion amongst strangers, bereft of many of their own officers, chilled by the bitter north wind. When the massed enemy infantry approached they ran away. Yet, as before, the absence of communications which hampered General Herr in his command post, hampered the enemy no less. Darkness fell upon the battlefield. The groups of defenders, strung out across the snow-covered ridges and in the deep re-entrants, prepared local protection by posting sentries upon the lips of such craters as they occupied. German patrols set out to probe amongst them for information as to numbers and dispositions but lacking identification marks on the ground – woods, houses, even roads had suffered change or destruction in the intense shellfire – their effective range of action was less than 1,000 yards. Even if this short sortie, encompassed at snail's pace over the torn ground – the men stopping every fifty paces to listen for the enemy, to check bearings – discovered a breach, their information had to pass through an attenuated chain before it reached a commander who had both the authority and the facilities to act upon it.

So the night 24/25th passed on the eastern Meuse heights, while the German artillery hammered such of the forward positions as it knew of, hammered the roads leading reinforcements in from the west. Those not on watch huddled in greatcoats, sacking or blankets in the dark, and even the hard frost was unable to deny sleep to many of the exhausted soldiers after four days of intensive battle. To the rear, regimental, brigade, divisional, corps and higher staffs had the comfort of shelter, light and warmth, but none of hope, as rumour and report spoke only of further withdrawals.

That night Joffre appointed General Pétain to take command of the battle to the right of the Meuse and despatched Castelnau to study at first hand the situation. Meantime the army group commander[54] advisedly pulled back his divisions from the Woevre plain into the wooded hills south-east of the battle zone. The 25th saw a series of fresh disasters as Castelnau hurried from one headquarters and one observation post to another and meditated upon the dispirited and ineffectual state of General Herr and his headquarters. The last of the forward trenches on the eastern heights fell during the day and, most serious of all, port Douaumont was taken by default.[55] The moral consequence of this loss of one of the great forts, standing on a key height and still mounting artillery in its turrets, was far-reaching: the troops in its vicinity began to scamper towards the rear. Detachments of weary, panic-stricken men mixed in growing confusion with wounded on stretchers going down, reinforcements and supply parties coming up. General Herr was prepared to see the whole of the eastern defences fall. Castelnau said they should not.

Late on the 27th Pétain took command of the entire Verdun sector.

---

[54] General de Langle de Cary, responsible for the centre group of armies, who took this important decision.
[55] See K. von Klüfer, *Seelenkräfe im Kampf um Douaumont* (Berlin, 1938).

During the course of the day the first movement towards the restoration of calm and stability had been completed successfully. Terror and despair had echoed back through the chain of local headquarters. The most effective means of dispelling this was to return an element of confidence downwards through the same chain. Castelnau made the decision that they would fight for and hold the eastern bank. More importantly, he convinced those commanders and staffs with whom he conferred that his order was a feasible proposition. Now Pétain reinforced his work.

From an empty room in the town hall [he wrote later[56]] I got into telephonic communication with General Balfourier, commanding the sector under attack.

'Hello! This is General Pétain speaking. I am taking over command. Inform your troops. Keep up your courage. I know I can depend upon you.'

'Very well, sir. We shall bear up. You can rely on us, as we rely on you.'

Immediately afterwards I rang up General de Bazelaire, commanding the sectors on the left bank, and I made the same announcement to him, telling him of the particular importance I attached to saving our positions west of the Meuse. He answered as General Balfourier had just done, in a tone of devoted and absolute confidence.

From that time on there was no doubt of sympathetic co-operation between the chief and his lieutenants.

A little later, towards midnight, Colonel de Barescut, my chief-of-staff arrived. I marked in charcoal on a large scale map, pasted on the wall, the sectors held by the army corps already in the field, and the front still to be occupied, after which I dictated the orders that were to be delivered to every unit the next morning. These were my first measures on taking command at Verdun.

They were enough. If these words, these gestures seem melodramatic half a century later, their effect at the time is overlooked. For next day, and thereafter as reinforcements arrived, the line was held.

With the slight easement of French anxiety there was a corresponding malaise amongst the victorious Germans. On 27 February – the seventh day of the attack – the offensive gained no ground. Pétain's resolute command, the arrival of reinforcements, and the flanking fire of the French artillery on the left bank of the Meuse, pouring its shells into the flank of the enemy as they advanced up the right, had all played their part;

[56] See Pétain, *op. cit.*, pp. 84-85.

but, as ever, chance had intervened in the battle and on this occasion in favour of the French. The improvement in the weather had brought about a thaw just as it was necessary for the Germans to bring forward their guns to support the advanced line. There would have been difficulties enough in negotiating the craters if the ground had been hard with frost. Now that it was soft the problems were multiplied. Many of the medium and heavy guns sank to their axles. And when at last they came into action they lacked the sheltered secrecy of the original positions among the Woevre forests. The long French 155s had a turn at counter-battery fire to good effect.

Against this background Falkenhayn conferred with the Crown Prince and von Knobelsdorf on the 28th. It was dear that any future movement forward on the right bank of the 'Meuse would be seriously hampered by the guns of the French batteries on the left. The left-bank positions must themselves be destroyed – no longer as a strategic measure but a tactical necessity. Falkenhayn could not disagree. On 5 March, while the fury of attack mounted once more along the eastern heights, German artillery lying back among the woods and re-entrant's behind the Montfaucon road began to pummel the forward trenches holding the west bank approaches.

Not surprisingly Pétain had maintained the original outpost line in this area. It ran amongst low hills – some little more than mounds beneath the eminence of Montfaucon – scrub-covered near the river, wooded to the west. The object of these posts was to act as a breakwater to the German assault waves, to reduce substantially the power and cohesion of the field-grey masses before they closed up to the main positions. For the main line lay upon a comparatively narrow obstacle chain: the heights of Côte 304, le Mort Homme and Côte de l'Oie. If these fell, the next defensible line was held by the forts 4000 metres in the rear. More important, the enemy might be able to drive down west of Verdun and cut the communications into the fortified region. The salient would be dangerously, perhaps fatally, affected.

The opening three hours of shelling demolished the outpost line. By the evening of the 5th the defences on the western heights, '...and the zone of batteries behind it looks like a foaming trough. Shell holes overlap one another. The trenches on the back slopes of Mort Homme and the Côte de l'Oie are completely wrecked.' At 10 am next day, twenty-four German battalions made the assault under a continuing bombardment, when they carried quickly the outpost line. Along the river, too, a surprise venture, involving the nice timing of assaults from either side of the Meuse, gained a swift local advantage. But the heights held, and without these the German attack was a failure. Time was gained to develop defences in rear. Thereafter, notwithstanding the French anxieties in summer-long battles ahead, it is doubtful if the Verdun position was in danger of collapse.

These views are based, of course, on the premise that the French would be willing to fight to defend the region – a premise shared, it will be recalled, by Falkenhayn. The disappointment of the Crown Prince, his eventual despair of taking Verdun was not shared by Falkenhayn. His concern arose less from the failure to take ground than the swelling number of German casualties *vis-a-vis* those of the French. On the last day of February Pétain's command had sustained 30,000 casualties, the Germans, 25,000. By the end of March the figures were 89,000 French and 81,000 Germans. The principle of employing massed artillery to save infantry in the break-in had proved, at best, a limited success. Once the initial surprise was lost it was no longer possible to fire an interdiction and counter-battery programme sufficient to guarantee the assaulting infantry freedom from defensive artillery fire and subsequent counter-attack by reinforcements. When the front of assault was extended to the west bank, the concentration of guns, howitzers and mortars was reduced while the French batteries, proportionately less harassed, were able to give greater support to their own men.

As time passed Falkenhayn could only hope that the gap between his own casualties and those of the French would widen in his favour. If it did not, he might bleed the French white but he would do the same for his own army. He maintained his tight control of reinforcements to the Crown Prince's weary divisions, releasing him Just sufficient to sustain the offensive, boosting the force from time to time with fresh formations from quiet sectors.

At Chantilly Joffre played a similar game but for a different reason. While he wished both to retain Verdun and to regain the ground lost in the fortified region, he had no wish to mount a major offensive there, for one prime reason amongst several: an offensive at Verdun would have been wholly French and be was now hopeful that the British were ready to take a substantial share in the summer campaign. Haig's plans for the Somme were progressing. As the spring advanced, however, it became clear that Verdun was absorbing at least a part of, the French force earmarked for the 1916 offensive. By May, with French losses there at 133,000, forty-two divisions had been engaged in the battle,[57] and the force to join the British on the Somme had fallen from forty to thirty divisions. Yet more fresh troops were called for. Joffre grew impatient with Pétain's persistence in dogged defence and, promoting him to command the centre group of armies, he appointed the brisk, aggressive Nivelle in his place at Verdun.

This phase of the war demonstrates well the strength and weaknesses of the two opposed supreme chiefs. Falkenhayn, who had so penetratingly appraised German war prospects,[58] is seen initially pressing his battle of attrition with an iron resolve. Yet, when it is plain that his own casualties are mounting beyond his expectations, he fails to take his own advice: '...for she is perfectly free to accelerate or draw out her own offensive, to intensify it or break it off from time to time, as suits her purpose...' He had the opportunity to threaten Verdun as he chose, and to entice the French into attack in continuation of his policy, especially after Nivelle – renowned for his offensive spirit – was appointed to confront the Crown Prince, Falkenhayn's novel and imaginative plan required, in its operation, a subtle flexibility which neither he nor his immediate assistants possessed.

Joffre read the battle of Verdun shrewdly, once he had been to see matters for himself. Wisely, he reinforced the region with a sparing hand – an early massive reinforcement would simply have provided a denser target for the German guns. He calculated the risks nicely, as a man may when he is far removed from the stress of the battle zone, so as to husband his resources for the Allied major offensive in the summer. Yet he could not bide his time for the *moment juste* when defence should end and offence begin. Even while Pétain was fighting the first grim holding battles on either bank of the Meuse with his spare force, Joffre was urging him to counter-attack on a wide front.

The two chiefs fought the battle on the basis of their previous experience. It would be unreasonable to expect that either might draw firm

---

[57] The German figure is thirty divisions but a number of these had been into battle four times, whereas many French divisions served one period only at Verdun before moving to a quieter sector.

[58] For an admirable summary of the matter, see Crutwell, *A History of the Great War* (Oxford, 1936), p. 289.

conclusions from the experience of Verdun until, say, the end of April, when the first German effort to break through the west-bank positions had failed. But by the end of that month the outcome of the fighting provided some clear lessons.

For example, however great its weight, a preliminary bombardment did not utterly destroy the enemy's resistance in his first line of defence, even when the garrison was incompletely protected as in the case of Colonel Driant's Chasseurs. In consequence, it was essential for the assaulting infantry to have communications to their own close support guns and howitzers to obtain fire on strong points continuing to resist.

Secondly, unless sure means of communication could be found to exploit a collapse of any section of the enemy defences, such as the flight of the North Africans on 24 February, the capture of the enemy's second line was not to be expected in the first phase of the attack. Having taken out the enemy's first line there must be, therefore, a pause to permit the infantry to study their next objectives by distant observation, patrols and the use of aids such as trench maps and air photographs; and the artillery to move forward, both to gain ground for the next bombardment and, not least, to reach out to the enemy rear with counter-battery fire. For whilst it was the isolated machine-gun which had delayed the first German assaults, it was the gun and howitzer which stemmed the advance of the Crown Prince's army during the spring and summer, enabling the hard-pressed infantry to hold the line. If the Crown Prince's gunners had been able to maintain their counter-bombardment successes of 21/22 February for ten days, even the astounding valour of the French line regiments would not have held Verdun.

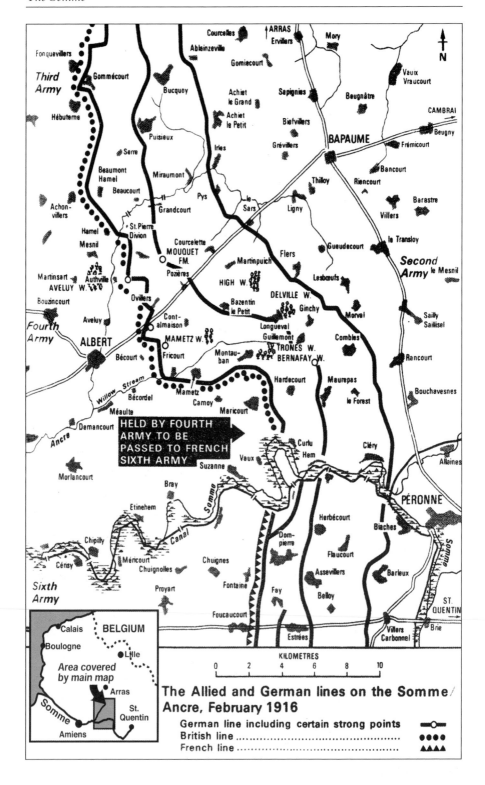

HELD BY FOURTH ARMY TO BE PASSED TO FRENCH SIXTH ARMY

The Allied and German lines on the Somme/Ancre, February 1916

German line including certain strong points •—○—•
British line .... ●●●●
French line .... ▲▲▲▲

PART II

GESTATION

THE RIVER

The entry in Haig's diary for 14 February 1916 makes it clear that the British Expeditionary Force was committed, on that date, to an offensive on the Somme in the summer ahead. At the end of the previous year Joffre had ordered studies of offensives in five different sectors; he was then by no means sure which would be the most suitable. Haig, too, had ordered similar studies, being well aware that he would be expected to approach quantitatively the French effort. But from 14 February onwards the die was cast for the Somme.

I am unable to discover any document in either the French or British archives which explains why the area of the Somme was chosen. Neither Joffre nor his staff appear to have made a comprehensive appreciation, weighing the merits of sectors. In directing General Foch[1] to study an offensive between the Somme and Lassigny, and in his letter to Haig suggesting British participation in such an operation,[2] Joffre's preamble is too vague to be worth serious consideration. For his part, and for sound

[1] Commander of the French northern group of armies. He was ordered to prepare an offensive on a thirty-mile front, employing forty divisions and 1,200 guns.
[2] See *British Official History of the War, Military Operations, France and Belgium, 1916* (hereafter referred to as OH, 1916), Vol. I, pp. 26-27.

reasons,[3] Haig favoured Flanders. But after receiving Joffre's request to cooperate with Foch he was obliged to consider the Somme. North of the river Allenby held the line with his Third Army. In January he was instructed to study an attack in the spring by fifteen British divisions acting alone or, alternatively, astride the river with the French in the summer, when the British contribution might be twenty-five divisions.

In seeking a reason for the selection of the Somme as a sector, it is probable that it is to be found in the simplest answer: the British and French armies joined on its banks.

An objection may be raised to this view in that British and French forces were also cooperating round Arras, where Joffre's Tenth Army was sandwiched between the British First and Third. An Anglo-French offensive centred on Vimy Ridge might have yielded useful results – particularly in conjunction with a blow struck in Flanders – but not without drawbacks for France. As we know, Joffre had been continually asking Haig to take over more of the trench line; and nowhere was he more anxious to see this done than at Arras. If a joint summer offensive should be mounted in that region, Tenth Army's relief would be indefinitely postponed – as unsatisfactory from the logistical as from the operational aspect – while the command of the offensive overall might logically have been demanded for Haig by the British Government in view of the preponderance of their troops. Joffre looked forward to a rising British share in the responsibilities on the western front in 1916 but he did not want it on those terms. Though there were no immediate strategic objectives on the Somme – such as the railway complex at Verdun – the British and French were side by side. Here Joffre could be sure of maintaining overall control of effort and extent, direction and date.

The Somme is a quiet river. From St Quentin it flows in a south-western loop to Péronne and then westwards to Amiens through Corbie. At Corbie it is joined by the thin stream of the Ancre. In these upper reaches the Somme follows a wandering, looping, rush-strewn course amongst marshy ill-defined banks. Its valley is wide and shallow amongst the chalk downs on either side. The river bottom is muddy, sometimes treacherously deep. Like the canal which runs parallel to its course, it is an obstacle to the

---

[3] *Ibid*, pp. 32-33.

movement of troops. But there were adequate roads amongst the pastures then, as now, connecting farms, villages and market towns, with a profusion of lanes twining amongst the beech woods and cider-apple orchards. Just north of the river the Roman highway ran straight from Amiens into Albert and east to Cambrai through Bapaume. Just south another connected Amiens and St Quentin.

There had been little activity in the area since the days of the Marne crisis. After the German withdrawal in the early autumn of 1914, the Somme line extended northward haphazardly from the Oise through the countryside of Picardy. Across the open downs the trench complex scarred the grass with chalk. Joffre commented at the end of 1915: '...For long months the reciprocal activity of the troops opposed to each other has been less than elsewhere.' He meant it was a quiet sector.

Whilst the trenches lay under snow in early February, Haig made use of a further agency for operational planning. The Fourth Army was in process of forming-up under Lieutenant-General Sir Henry Rawlinson, whose headquarters was in being from the 5th, in readiness for the arrival of its troops in March/April. Haig put the army commander and his staff to work to review three plans, one of which was the projected Somme offensive. From the 14th, as we have seen, this became a prime task. Rawlinson was disappointed to discover, when he visited GHQ after breakfast on the 17th, that he was to be subordinated to Allenby, but other events were to relieve his regret. The assault at Verdun on the 21st by the Crown Prince's army had far-reaching effects. In so far as the BEF was concerned, the most immediate consequence was an urgent request by Joffre for the relief of the Tenth Army, post haste. Haig loyally agreed, passing half of its sector to First Army on the north side, half to Allenby's Third on the south. In effect Third Army side-stepped to its left. On the Somme front Rawlinson took command of the three corps *in situ* and at once Fourth Army came into being.

It was now 1 March. With that habit of method and thoroughness which contrasted so strangely with his love of gossip and gerrymandering Rawlinson made a complete personal reconnaissance of his front. His trenches ran for twenty miles. In the south they rested on the river itself, in the north they shared the village of Hébuteme with the revised right flank of Allenby's army. But these bare facts had little significance in the preparation for a mighty attack. What mattered primarily was the nature of the ground and the positions which the enemy had chosen to occupy upon it.

Hébuteme village lay upon a ridge of high ground extending four to five miles south towards the hamlet of Hamel on the bank of the Ancre. On the ridge the trenches were generally well-concealed on forward slopes running gently downhill to the east where, lower down, the German positions, also well-concealed amongst villages, re-entrants, woods and copses, were under a degree of observation by the British. South of Hamel, however, the position was reversed. The Ancre stream divided the front to British disadvantage. Whereas their line lay west of the river on the Hébuteme-Hamel ridge, it now crossed over to the east and ran across the lower spurs of a ridge held by the Germans. From this high ground, running roughly south-east from Thiepval village through Pozières to Guillemont, the German defences extended west down the spurs and re-entrants in a cunning pattern. The observation posts could watch Albert and the traffic approaching it from Amiens and see the whole length of the Ancre valley between Albert and Corbie. The first defence line – in itself a comprehensive position of outpost, support and reserve trenches – covered potentially with fire every approach upwards from the British position. The second defence line, no less comprehensive, gave direct artillery observation upon an enemy reaching the first and, in certain places where the two were close, offered machine-gun support. Field batteries were deployed between the two main lines. In the forward trenches, whilst light machine-guns backed by rifles might sweep away an enemy directly approaching the outposts, others on heavy mountings were nicked out of direct view in hollows and re-entrants from which they might release a deadly stream in enfilade upon an advancing foe.

Guillemont, the southernmost village of the ridge, lies at the head of a rivulet – the Willow Stream – which winds up to the village from the Ancre. Between the Willow Stream and the Somme a long spur rises sinuously from Corbie, reaching its highest point fifteen miles to the east at Maricourt château before turning north through Montauban and east again through a high ring contour to Guillemont. The long feature constituted a third sub-division of the Fourth Army's sector. The German line, running approximately north-south from Hébuteme to the Willow Stream, swung sharply to the east across its narrow valley, disclaiming but observing the ground from Maricourt to Corbie, while holding the high points Montauban-Guillemont.

This was the ground which Rawlinson quartered with his binoculars in the course of a detailed reconnaissance in February.

FROM THE GENERAL TO THE PARTICULAR

Haig's headquarters was located at St Omer, close to the Channel coast by Calais.[4] A splendid collection of motor cars concentrated near the house of the General Staff on 4 March, each bearing an army commander's coloured rectangular flag. In the conference room, with his principal staff officers, 'DH' met his army commanders to acquaint them with his firm policy for the summer offensive.

They began, customarily, with an intelligence briefing. The latest news from Verdun was given by Charteris,[5] followed by a summary of other information gained by political agencies and espionage, and the latest battle intelligence flowing back from the Royal Flying Corps, artillery observation posts and the battalions in the line. Haig then spoke of his own intentions. Plumer, as commander of Second Army, was to pursue plans for an offensive in Flanders, reporting in April on the merits of each of three sectors suggested. This was prudence. Haig could not be sure of the outcome at Verdun, particularly in consumption of French reserves. If matters went badly for their ally, the offensive might become wholly a British responsibility, in which case it would be in Flanders. As things stood however, both allies were still committed to the Somme, where Rawlinson must now proceed to detailed planning, accepting a certain amount of give-and-take with the French Sixth Army on his right flank in the junction of the common assault.

Rawlinson returned to his own headquarters at Querrieu, near Amiens, that night and gave orders for the assembly of his corps commanders and heads of staff branches on the 6th. Though the spring was only just beginning, he recognised that he would need as much time as possible to make ready.

They all met at Querrieu: Hunter-Weston – known widely as 'Hunter-Bunter' – who had brought his VIII Corps headquarters back from

4 It was moved on 31 March to Montreuil, a more central position, where it remained until the end of the war.

5 Haig's senior intelligence officer (Brigadier-General, General Staff Intelligence).

Gallipoli, but had only one division under command as yet; Morland, X Corps, who had proved himself in battle as a brigadier in the anxious autumn of 1914 in Belgium; Congreve, XIII Corps, whose precise skill under fire south of Armentieres had saved his brigade from piecemeal destruction during 'First Ypres'. None fits the image of the hearty, compassionless chief, ignorant of battle conditions and too fearful of fire to remedy his inexperience. Beside Rawlinson and these three, two other principals attended: 'Curly' Birch, the chief gunner, said to measure two metres in height; and his equal in stature, Major-General A A Montgomery, Rawlinson's chief of staff.

In his usual way Fourth Army commander had made meticulous preparations for the meeting. He had written out notes in careful sequence – main headings for each subject supported by an *aide-mémoire* of ordered phrases. Beginning at once with the prospective Somme battle Rawlinson laid out his programme. The army would attack in June or July – unless pressure at Verdun compelled an earlier and more limited relief venture in April. A fourth corps would join them shortly and all corps would consist of four infantry divisions for the assault. The artillery would be reinforced by heavy howitzers sufficient to provide one to every 100 yards of the German front, and there would be no stinting ammunition. From left to right, the corps would be VIII (Hunter-Weston), X (Morland), the corps to come, XIII (Congreve). The initial phase of the operation would surely be the capture of the enemy first line and on this premise they might begin such preliminary work. Sites must be found for the guns of the many reinforcing batteries expected and observation posts agreed upon from which to control their fire. The immense problem of laying cable must be overcome – a problem which entailed the burying of the cable to a depth of six feet, where it should survive all shell fire other than eight-inch heavies and grosser weights. To guard against these disruptions, a complex of switch lines must be installed, adding to the digging task. The programme of road maintenance, the cutting of new routes and the extension of the railways would be amplified. In so far as labour for defences and communications was concerned, the men holding the line could not be drawn upon; all their spare effort would be needed to keep the trench works in repair. But there were three divisions in reserve and some 4-5,000 men amongst the ammunition columns of the Service Corps who might be spared to work with them under the skilled supervision of the engineers. They must use every available hand; for shortly they would need to build an immense complex of camps for the new divisions and to extend the defence works with forward command posts, mines, saps, and assembly trenches. In addition to meeting this huge requirement for physical effort, they must find time to train for the battle ahead. They could not begin their work soon enough.

While the corps commanders and their operational staffs put these matters in hand, the administrators began to feel the burden of their work. The strength of Fourth Army and the GHQ reserve would double the number of men in the area to 500,000. With them would be 100,000 horses and a multitude of vehicles. Fortunately the summer was coming. Neither men nor beasts would require elaborate accommodation but the soldiers must have shelter from rain storms. All would need feeding and water. There must be petrol or fuel oil and lubricants for the trucks. For the forthcoming battle they would need reinforced dugouts for the dressing stations; in the divisional camps beforehand, medical centres for the sick and those wounded by long-range shellfire. Dressings and drugs must be stocked against the blood-letting. Latrines had to be dug, washplaces made – more water needed here in an area already short of it. Pumps must be brought in for the deep boreholes; and for the pumps, repair arrangements. Workshops, too, for the vehicles, the arms and equipment of this host of men in assorted units: cavalry, infantry, gunners, sappers and signallers, drivers, blacksmiths, butchers, bakers, clerks, medical orderlies, storemen of all types, cobblers, tailors, mechanics, veterinarians, police, postmen, labourers.

In order to ensure that ammunition and supplies of all kinds would be to hand through every stage of the battle, so that operational deployment should never be checked for want of any commodity, it would be necessary to establish a series of dumps from front to rear, each being filled from its neighbour behind, each sending forward to the dump next in front. So, too, there must be reserve depots of arms and equipment. For this great enterprise the roads were inadequate, being neither sufficiently comprehensive for the area of assembly nor metalled to withstand the ceaseless traffic of vehicles and horses. The chalk downs were easily cut as the surveyors demanded but there was scarcely any stone nearby for road metal and the need to import this commodity added to the burden of effort. The railway system might have eased matters but the forward lateral line was already cut by the German trenches between Amiens and Arras so that new rail beds were needed. Beside these through lines, special loops, sidings and spurs were in constant demand by those in charge of store complexes, and for the deployment and ammunition supply of the heavy guns.

Viewing this gigantic administrative problem in retrospect, what is remarkable is not that there were minor muddles, shortages and delays, but that almost everything was ready for the men and their gear when they arrived, and complete for the moment of assault when it came.

Rawlinson caught 'flu on 8 March. He was sent south to convalesce in the sunshine at Nice, from which he returned on the 29th. In his absence, Archie Montgomery, the chief of staff, had received a definite statement from GHQ of resources which would be available to Fourth Army. These included reinforcement by the new corps, III, under Lieutenant-General Pulteney.[6] Their force would therefore total seventeen divisions, excluding the GHQ reserve of three. Rawlinson and Montgomery now surveyed their position.

It was a curious situation, even for those times when command and staff procedures were relatively undeveloped. They knew with what they had to fight but were not sure exactly what they were expected to do with it. As we have seen, the battleground had been chosen for reasons of military politics rather than strategy. No immediate objectives tempted them behind the German lines; and although the enemy positions formed a salient between the river and Arras to the north, it was but a shallow disc which extruded, threatened clumsily on one side. Even Haig was not sure what he intended at this stage; talk of a breakthrough as a preliminary to turning northwards, taking the enemy lines in flank and reverse'[7] came later. At the end of March, therefore, Rawlinson and Montgomery had to make a plan for an offensive without a specific object in mind. Notwithstanding his subsequent directions Haig must bear the blame as an

---

[6] The headquarters of III Corps under Lieutenant-General Sir William Pulteney with one of its divisions, the 8th, came under command of Fourth Army on 24 March.

[7] See p. 77.

experienced professional chief for this condition of affairs.

Looking at the ground and the enemy for the umpteenth time, one thing at least was clear: wherever the attack might lead, the prime target must be the feature dominating the Ancre valley – the feature running south-east from Thiepval through Pozières, High Wood, and Longueval to Ginchy and Guillemont. With this in Fourth Army's possession, the enemy positions on either flank could be made untenable. Moreover, since the feature as a whole carried both the German first and second lines, its capture would mean that the enemy defences were almost breached, for the third line in rear was still only in the early stages of construction. This feature, this dominating ridge above a succession of spurs leading up from the Ancre, must therefore be their main concern. Ideally, to ensure its capture, they would need to mount substantial operations on either flank: on the left, north of the Ancre, to include the high spurs running east from Gommecourt; on the right, the tortuous spur running parallel with the Somme above Corbie, at the head of which lay Montauban and the ring contour overlooking Guillemont. Ideally it was so, but was it practicable? From Gommecourt in the north to the tortuous spur in the south was a frontage of attack of 26,000 yards. Bearing in mind that they were planning for a sustained offensive over several weeks, and that the prepared enemy defences ran back as much as 5000 yards, Rawlinson and Montgomery were clear that this frontage was too much to take on. As a fair estimate, they were reckoning on eight to nine men per yard of front to carry them through the weeks of assault ahead. This meant that the maximum frontage should be about 20,000 yards. Rawlinson made another reconnaissance from his northern observation posts and reached the conclusion that they might safely contract the northern flank to the Serre feature.

Having decided on the overall objective, the next question was: how to take it? There seemed to be two methods. The first was the Verdun type: the sustained assault which aimed to hurl attack after attack upon the enemy with the aim of exploiting to the maximum the initial surprise, thereafter keeping the enemy unbalanced by incessant assault. Both Rawlinson and his chief of staff were dubious that this would succeed. 'The trouble is,' the army commander commented to a member of Haig's staff, 'this method frequently exhausts the attacker first.' The depth and position of the enemy second line justified his view. North of the Albert-

Bapaume road, the first and second lines were only 1,500 to 3,000 yards apart and much of the second line was in view to British OP's. South of the road, however, the lines were as much as 5,000 yards apart, while scarcely any of the second line could be seen from Fourth Army positions. It was, in any case, beyond the range of field guns and mortars. Thus a sustained assault would have to be made blind upon at least half of the enemy's front after the capture of the first line. The field artillery and mortars would have to be moved forward over the crater field at a critical moment of the battle; the medium and heavy guns and howitzers would be compelled to rely solely upon the Royal Flying Corps to register and fire their equipments for effect. Having seen from air photographs the strength of the enemy position – his earth-work redoubts, his fortified villages, his gigantic belts of barbed wire – the disadvantages seemed to outweigh the superficial attractions of essaying a sustained assault.[8]

The alternative as they saw it was to capture the feature in two stages. The first of these would entail the occupation of the entire enemy first line, certain fortified villages whose possession would assist movement on to the second line, and strong positions on either flank to prevent the enemy from interfering with the second stage either by fire or counter-attack. This achieved, the second stage would embrace the capture of the enemy second line, when the way would be open for strategic exploitation.

Finally, a choice of method had to be made in preliminary bombardment. Were they to use a short, sharp concentration of fire over five to six hours and then assault, catching the enemy by surprise as he lay under cover in his deep dugouts, expecting hours more of attention from the allied artillery? Or should they bomb and shell him for several days at set times for sustained periods? Using the latter, they would not only expect to drive the enemy underground, but deny him ammunition and hot food, prevent the evacuation of his wounded – this consequence was appreciated – and crush his defence works in the process of wearing down his nerves.

Haig was known to favour the short bombardment because it offered surprise. Rawlinson proposed the lengthy preparation. He did not believe they could cut the enemy wire or sufficiently soften the enemy with less, a

---

[8] Rawlinson and Montgomery were, of course, aware of French failures using this method. As a corps commander, Rawlinson had discussed the Champagne offensive of 1915 with Haig (then his army commander). GHQ and army HQ's had also had some details of the German difficulties at Verdun, including *inter alia* the movement forward of field artillery and mortars in the middle of the battle.

view in which he had the support of Birch, the chief gunner. To sustain an element of surprise, it was planned to conclude the bombardment at dawn, having formed-up the infantry in darkness.

In presenting his views. Haig in writing on 3 April,[9] Rawlinson almost compromised his case. The following appears in his paper, contrasting strangely with his otherwise direct approach to the capture of the main feature:

> It does not appear to me that the gain of two or three more kilometres of ground is of much consequence, or that the existing situation is so urgent as to demand that we should incur very heavy losses in order to draw a large number of German reserves against this portion of our front. Our object rather seems to be to kill as many Germans as possible with the least loss to ourselves, and the best way to do this appears to me to be to seize points of tactical importance which will provide us with good observation and which we may feel quite certain the Germans will counter-attack. These points to be, not only ones of special tactical importance with a view to a further advance, but to be such that the Germans will be compelled to counter-attack them under disadvantages likely to conduce to heavy losses, which we can only ensure if these tactical points are not too far distant from our gun positions...

To my mind this extract characterises Rawlinson as a soldier. He was an expert at laying bets on and off any project for which he was responsible – in covering himself against failure. The more he looked at the task of breaking into the German defences, the more his imaginative mind saw the difficulties. From the inception of planning, he apprehended that, at best, his army would succeed in taking limited portions out of the enemy line. Yet, clearly, great things were expected of him – spectacular results indeed. Successive references by GHQ to the magnitude of his resources- compared with Loos, for example – made this attitude plain. Reference to the unimportance of ' ...two or three kilometres of ground...' more or less safe-guarded him. If they failed to break in, he might subsequently point to the fact that he attracted large numbers of the enemy and destroyed them.

Whether my opinion is correct or not – and Haig had no illusions about

---

[9] OH., *1916*, Vol. I. Appendix 8.
[10] See Haig, *op. cit.*, p. 289.

Rawlinson's character[10] – the commander-in-chiefs reaction to the Fourth Army plan was far from approbatory. Rawlinson and Montgomery reported to GHQ on 5 April to receive a verbal critique of their proposals which smacked of the staff college teacher discussing the paper of a misguided student.

Haig remarked that the plan lacked strategic purpose and seemed to have overlooked the importance of gaining surprise. The nature of the ground appeared to have been largely disregarded. All that had been achieved was to spread out the forces allotted more or less evenly along the line with the aim of making a general push forward, regardless of the enemy positions and the features of tactical importance.

These were damning comments and scarcely fair to Rawlinson. If there was a lack of strategic motivation, this was Haig's fault; he had failed to give Rawlinson an aim or task. The criticism concerning appreciation of ground was also ill-founded; the Fourth Army paper analysed this closely. It is only in the remarks concerning troops and ground relative to strategic surprise and tactical opportunity that we see, for a moment, a flash of inspiration, a prospect of achieving those spectacular results for which all so sincerely wished.

No one doubted the importance of the main feature. What was lacking was a subtle approach to its reduction. For example, a major thrust from the high ground Hannescamps-Fonquevillers-Hébuterne – in concert with feints along the whole army front – might have had success by penetration to Bapaume behind the Thiepval-Longueval-Ginchy ridge; and this ought to have been considered. In the same way the prospect of breaking the enemy line by a strong thrust north-east through Montauban-Guillemont-Ginchy, again using the advantage of a start on high ground while feinting along the Ancre, had been overlooked. Either would have offered that chance of strategic surprise for which Haig correctly looked.

There were other objections, probably contrived by Haig as spurs to press Rawlinson towards a comprehensive review of his plan. But if the commander-in-chief was successful in getting him to do this, Fourth Army commander obtained some profit in return. A fifth corps was added to his command, XV under Lieutenant-General Horne, without the full extension of front being insisted on. Indeed, there was a shortening not altogether to his liking. In the north.,Third Army took on responsibility for

Gommecourt, a happy arrangement for Rawlinson; but in the south, he learned, French encroachment on his side of the Somme would be on the scale of several divisions, which must surely overload and confuse traffic on roads and railway down by the river.

The French plan for their part in the offensive was gradually hardening. On 27 March Joffre had written to Haig concerning the common boundary between the two armies and the timing of their attacks. In his view the British, together with the French divisions north of the Somme, should attack first, the French forces south of the river later – 'some days' later being the proposal. Once more Joffre was attracted to the clear advantages of a consecutive double blow in which the first would attract to it the enemy reserves so that the second might the more easily break-in and then through. Haig was also clear, however, that this offered the hard work to his own force and the probable rewards to the French. Not unnaturally, he found himself unable to agree. On 14 April Joffre suggested that the objective of the offensive should be the road Bapaume-Péronne-Ham, the principal point of breakthrough being Péronne-Bouchavesnes for the French, Rancourt-Combles for the British. His concept was one in which the French Sixth Army played the main part: '...The mission of the British forces should be to cooperate in the action of the French forces, notably in facilitating their passage of the river south of Péronne...' Despite Verdun, it still seemed that Foch, as commander of the French northern army group, could persuade Joffre to find him sufficient forces for the major share of the battle. Whilst continuing to insist on a simultaneous attack north and south of the river, Haig made no objection to this second proposal; it would bring the Allied forces through the German lines at the eastern end of the high ground he himself wished to capture and hence offered strategic possibilities for a break-out. His reply to Joffre's letter gave him the opportunity to press again two other aspects: the crowding of the north bank of the Somme by French divisions, to which Rawlinson had objected, reinforcing Haig's own opinion of its undesirability; and the matter of timing. He asked for a minimum of four weeks' notice of the day of the attack.[11] Joffre promised at least three weeks but hoped that in any case preparations would be ready by 1 June. Haig wrote again to say that this was satisfactory, but reminded his colleague that the longer they waited, the stronger he would be.

[11] OH., *1916*, Vol. I, pp. 42-43.

Thus the two chiefs communicated throughout late March, the whole of April and into the first two weeks of May. While Joffre's letters were couched still in the language of a supreme commander whose own national army would be making the running, Haig was well aware not only of his colleague's rising difficulties in finding men for the raging Verdun battle but in the pressures upon him from Paris by Government and Opposition. All the Allies – French, British, Russian and Italian – had agreed at Chantilly[12] to attack the enemy in the summer; yet now that the summer was upon them, the French losses had exceeded all expectations owing to Verdun. In Chamber and Senate many feared that another offensive now must exhaust their armies. Some thought this might be avoided by waiting until the Allies were strong enough to bear the brunt of the fighting. The advocates of offensive action were chilled when on 14 May the Italians were attacked in the southern Tyrol and fell back eight miles, losing heavily in men and guns to the Austrians.

On 24 May Joffre's reaction to these circumstances became known to Haig. General des Vallières, chief of the French liaison staff at GHQ, returned from a visit to GQG, bearing a letter from Joffre which he had instructions to amplify. The French contribution to the Somme offensive would now be something between twenty-two and twenty-six divisions. The longer they waited, said des Vallières, the more reserves would Verdun consume. If for no other reason, the Somme attack must begin, soon, to relieve the enemy pressure on Verdun and – now – on the Italians. The Russians would attack in the east on 15 June. Would the British commander-in-chief receive General Joffre on 26 May to discuss an early date for opening the offensive?

The two men met at Haig's chateau at a little after 11 o'clock on that morning, the principals withdrawing to the writing-room. Almost at once, according to Haig's diary, written up that evening, Joffre began to re-state the case which des Vallières had patiently explained two days before.

Friday, May 26... The French had supported for three months alone the whole weight of the German attacks at Verdun. Their losses had been heavy. By the end of the month, they would reach 200,000. If this went on, the French Army would be ruined. He (Joffre), therefore, was of the opinion that 1st July was the latest date for the combined offensive of

[12] 6-8 December 1915 (see also p. 25).

the British and French. I (Haig) said that, before fixing the date, I would like to indicate the state of preparedness of the British Army on certain dates and compare its condition. I took 1st and 15th July, and 1st and 15th August.

The moment I mentioned August 15th, Joffre at once got very excited and shouted that 'The French Army would cease to exist if we did nothing till then.' The rest of us looked on at this outburst of excitement, and then I pointed out that, in spite of the 15th August being the most favourable date for the British Army to take action, yet in view of what he had said regarding the unfortunate condition of the French Army, I was prepared to commence operations on the 1st July or thereabouts. This calmed the old man, but I saw he had come to the meeting prepared to combat a refusal on my part, and was prepared to be very nasty...

After a good lunch, they parted friends, '... Joffre enjoyed himself so much that it was 2.20 pm before he went...' They agreed to meet again on the following Wednesday, the 31st, to discuss the offensive with representatives of the French Government; in particular, Haig noted, '...Joffre explained that the Minister (of War) wished to have the views of the Generals and hoped I would support him in the matter of making an early attack to extricate the French at Verdun. I, of course, replied in the affirmative.'

Wednesday, May 31. The President (Poincaré), M Briand (Prime Minister) and General Roques (Minister of War) came by train from Paris. They arrived at 11.30 and we at once assembled in the Presidential railway carriage – seven in all.

General Castelnau read over the Memorandum of which I received a copy last night. I took exception to a para. which said that the 'British Army had not been attacked' and pointed out that our losses in killed and wounded since December amounted to 83,000 – and 653 mines had been sprung during that time. Castelnau explained that para. meant English had not been attacked like the French at Verdun. The main discussion arose over the necessity for making an attack at an early date. Poincaré said that he had just returned from Verdun where he had seen the senior Generals – Pétain, Nivelle and another General. They told him 'Verdun sera prise' and that operations must be undertaken without delay to withdraw pressure from that part. He asked my views. I told him that I had visited London in February when fighting at Verdun began, and had got the approval of the Govt, to make arrangements and support the French in case of necessity. That, on my return to France, I had written a letter to CIGS and got the approval of the Govt. confirmed by letter.

...when is the most favourable date for attacking. General Joffre, who alone knew the situation fully (at Verdun and in Russia, Italy, etc.) had asked me to be ready by the beginning of July. I had arranged to comply with his request.

We next discussed the paragraph which stated that we must foresee the probability of the French Reserves diminishing, etc. The slow output of French heavy guns was pointed out and the need for supplying Verdun with everything necessary was recognised, and I said that *in view of the possibility of the British having to attack alone,*[13] it was most desirable to bring to France the Divisions which the Allies held at Salonika. I pointed out that this theatre (France and Belgium) was the decisive point, and that we ought to have every available Division here ready to strike in at the *decisive* moment. Briand enlarged on the possibility of the Servians making a separate peace, if they were not led forward to the attack against the Bulgarians. I said that would be preferable to our lacking the necessary superiority to exploit any success we gained here. Beat the Germans here, and we can then make what terms we like!

Foch came in for a reprimand from M Briand because he had stated to the politicians that he was against the offensive this year. His excuses seemed very lame, he ate humble pie and I thought he looked untrustworthy and a schemer. He had evidently spoken very freely to Clemenceau recently. Briand also compared Pétain to a motor engine in that he went tap tap tapping out all kinds of opinions to parliamentarians who went to Verdun expressly to get facts with which to fight the Government. 'The generals,' he said, 'must be united.' From what he said I formed the opinion that Pétain had the 'wind up'.

While Haig sought to reconcile the struggle between his natural wish to delay operations until the maximum resources were to hand and trained,

[13] The French President's brief for the meeting prepared by GQG, contained the words '...*on peut et on doit même envisager le cas ou l'Armée anglaise devrait enterprendre l'offensive preparée*'.
[14] Leader of the French parliamentary opposition.

and his loyalty to Joffre and the allied cause, Rawlinson had continued with his studies and preparations. Throughout the remainder of April and the first three weeks of May he had five private discussions with his commander-in-chief, much of the substance of which was confirmed in their formal correspondence. During the same period Fourth Army commander made personal contact with Foch in his headquarters at Dury and, through him, with General Fayolle, whose Sixth Army occupied the Somme basin and the high ground to the south. It was his XX Corps (Balfourier) which would crowd in upon the north bank to attack alongside the British XIII (Congreve). On 27 May, when it was still said that the French contingent would number well over 20 divisions in the joint battle, Haig had the following sent to his army commanders:

INSTRUCTIONS AS TO PREPARATIONS FOR THE BATTLE

1. Preparations for taking the offensive on a large scale are being made on two sections of our front, viz:

(a) By the Second Army, and
(b) By the Fourth Army and a portion of the Third Army.

2. It is not yet certain which of these attacks will be launched first. In the event of (b) being decided upon, then the First, Second and Third Armies will take steps to deceive the enemy as to the real front of attack, and wear him out and reduce his fighting efficiency both during the three days prior to the assault and during the subsequent operations. On the other hand, if (a) takes place first, then, of course, the role of the flank Armies will become changed. But preparations for deceiving the enemy should be made without delay on the supposition that (b) attack will be made first. This will be effected by means of:

(a) Preliminary preparations such as advancing our trenches and saps, construction of dummy assembly trenches, gun emplacements, etc.
(b) Wire cutting at intervals along the entire front with a view to inducing the enemy to man his defences and causing fatigue.
(c) Gas discharges, where possible, at selected places along the whole

British front, accompanied by a discharge of smoke, with a view to causing the enemy to wear his gas helmets and inducing fatigue and causing casualties. (See attached paper marked 'A' on use of gas.)[15]

(d) Artillery barrages on important communications, with a view to rendering reinforcements, relief and supply difficult.

(e) Bombardment of rest billets by night.

(f) Intermittent smoke discharges by day, accompanied by shrapnel fire on the enemy's front defences with a view to inflicting loss.

(g) Raids by night, of the strength of a company and upwards, on an extensive scale, into the enemy's front system of defences. These to be prepared by intense artillery and trench mortar bombardments.

The above means should be so combined as to produce the greatest effect. A note on wind, together with charts showing the direction of the wind during June, July and August, for the past 10 years is attached marked 'B'. Arrangements should be based on utilising any wind between WSW and SSW.

3. Armies should make arrangements to carry out operations as indicated above on the basis of resources being made available as in attached table marked 'C' for attack.

The allotment in ammunition for the Third Army includes that required for offensive operations at the Gommecourt salient, and for 13 days subsequent to the delivery of the attack.

The allotment in ammunition for the Fourth Army includes preliminary operations, bombardment, day of assault, and 13 days subsequent fighting.

As regards the amounts allotted to Third and Fourth Armies for offensive operations, it is to be understood that ammunition should be expended during the opening stages of the operation as required, irrespective of allotment. The figures represent an expenditure which it is anticipated will meet all requirements for the period named.

A further allotment of ammunition will then be made for the continuance of the battle.

The first draft of this instruction was made on the afternoon of 26 May, just

15 I have not included papers marked 'A', 'B' and 'C'.

after Joffre and his party had left at 2.20 pm, full of a good lunch and 1840 brandy. All else apart, it was clear to Haig that the prospect of French participation was dwindling. He wanted to keep the choice of sector for the offensive in his hand until the last possible moment and Flanders remained his favourite. The Messines-Wytschaete ridge, on the south side of the Ypres salient, had been selected for a possible offensive by Plumer's Second Army; plans were complete and five miles of mine galleries had been dug under the enemy lines and filled with 1,000,000 pounds of explosive. Some time was needed to extend roads and railways – the mines had attracted a great deal of labour – and to complete dumping of ammunition and supplies, but the essential work could have been completed by the combined resources of First and Second Army in about a fortnight. With the conclusion of the meeting in the French President's railway carriage at Salieux, however, events were already running towards the Somme as the offensive sector.

For one thing, Joffre had lingering doubts that the British Army would attack if his own men were altogether absent. To tie matters down yet more firmly, he wrote to Haig on the day after his return from Salieux railway station stating that the combined Anglo-French assault would be made on 1 July. The finality of the date was not absolute, however. He added the question, how long a period of notice would be required to complete arrangements if it should be necessary to alter the day? Haig asked for twelve days' notice in confirmation of '1st July or later'. He also wished to confirm his own doubts concerning French participation. How many French divisions will be cooperating, he asked in his reply, and what will be their objective? His concluding remarks stated fairly that he could not take his own final decisions until he knew exactly what action was to be taken by Foch's army group both in the offensive and in subsidiary and deception measures.

Joffre's response, next day, 6 June, did not answer directly on the matter of strength. But the information he gave spoke for itself. The principal mission of Fayolle's Sixth Army would now be to 'support the British'. Its task would be to make good the line Maurepas-Hem,[16] a frontage of 4,500 yards, to a depth short of the German second line. There was no further mention of striking for Péronne and the main road north to Bouchavesnes

[16] The village of Hem, not to be confused with the town of Ham, twenty miles to the south.

and south to Ham. The right-hand boundary of the French assault would be the Amiens-St Quentin road. It was evident that the twelve divisions in Fayolle's army were all that might be expected.[17] Nonetheless, it was enough that the French were to join in the offensive, to which Haig had again given his solemn promise by acceptance of a date. The Somme it would now be.

As the two chiefs negotiated by compromise towards an agreement in their plans, two incidents, each outside their control, prolonged their discussions. On Sunday, 4 June, the expected Russian offensive began – yet not at all as the Tsar's General Staff had predicted. In Galicia General Brussilov opened a subsidiary offensive with his four armies using ammunition which he had saved from his daily allocation for harassment and defence. He attacked on a front of 300 miles and, astonishingly, broke through. At Verdun the Germans renewed their assaults and took Fort Vaux. This second event was earlier and nearer home. By 12 June Clemenceau was again bidding to bring Briand's Government down, the latest crisis at Verdun being one of the tools in his hand. Des Vallières had to tell Haig that GQG were asking him to begin the offensive on 25 June. Would he agree? Many of the reinforcing batteries had yet to come into position and several of the divisions had not arrived in their assembly areas. Haig rejoined that a British assault on the 25th would scarcely be in time to relieve the urgent crisis at Verdun. Nonetheless, he would give orders to begin the battle as requested. The operations staff began to draft firm orders for the armies.

When these were ready, there came a telephone call on the evening of 16 June. The crisis was over – at Verdun and in the Government. Nivelle's force[18] had halted the Germans; Briand had won a vote of confidence in secret session of the Chamber. A message from Joffre suggested 29 June or perhaps even 1 July for the assault. Haig demurred. Next day, Joffre came to see him, the positions reversed from 26 May. Now it was the British commander-in-chief who urged that they should get on with their business. His preparations had been hurried on and, despite their mastery in the air, he feared betrayal of their plans if they delayed matters. It now appeared that Foch's arrangements were incomplete. They agreed to the

---

[17] Sixth Army comprised thirteen divisions on 1 July 1916, of which five were in the line.
[18] He had assumed command at Verdun *vice* Pétain on 2 May, when the latter became central army group commander.

29th but accepted that Rawlinson and Foch must have power to delay day by day thereafter if the weather should prove unsuitable. Summer rainstorms were to be expected.

Just before they parted, Joffre spoke optimistically of advancing beyond Bapaume, some ten miles beyond the British line; Haig more cautiously mentioned that he intended to turn north towards Arras 'if all goes well and we reach Bapaume'. He did not mention that he still had in mind the possibility of switching the offensive to Flanders if they failed to break through on the Fourth Army front. He had made this clear to his own command in an instruction issued the previous day.[19]

THE OBJECTIVES

1. The Third and Fourth Armies will undertake offensive operations on the front Maricourt-Gommecourt, in conjunction with the French Sixth Army astride the Somme, with the object of relieving the pressure on the French at Verdun and inflicting loss on the enemy.

    The First and Second Armies, and the Third Army North of Gommecourt, will operate at the same time, with a view to misleading and wearing out the enemy and preventing him from sending reinforcements to the scene of the main operations.

2. The various objectives of the Fourth Army operations are described below:

    (a) *First objective*. To seize and consolidates position on the Pozières ridge extending from the vicinity of Montauban to the River Ancre, so as to secure good observation over the ground to the eastward of that ridge. Simultaneous with the above, to seize and consolidate a good position between the River Ancre and Serre, so as to cover the left flank of the operations south of that river.

    (b) *Second objective*. Having secured a position on the Pozières ridge, as described above, to turn that position to the best account against hostile troops, This may be accomplished in different ways, depending on how the battle develops:

    (i) The enemy's resistance may break down, in which case our advance will be pressed eastwards far enough to enable our

---

[19] GHQ, OAD, 12 of 16 June 1916 (*OH, 1916*, Vol I, Appendix 13).

cavalry to push through into the open country beyond the enemy's prepared lines of defence. Our object will then be to turn northwards, taking the enemy's lines in flank and reverse, the bulk of the cavalry cooperating on the outer flank of this operation while suitable detachments should be detailed to cover the movement from any offensive of the enemy from the east. For the latter purpose the line Bapaume-high ground east of Mory – high ground west of Croisilles – Monchy-le-Preux is of tactical importance. The front gained between the Rivers Somme and Ancre must meanwhile be maintained by part of the forces available.

(ii) Alternatively, after gaining our first objective as described at (a) above, we may find that a further advance eastwards is not advisable. In that case the most profitable course will probably be to transfer our main efforts rapidly to another portion of the British front, but leaving a sufficient force on the Fourth Army front to secure the ground gained, to beat off counter-attacks, and to keep the enemy fully employed. For the last-mentioned purpose further local offensives will probably be necessary in order to continue the battle, to compel the enemy to use up all his reserves, and to prevent him from withdrawing them elsewhere. Such local offensives might take the form of attack on hostile strong points in the front of the Fourth Army with a view to improving the position held, or of a move northwards in cooperation with the right of the Third Army against the enemy still holding the defences in front of the latter.

3. The dates of the commencement of the bombardment and of the day of assault will shortly be fixed and will be notified to Armies.

There was to be no further wavering concerning time and place of the offensive; or, for Rawlinson, doubt as to the features his army was to capture. Almost fifty years later, with a second world war between us and the event, Haig's OAD 12 may strike us as being too late in its strategic direction, too detailed in its tactical instructions to Fourth Army Commander. But we should bear in mind that this was the fashion of the time; above all, an inheritance of the British military whose commanders-in-chief had had no experience whatsoever of handling large forces in the field so that the task of giving tactical – as opposed to strategic – orders normally fell within their purview. Thus we may excuse Haig for telling an army commander to capture a spur or a ridge. At the same time his protagonists must accept that, in the giving of such orders, Haig bears the responsibility of their consequences.

One other point should perhaps be stressed here: the prospect of switching the offensive to Second Army sector if Fourth Army failed to achieve a breakthrough. Again, there is a flash of strategic imagination. 'Alternatively, after gaining our first objective... we may find that a further advance eastwards is not advisable. In that case the most profitable course will probably be to transfer our main efforts rapidly to another portion of the British front...' *'Rapidly'* – the italics are mine – here is the sign that Haig recognised his ability to keep the strategic initiative, to deliver the powerful second blow while the enemy reserves were still flocking to parry the first. The labour was there in First and Second Armies to complete the road and railway construction and the dumping of ammunition and supplies. The French railway system was adequate to the task of moving swiftly British reserves from Picardy to Flanders. The possibility of an exceptional strategic success was maturing; and was recognised.

With these high considerations in Haig's mind, it is time to study the soldiers whose destiny furned on his decision.

CANNON FODDER AND CANNON

We hear it said often of the Great War that 'the flower of British manhood fell on the Somme.' Remarkably, for a popular generalisation, this is true.

On 7 August 1914 – the day after he took office as Secretary of State for War – Kitchener issued his famous call for volunteers. He planned to raise immediately 200,000 men, ultimately not less than 1,000,000, while the Regular Army held the line.

He repudiated much of the reserve army structure so painstakingly prepared by Haldane. He ignored the necessity for a controlled inflow of men which maintained posts essential to industry, agriculture and communications. He overlooked the problem of housing, kitting, feeding, training this colossal recruitment.

Perhaps even he was surprised by the immediate response to his appeal. Recruiting offices were choked by men of all classes, ages, shapes, sizes and standards of fitness, overtaken for the most part by a passionate patriotism. The majority had to be sent home to come back later. Faithfully they returned. Although many were discarded on account of age or physique, a host remained, eager to serve their country on the battlefield. Yet the means were not to hand to prepare them. The regular units of the BEF could not find enough trained men to make good their losses in the field; thus there were few to spare as instructors for the 'New Armies'. A valuable supplement was found in officers on leave from India, who were commanded to remain at home. Officers, warrant and non-commissioned officers long since retired or invalided were able, after personal agitation, to make a contribution – Kitchener had initially rejected their services – former cadets of the Officers Training Corps at public schools were commissioned *faute de mieux*, and a few cadres were obtained from the Territorial Force which remained otherwise under-employed. One of the more fortunate of the new infantry battalions had three 'trained' officers – a commanding officer of sixty-three (he had retired well before the Boer War), a regular subaltern with one leg badly broken in a riding accident, and a quartermaster retired in 1907 who was stone deaf. Another was commanded by a warrant officer for seventy days, there being no other trained soldier in a unit of 600 men. A battery of artillery was formed up under command of a former infantry major of the militia whose only NCO was a band sergeant. Barrack areas, sheltering almost double their schedule of numbers, could accommodate only a fraction of the recruits; the mobilisation stores could not provide tents; everywhere, billets were requisitioned amongst shops, houses, institutions, even factories. Lacking uniforms and equipment, lacking arms but drilling with broom handles, the devoted trainees were sustained by enthusiasm.

By the beginning of 1915 a measure of order was emerging from the muddle created by Kitchener's precipitate hand. The first officer training units were teaching the rudiments of command and administration in the field to young men of secondary education. Arms schools were giving instruction to men selected as cadres. Within units, courses were being run for junior NCO's, though often amongst the earliest of these the blind were leading the blind. Men of natural administrative talent had come forward to fill such posts as orderly room or quarter-master sergeant. But amongst them all in this welter of hasty, crowded activity there were inevitably some who were not so good and some who were not only bad but vicious. Fortunately, many of this latter minority saw to it that they did not leave the home shores for active service overseas.

The paucity of trained leaders and instructors was the most serious of the many shortages during the inceptive winter of 1914 and the preparatory months of the following year. For the consequence was acceptance of a debased standard of training in every arm and at every level. In peace time, it had taken about one year to bring a recruit towards that high proficiency seen amongst the men of the BEF at Mons, on the Marne and the Aisne and, finally, at 'First Ypres'. In war, with a high level of intelligence amongst the eager recruits and the dynamic of unbounded enthusiasm, the same should have been achieved in six months, given the instructors and the equipment. If Kitchener had asked men to register with a view to being called forward when needed – as ultimately he was obliged to do – and had reinforced the BEF in France with units of the Territorial Force – as ultimately he was obliged to do – he would have created a breathing space in which to use the limited numbers of instructors, the limited quantity of warlike stores to train cadres of officers, warrant and non-commissioned officers for every type of new unit required. If this had been done, the BEF would have become by the end of 1915 a great and formidable force whose technical quality matched the moral and physical excellence of its men at the very time when the edge of German and French arms was growing blunt.

But it was not so. The men of the new divisions who began to take their place in France in the late autumn of 1915 were scarcely trained recruits. Many of their gunners owned not a single equipment – gun or howitzer – until they reached France, having performed their training on borrowed weapons. Many of the infantry had received their personal rifles in the week before departure. Now, with the French daily demanding that the British should take a greater share of the line, with the progressive break-up of the old Regular Army after 'First Ypres' due to casualties, and due to French's and Haig's prodigal habit of occupying forward trenches with swollen defensive garrisons, it became necessary to commit the new divisions to the line. Whilst it is true that they learned something of how to survive in contact with the enemy during the bitter winter, something of how to protect themselves, there were many who did not survive; and those that did learnt little else. More important, confined in these blind conditions of perpetual hardship and intermittent terror, they began to question the use made of their services towards victory.

In so far as he was able to do so in the three months preceding 1 July, Rawlinson rotated his infantry through three occupations: holding the line, labouring amongst the dumps and defence works, training.

Of all arms, the infantry and cavalry had the most time for training. It was felt that the gunners could not find better practice than in firing their equipments against the enemy – a superficially reasoned view which is open to question. Sappers of all kinds could hardly cope with the many demands on the diverse services they provided.[20] But amongst the infantry and cavalry, there were few units in location by 1 May who did not receive two to three weeks for training prior to the battle.

It is interesting to see what use was made of the time.

Both GHQ and Fourth Army Headquarters issued special tactical notes in May[21] to assist subordinate commanders in training their men for the offensive. Some of their advice was sound; much of it was not. The precepts were a paradox. On the one hand they emphasised the importance of limiting objectives for battalions and companies so as to permit their speedy capture. On the other, they persisted in the use of formations for movement which would both delay the advance and offer a prime target to the enemy. They advocated the perfection of skill-at-arms for riflemen, bombers, light machine-gun (Lewis) and, medium machine-gun (Vickers) teams towards the most effective use of these weapons while denying, by prolonged centralisation, their timely deployment to engage the enemy.

This is hindsight: so it is. It is a wisdom in the basic art of fighting which they did not possess at GHQ or in the army headquarters along the front because the senior men had no first-hand experience of company or even battalion warfare in the trenches. Some had never commanded a rifle

---

[20] The Royal Engineers in the battle zone were employed both in assault engineering and 'works' functions: camp structures, water, etc. They also ran the Army Signal Service.

[21] *OH, 1916*, Vol. I, Appendices 17 and 18.

[22] Lieut-General H H Wilson, commanding IV Corps, was a notorious example.

company in peace[22]; many of those busily engaged in giving advice were not infantry soldiers at all. We cannot blame the masters for not knowing, but must regret that none was great enough to break out of the bonds of his past to analyse what was going wrong, what was needed to put matters right,[23] Thus many of the precious days given over to training were used in teaching men to form up in ordered, dressed ranks in line, column or mass. First would come the assault wave, then the supports, ready to consolidate the gains of the assault, last the reserves to exploit success or guard the flanks. Distances between men in a rank would be two to three paces, between ranks in the assault wave at most 100 yards. The importance of the troops remaining 'above ground' once they had left their own forward trenches was mentioned on a number of occasions. The two most important tips were touched on briefly and but once.

> ...occasions may arise where the rapid advance of some lightly equipped men on some particular part of the enemy's defences may turn the scale.[24]
> ...small columns, which can make full use of the folds of the ground to cover their advance, are preferable during the preliminary stages of the advance.[25]

In many cases, divisions dug trench works behind the line to resemble the positions which the close study of maps and air photographs warned them they would meet in the offensive.

Despite compensation French farmers protested angrily at this misuse of their fields and woods. Some brigade and divisional rehearsal exercises were carried out on replicas of the German defence system marked out in white tape.

In between these events the soldiers practised their weapon skills. But a man does not acquire expertise by odd hours here and there in instruction, interspersed by occasional bursts of frenzied firing in a trench attack. It takes months of careful, progressive training before he has that feel for the weapon so that, however dark the night, when he picks it up it settles instinctively into his hand where he knows the weight and balance of it as

[23] A tactical investigation staff had been established at GHQ in December 1915, but its terms of reference were too narrow.
[24] *OH, 1916*. Vol. I, Appendix 18, para. 2.
[25] *Ibid.*, para. 23.

if it were one of his own limbs – so that, however critical the moment, he holds the weapon steady, aligns his sights, operates the trigger with sure unhurried movements to project the bullet unerringly into the mark. During these last few days a rapid-fire competition was held for individual shots. The winner succeeded in firing twelve rounds into the target at 200 yards in one minute. Before the war, recruits were able to fire fifteen rounds per minute into the target at 300 yards at the end of their course; first-class shots and marksmen often reached thirty. The training of the 'New Armies' had been too little and now it was too late.

In the matter of cannon, the BEF were better provided for in the Somme offensive than at any time previously. This is not to say that their problems in the matter of artillery support had been solved by the beginning of the offensive.

The four British divisions had come to France armed with 18-pounders – field guns firing 18-pound shells[26] – and 4-5-inch howitzers. These were backed up by a medium gun, the 60-pounder. There was no general provision for heavy guns or howitzers with the field army; no case had been made for their inclusion by the General Staff. This was not entirely a matter of the uniformed element in the War Office being blind or careless; as ever, in peacetime, they were hindered by lack of money. In order to obtain funds for mobilisation stocks of all sorts, it had been necessary to obtain agreement with the Treasury and the Foreign Office as to the sort of war which might involve a British expeditionary force in Europe. The final agreement foresaw four infantry divisions and one of cavalry in the field for at least two months during which four major battles might be fought, each lasting three days. Arms, ammunition, equipment and supplies were stockpiled against this contingency.

In the matter of artillery ammunition, the Treasury had earlier accepted the recommendation of Sir Francis Mowatt's committee on war reserve stocks and manufacturing capacity.

This had sat in the latter stages of the second Boer War to suggest what provision should be made for an expeditionary force of six infantry divisions and one cavalry division overseas – not necessarily in Europe – and their modest recommendations became official policy in 1904. It remained policy despite the possibility of British participation in a

---

[26] The RHA batteries, which supported the cavalry, were equipped with the 13-pounder.

European war, when a massed enemy army of the most modern type would be encountered, and the introduction of the quick-firing field gun which offered a means of dealing with such a foe. In reply to demands for an increase in reserves of shells, the finance branch thought it reasonable to say that whilst they realised the enemy in Europe was more formidable than a colonial savage or a *voortrekker*, the provision they had agreed upon had been for a force of six divisions whilst the new contingency would employ four. Notwithstanding the nature of the foe and the quick-firing gun to help deal with him, the War Office still had two divisions' complement of shells to redress the balance. Faced clearly with a prolonged argument, the General Staff did not pursue the matter, deciding to pursue another urgent need: small arms ammunition reserves for war in Europe. Of course, the war did not begin or continue as any of the belligerents had foreseen, not least in the expenditure of artillery ammunition. The German General Staff were as much surprised by the heavy consumption of shells as the French and British. All had drastically to revise their system of production.

In 1915 supply of shells was for a time exceeded by expenditure, and the buffer of reserves dwindled alarmingly. The protests of Sir John French and a newspaper campaign in London gave rise to a complete rationalisation of heavy industry at home, when at last production was geared to the needs of a nation at war. The dynamic Lloyd George, the first Minister of Munitions, promised to end shortages once and for all.

Yet it was not only a matter of more shells. Thanks to Lloyd George's genius in the selection of subordinates, his energy and talent for organisation, shell production soared. There was less success in the production of fuses; often tens of thousands of shells lay idle in a stock-pile awaiting these engines of calculated detonation. And there was an urgent need to produce the types of shell – high explosive or shrapnel – in the correct proportion. In this context, the output of heavy and very heavy guns and howitzers was far from adequate. It is scarcely credible that, for a time in 1915, the War Office attempted to hinder the Ministry of Munitions in its endeavours to expand the production of heavy ordnance.[27] Perhaps because of the departmental squabbles, both ministries overlooked the fact that the new guns in production were consistently outranged by

---

[27] See D Lloyd George, *War Memoirs* (Ivor Nicholson & Watton, London), Vol II, pp. 557-564.

those of the enemy. Thus, British counter-battery fire could never be wholly effective.

At the other end of the scale, the Minister and his staff were able to hasten the acceptance and production of the Stokes light (3-inch) mortar. Prior to October 1914 the British Army had not possessed such a weapon. The demands from the trenches for a simple bomb-throwing device were urgent and insistent, however, and a variety of inventions were tested before the end of the first year of war. The most satisfactory was the conventional steel tube into which the bomb was dropped tail first. At the enclosed bottom end, a striker pierced the firing cartridge in the base of the bomb, throwing it up and out of the tube at a high angle, from which ultimately it dropped; directly into the enemy trench. Strictly speaking, it was not an artillery equipment at all but, as a sensible working arrangement, the gunners took on the heavier calibres, the infantry the Stokes 3-inch. Unfortunately it was decided to organise the latter by companies, one being allotted to each infantry brigade headquarters. Whilst sections were certainly sent into the forward trenches, they were not directly available to the battalion or, better, company commander for training as an integral part of his force. Instead of supplying a crude but intimate form of immediate artillery support to the infantry sub-unit, they tended to be a part of the overall fire support organisation – something supplied by 'them' rather than 'us'.

Behind the trenches along the Ancre and above the Somme, the diverse reinforcing batteries came into line through May and June. There was no problem in deploying the field guns and howitzers – indeed, they were used to frequent changes of gun line to avoid counter-battery fire – they were light and manageable behind the horses. Provided that the ground was reasonably firm, there was little difficulty with the mediums.

But the movement of the heavies required much care and forethought. Those concealed amongst the woods behind the Ancre needed open rides to drive in. Some of the very heavy guns required the services of a light railway. By mid-June twenty 6-inch, one 9.2-inch and one 12-inch guns were in position with 104 6-inch, sixty-four 8-inch, sixty 9.2-inch, eleven 12-inch, six 15-inch howitzers in or moving into their final places. Close by, the first requirement of shells was rising in stacks on the gun line.

The gunners were under no illusions as to the work ahead of them.

Whilst the forward observing officers with their signallers might be in the more immediate danger in the foremost line with the infantry, those on the gun line would be preparing, moving, loading shells into the breech hour after hour for many days. The 18-pounder projectiles would be fed in by hand, the heavies by chain and pulley. It would be exhausting work, with the ever-present hazard of a premature dropping just short of the muzzle or bursting in breech or barrel.

At last all was ready. All signal cables had been tested to the forward telephones, all observing stations and posts were manned. The fire plan, issued by Fourth Army on 5 June, had been broken down to corps and divisional artillery tasks, related carefully to a programme of tactical times and ammunition expenditure. The night of 23 June was quiet, the air cool after an afternoon of thunderstorms. Most of the batteries were able to rest in their bivouacs amongst the trees or in the shelters made amongst ammunition boxes. Reveille was before dawn on the 24th but the light was long in coming up: heavy rain clouds obscured the sun. By 7 am, the first of the heavies was loaded and at that hour the gun position officer gave his order: 'Fire!'

A 200-pound shell sped, spinning, across the wire.

THE OTHER SIDE OF THE WIRE

'At first,' wrote Falkenhayn, 'we had practically no explanation of the total absence of relief offensives on the part of the enemy on the Western front during the first weeks of the operations on the Meuse [at Verdun].'[28] All the same, he had no doubt that a relief offensive would be mounted sooner or later and, since almost all his resources free of the trenches were committed to the Crown Prince's battle, he was anxious to divine where the blow would fall and when.

He was attracted to the view that the French would attack in Alsace-Lorraine; but this was contested. His attention was directed to the Arras sector, partly because of the continued identification of new divisions in the line there – some of the 'New Army' formations obtaining battle experience – partly because he was sensitive concerning Lille and Flanders. At midday on 6 April Falkenhayn telephoned Crown Prince Rupprecht of Bavaria, whose Sixth Army held the sector, concerning a disruptive attack

[28] Falkenhayn, *op. cit.*, p. 239.

against British preparations. He '...offered us heavier artillery than we'd asked for but ...only four divisions, instead of the eight we had requested. Does he think he can haggle with us...?' asked the Prince in his diary. The matter rested.

In May, while Falkenhayn watched developments reported by Sixth Army, General Fritz von Below, commander of the Second Army to the south, began to feel that the offensive might be directed against his front. As this stretched from Noyon on the Oise to Gommecourt inclusive, and was held with only three corps, he was naturally sensitive concerning enemy movements. Now his aviators reported construction of new broad-gauge railway lines, several new highways behind Albert and what looked to be new battery positions close to the Ancre. Significantly, too, aerial scouting was becoming difficult due to concentrations of British attack aircraft against them.[29] Von Below emphasised the weakness of his position, which allowed of no divisional reserve worth the name along his front. Preoccupied with Verdun and inclined to believe in Arras as the sector of attack, Falkenhayn sent him additional labour to construct his third line of defence and a detachment of 8-inch howitzers captured from the Russians.

The lack of divisional and corps reserves on Second Army front was due principally to Falkenhayn's concept of the defence. Warning army commanders in February that the Verdun offensive must stimulate allied counter-attacks elsewhere, Falkenhayn advised, since he had no reserves to offer them, that they should not surrender a metre of ground to the enemy.

If a position was lost in the first rush of an attack, it must be retaken instantly. The Chief of the General Staff believed that soldiers would fight the more tenaciously in defence over a long period if their orders were to hold on to the last man and the last round. Because of this policy the trenches of the first line were heavily garrisoned.

Having the bulk of their men within range of the enemy's divisional artillery, the German commanders were more than ever concerned with defence works. It was for this reason that the chalk beneath the complex of trenches had been honey-combed with shafts and galleries leading to deep dugouts.

Gradually, during the long period of quiet, huge dormitories had been

---

[29] See OH, *The War in the Air*, Vol. II, pp. 200-201.

cut beneath the first and, to a lesser extent, the second line defences along the front. For the officers single rooms were provided, often with planked floors, bed, chair, table and sometimes a chest of drawers. The steep stairways leading up to the surface provided a supply of fresh air complemented by narrow ventilation shafts, reinforced with steel piping. All subterranean roofs were heavily propped and trussed. Within the depths, iron rations and mineral water were stored against a prolonged bombardment.

During the third week in May, Below and his chief of staff, Grünert, became convinced that some form of offensive was in preparation against them. On the 25th they proposed a 'preventive attack' along the high ground immediately north and south of the Somme; and when this was rejected as being beyond their resources, they amended it to an attack across the Ancre valley between Ovillers and St Pierre Divion. While Falkenhayn approved preparations being made, he could send nothing more than an artillery regiment in reinforcement. On 6 June Below gave Falkenhayn his firm view that: 'The preparations of the British in the area Serre-Gommecourt, as well as the increase by twenty-nine emplacements of artillery in the past few days, detected by air photographs, lead to the conclusion that the enemy thinks first and foremost of attacking the projecting angles of Fricourt and Gommecourt. In view of the ground and the lie of the trenches, it is quite conceivable that he will attempt only to pin the front of 26th Reserve Division[30] by artillery fire, but will not make a serious attack. This possibility is already provided for by the disposition of the forces of XIV Reserve Corps.'

South of the Somme, he reported the appearance of three new French divisions in the line. 'To oppose them, XVII Corps is too weak, both in infantry and guns. Even against an enemy attack on a narrow front made only as a diversion the Guard Corps (the southernmost) is also too thin; it is holding 36 kilometres with twelve regiments, and behind it there are no reserves of any kind.[31]

Brussilov's offensive had now opened with such surprising success in the south-east and Falkenhayn had to send five divisions from the western front to Galicia. There was nothing to spare to permit Below to test his supposition.

[30] In view of the strength of their defences in this sector.
[31] H Wendt, *Verdun, 1916* (Mittler & Sotm, Berlin), p. 173.
[32] See *OH, 1916*, Vol. I, pp. 81-85.

Yet testing was hardly necessary. Despite the extensive efforts of Haig's camouflage department,[32] the evidence began to accrue. German scout aeroplanes were slipping through the aggressive patrols of the Royal Flying Corps, and evading the 'archie' shells thrown up by the 13-pounders below. The sausage observation balloons still flew daily, though attacks against these were intensifying. The German observation stations along the high ridge, equipped with powerful telescopes, swept much of the Ancre valley. The accretion of men, animals, guns, vehicles was not to be hidden.

Espionage corroborated the suspected imminence of a great offensive. An agent in the Hague reported the British military attache as saying that the offensive in the west would begin next week. This was received on the 14th. Earlier there had been a report from England that a member of the Government, Mr Arthur Henderson, had asked the staff of a munitions factory not to query why the Whit holiday was being stood over. 'How inquisitive we are! It should suffice that we ask for a postponement of the holidays and to the end of July. This fact should speak volumes.' Curiously, this speech was reported in the censored national press next morning and hence became public knowledge in Europe. Crown Prince Rupprecht whose diary displays his interest in British newspapers, noted on 10 June, '...'This fact should speak volumes'. It certainly does so speak, it contains the surest proof that there will be a great British offensive before long.'

His entry for the 15th notes that Falkenhayn continued to look towards Alsace-Lorraine for a joint Franco-British offensive. The Chief of the General Staff had accompanied the Emperor to Crown Prince Rupprecht's headquarters on that day, when Falkenhayn explained that he could not see the French and British turning north to devastate Artois and Flanders – the logical outcome of success on the Somme. Hence, they would prefer to attack into German territory in Alsace-Lorraine. The operations branch of Supreme Headquarters thought that the enemy would launch a secondary attack at Lens. 'Why just at Lens?' the prince asks. 'According to our information, there is no basis for such a view.'

On the 19th he noted that four British divisions had been shifted from his own front to that of Second Army, and that the French XXX Corps had come up from Belfort to reinforce XX Corps on the Somme.[33] He closed with the remark that, 'There can be no further doubt that a great French

---

[33] In fact, XXXV Corps.

offensive is about to begin against Second Army.'

'A particularly reliable agent' reported on 23 June that the offensive was imminent, though his Sixth Army would be subjected to a demonstration and artillery fire. Early the next morning the barrage began, continuing at intervals through the day.

91st Reserve Regiment took prisoner a wounded soldier north-east of Gommecourt on the night 23rd/24th who told them that an attack was due in a few days. At the same time the German military attache in Madrid reported that the offensive would begin on 1 July – a date confirmed by another agency. None of the senior commanders were surprised therefore when the Allied bombardment began on the 24th, though to deceive the enemy, preparatory activity continued intermittently up and down the entire front of the BEF. Gas and smoke clouds were released from cylinders as the wind offered opportunity; digging and deployment of men and vehicles were demonstrated in some part of every sector from Flanders to the Somme. The Royal Flying Corps began systematically to attack German observation balloons with rockets and phosphorus bombs, and to fly an intensive sortie rate in scouting, artillery spotting and fighting to prevent the passage of enemy aeroplanes over Allied trenches. But the flying programme was hampered by the deteriorating weather. Prince Rupprecht and Below made careful comparison of the British activity day by day, noting that each was being raided by night regularly, but agreeing that the balance of evidence was for an offensive against Second Army from Fricourt salient to Gommecourt inclusive. Falkenhayn was perhaps the only principal misled by Haig's deception plan but he was also misled by his own appreciation. For although he inclined now, under the weight of evidence, to the expectation of an attack north of the Somme, he reaffirmed almost daily that it would be on Sixth Army front. Even so, he made no effort to place a general reserve of any sort in its rear. Neither Second nor Sixth Army were covered.

These high matters were unknown to the German soldiers manning the line. By day those responsible for open trenches remained in their deep dugouts while the drumfire of the enemy guns throbbed and roared overhead. When it ceased, they had to hasten upwards, expecting to meet the enemy assault. By night, when the guns were not firing at them, they manned their positions with about one-third of the men permanently on watch against patrols and raiders while gaps in the wire were patched up to the limit of the stores held forward and the worst of the shell damage was repaired in the trench lines. Often they could do no more than pile up the loose chalk and earth along the original parapet or connect one great shellhole with another to maintain a continuous defence. In the village fortresses, and in the extensive redoubts carved from the earth at other key points, sandbags, timber and steel sheeting withstood a great deal of the fire. The most serious consequence to all was the fearful din and danger all around them which caught, day after day, the unwary and the unlucky in death or wounds, the inability to evacuate many of those needing medical treatment from the fuggy dugouts; the inaccessibility of the battalions to the ration and ammunition parties – as yet there was adequate ammunition but rations began to run out on the 27th – and the added tension of waiting, waiting, waiting for an offensive and wondering whether, in the clash of battle, one would survive.

Behind the first line of trenches, the field gunners shifted their battery positions by night as often as possible when sure that the circling British and French aircraft had spotted their lines. Others remained quiescent. Behind the second and, in a few cases, the pegged but undug third line, the long-range guns of the heavy artillery swelled the fire upon British trenches, roads, railways and billets; more especially upon the British batteries which, outranged, could not effectively destroy these tormentors across the wire.

OVERTURE AND BEGINNERS

Throughout June Haig's doubts of success waned. He was restored to his characteristic optimism.

He was delighted, though no less surprised than others, with the success of Brussilov's offensive. The spectacular feat of two wide gaps broken open on a front of 300 miles made Third and Fourth Army's 20-odd seem small beer; and the Russians had done this with minimal artillery support, far less than, yard for yard, Rawlinson had available; though admittedly the enemy in the Carpathians was second-rate. Then Joffre and, later, Foch, contributed to Haig's rise in spirits. The former pointed out that they were about to do to the enemy what he had himself inflicted on the French at Verdun: the blasting of his defences out of existence as a prelude to the infantry advance. The French commander-in-chief made it clear, once more, that these tactics had almost succeeded against the fortress region. Here, on either side of the Somme, the ground offered greater tactical opportunities than the Meuse heights – this questionable assertion was not challenged, so far as I can discover – and the enemy had no natural line of defence on which to fall back behind the Bapaume-Péronne road. Foch seems to have regained his former ebullience after seeing General Fayolle's final preparations unfolding. Certainly, he had provided the French Sixth Army with excellent resources in artillery, 117 heavy batteries being on line to support an initial assault by five divisions. South of the Somme the enemy was believed to be both weak in infantry for defence and in artillery. The enthusiasm of his old corps, XX,[34] which was to operate immediately on Rawlinson's right on the north bank, matched that of I Colonial Corps and the XXXV to the south. Foch was able to offer Fourth Army sixteen 220-mm howitzers, twenty-four 120-mm guns and sixty of the famous quick-firing 75's, the latter being disposed to shoot gas shells of which, as yet, the British had none.[35]

Looking back to Loos, the operations branch at GHQ saw that the ammunition allotment for the battle in 1915 was less than a fifth of that available for the Somme. But when Kiggell, the chief of staff, mentioned this to Haig, he was reminded by the commander-in-chief that they had failed to make the best of their opportunities there. With the immense resources now to hand, there must be no question of missing the chance, however fleeting, of a real breakthrough.

Rawlinson and Haig had seven or eight conversations on this subject between 11 and 28 June. Two formal memoranda were issued besides.[36] Haig kept on thinking of new contingencies which he should discuss with Rawlinson; the vulnerability of the Fricourt salient and Montauban spur was under-estimated by Fourth Army, he feared; would they be able to follow up success quickly enough here, or elsewhere, to engage the enemy second line without respite if opportunity offered? The matter of control of the mobile forces for the break-out was not going to be easy. Could Rawlinson command his army effectively with corps pushing open flanks

[34] The 'Iron Corps', commanded by Foch at Nancy at the out-break of war.
[35] Gas shells – as distinct from containers – had been asked for by Sir John French in 1915. The first 10,000, filled with tear gas reached France in April 1916. The great majority of gas shells fired on the Somme front throughout the battle were of French origin.
[36] See *OH, 1916*, Vol. I, Appendices 14 and 15.

in different directions and several others moving out into open country? It was agreed between them that it could not be done: an intermediate headquarters at least must be available for the mobile elements. Haig decided that this should be styled HQ Reserve Army, and Gough should be the commander.

Aged forty-four, a man of quick wit and a great deal of gay charm, Hubert Gough seemed to many of his contemporaries to be marked for high military office. He was a cavalryman, his force would be primarily cavalry, and he had already been training a reserve corps behind the front for a break-out. A small supplement to his headquarters was allowed, principally in communications as so much would depend upon speed of information and the passing of orders. The commander-in-chief was confident that Gough's quick brain and acknowledged impatience with laggards would minimise delays in response to opportunities. Less optimistic, Rawlinson suggested that he might, in any case, make good use of Gough and his staff. Should the long Fourth Army Front become staggered, it would assist control if HQ Reserve Army should take responsibility for the two corps on the northern wing, on either side of the Ancre, though acting under Rawlinson's orders.

Saturday 17 June was the day on which Joffre came to suggest 1 July for the attack; and accepted finally that they could not postpone it further – weather apart – beyond the 29th. Next day, Sunday, Haig saw Rawlinson after church to suggest that they were being prodigal perhaps in the expenditure of ammunition in the preliminary bombardment. There was a further study of the map relative to the cavalry. On Wednesday the 21st Haig confirmed their previous discussions and the system to be used in the break-out. He was away for a day or so then, visiting other sectors, but returned to meet the French Prime Minister who came from Paris on the Saturday evening. Did they still think the British would hold back? The object of M Briand's visit seemed to be to urge the opening of the offensive to relieve Verdun, and Haig reassured him. On Sunday 25 June 'DH' went to his Church of Scotland morning service to hear Padre Duncan preach. His text, Haig's diary records, was '...a verse from Chronicles 'Yes, I will go in the power of the Almighty God'. He pointed out that we must look upon God as ever present with us, and that His plans rule the Universe. Consequently, whatever we do, we must try and go with the Lord. We are merely tools in

His hands, used for a special purpose. And he quoted a saying of Abraham Lincoln's when asked if he was sure the Lord was with him.

He replied that the important point was that 'he should be on the side of the Lord'. Mr Duncan also told the story of how before the attack began, the Scots knelt down in prayer on the battlefields of Bannockburn in 1314...'

Forward, the guns were rumbling for Haig's own battle. After two stormy days, Sunday the 25th was a fine, warm day, the sun scarcely obscured at all by cloud. Overhead, the airmen of IV Brigade, RFC scouted and spotted continuously for the guns. German intruders did not slip past and it was on this day that they set fire to three enemy observation balloons watching Fourth Army front. Others, as yet undamaged, were hastily drawn down to earth. From the circling Moranes and BE2c's came details of 102 enemy batteries. The British gunners earmarked for counter-bombardment made reply. Monday the 26th was a day of showers with bright intervals. The wind favoured gas and smoke which drifted over the enemy trenches from varying points of the British lines from before dawn until the late afternoon. Some of the enemy guns brought down defensive fire in front of their wire, perhaps fearing a local attack but there was little other apparent reaction. In the afternoon the RFC flew photographic sorties extensively, seeking information as to the damage wrought by the bombardment on trenches and wire.

Dull days followed. Starting on 'U' day the 24th, the 27th and 28th were 'X' and 'Y' respectively. Next morning, they should assault. But the evidence of night raids and patrols, daylight observation and aerial photography tended to indicate that the heavy bombardment had yet to achieve its object. The gunners admitted their dissatisfaction. They depended so much for correction of fire on the RFC; and the pilots and observers had been hampered by low clouds on Saturday, Monday, Tuesday and now again on Wednesday. On 'U' day, for example, they had registered only forty targets against a requirement of 117. The programme had remained progressively in arrears.

In such circumstances, there was no choice but to postpone 'Z', the assault day. The decision was taken at 11 o'clock on the sombre Wednesday morning and the French, who had proposed 1 July as their choice, were not ill-pleased. Thursday and Friday would now become 'Y1' and 'Y2'.

They would assault on the Saturday.

The news of the change of date took some little time to disseminate. Its consequences were felt most by those men who had already spent several days under shellfire in wet trenches, where chalky walls crumbled into slime with every fresh shower. Fortunately, many forward battalions had been able to withdraw, leaving a reserve rifle company in the line. In some cases mortar or machine-gun companies did duty, but even those out were not far removed from the gross discomfort of the firing line.

Their shelter was in groundsheet bivouacs or cramped, leaking buildings in the villages behind the Ancre. Yet the sick rate actually dropped during this period; not only were fewer men sent back for sick treatment but fewer men reported sick to their regimental medical officers. Though the actual day selected as 'Z' was not known to everyone it was an open secret that it was 'any day now', and the great majority wanted to be there when it began.

'Any day now', wrote a West-Country soldier in his diary. 'This is what we expected when we joined up. A bit different from sitting in the trenches in Flanders, waiting for Jerry to shell us.'

'You may not hear from me for a bit', a corporal wrote home to Staffordshire. 'We'll be pretty busy any day now.'

An officer of 34th Division, a part of the 'New Armies', wrote: '...When one thinks about it all, or stops to analyse it, it seems an extraordinary game – the awful waste – but the only thing to do is to go on and try to biff the Boche. We are all very cheerful and confident that we shall do him in the end, and may it come soon.'

In the same division, from a field battery commander's diary:

Saturday, June 24th to June 30th, Friday. Wire cutting every day for an average of five hours per day. Also at least one special bombardment each day, and several abortive attempts to loose gas. The latter eventually went over one morning, about Wednesday. Shooting all night on approaches and wire cutting. Am living in the OP on sardines and bread

...The seven guns averaged nearly two thousand rounds per day, and are beginning to give buffer trouble; seldom more than five in action at the same time.[37] Boche prisoners say they are finding great difficulty in

[37] This refers to the buffer springs which had not been designed for such prolonged intense activity. There were insufficient spare springs to meet the demand for replacements – a situation which grew worse until January 1917.

getting food and other supplies...

At Billon Farm, behind Maricourt, a medical sergeant remarked to a doctor in the divisional advanced dressing station: 'Well, if we don't get any customers from our own men, there'll be plenty from Jerry after all these whizzbangs on him.'

Day after day they had watched 'these whizzbangs' passing over, rushing and hissing through the air to burst with a crump and a cloud of smoke in endless succession on the enemy's forward slopes or with a more distant thump behind. So many who were there remark how they were cheered by the unceasing rain of shrapnel and high explosive – chiefly the latter – upon the enemy. For they all knew in their hearts, the scattered remnant of the old Army, the Territorials, the men of the 'New Armies', veteran and novice, that at some stage they would have to get out of their trenches and go forward up on to the naked spurs north of the Ancre, or the long ridge that hung above them. Whatever their reason for being there, whatever the measure of their courage, they wanted Jerry to be thumped to pieces first.

The hours were closing to zero.

Daily the fires had grown upon the enemy ridge and behind, towards and beyond Bapaume and Combles, where the aeroplanes and kite balloons could see smoke and watch ammunition exploding.

There had been lucky shots by the enemy guns, too. Those British dumps hit by German shells had been abandoned but their stocks had been made good elsewhere; some of the stores immediately required were hidden in brigade caches in woods, half-ruined houses, hollows a few hundred yards behind the forward trenches. This work accomplished, the supply and repair services were already working shifts to keep the batteries serviced. Those sappers required for assault work left their duties on roads and bridges, by pumps, in trenches, saps and shallow galleries. Their fellows in the signal service stood ready at their telephones, with their lamps, their pigeons or their crude wireless stations, ready to tap messages to the rear or to aircraft next day, or in liaison to the French army on the right flank. The doctors and dressers sat about in the collecting and dressing stations, gauze, lint, bandages, splints, instruments, antiseptics – but no antibiotics – ready to hand. Behind, the silent empty ambulances, hidden occasionally by tactful hands from the infantry's approach routes. Along the roads the provost staff were posted beside their traffic signs, or out in security patrols looking for enemy agents disguised as peasants, seeking to redirect stragglers or to catch the occasional deserter from the line. None were reported in the returns to the provost marshal for the night 30 June/1 July.

That Friday night the fitters, riggers and armourers, RFC, serviced and patched the machines and the balloons from the day's operations – there had been a brief combat over the lines but the main damage had been caused by small arms fire from the ground – while the squadrons were briefed for next day, 'Z' day. Certain officers had been called away from IV Brigade to discuss the air photographs developed from sorties in the afternoon. These pictures, particularly those of the redoubts north and south of Thiepval, of Ovillers and its little neighbour, la Boisselle, were searched throughout the evening for scraps of new information. But it was not only in these areas that uncertainty existed. There are fears and doubts before every major attack; facts or situations, more or less important, which remain undetermined. But so much of the conflicting information here was ominous. On the bright side, they had taken prisoners from Ovillers area, from Pricourt, Mametz and the road up to Montauban, with deserters swelling the numbers. From these positions, the central and southern portions of the army front, they knew that the strain of the bombardment was telling on the enemy; iron rations and mineral water had been broken into; wounded were mounting as the gunners enticed the garrisons from the dugouts by lifting their fire, only to drop back again unexpectedly to find them lining the parapets in expectation of attack. Trench works and gun lines alike were being eroded by high explosive beyond possibility of repair. Clearly, the additional two days before 'Z' was no less of a strain on the enemy than on friends. None of the prisoners admitted to knowing the day of attack, but all wished it would come soon. On the bright side, too, great gaps had been found in the wire in the area of the Fricourt salient to the south. Through these, raiding parties had passed on several nights to find portions of the enemy trenches unoccupied. On the central position, however, immediately east of the Ancre, observers could see that many of the original belts of wire – often 40 yards deep with barbs 'as thick as a man's thumb' – remained untouched. In other places gaps had been filled

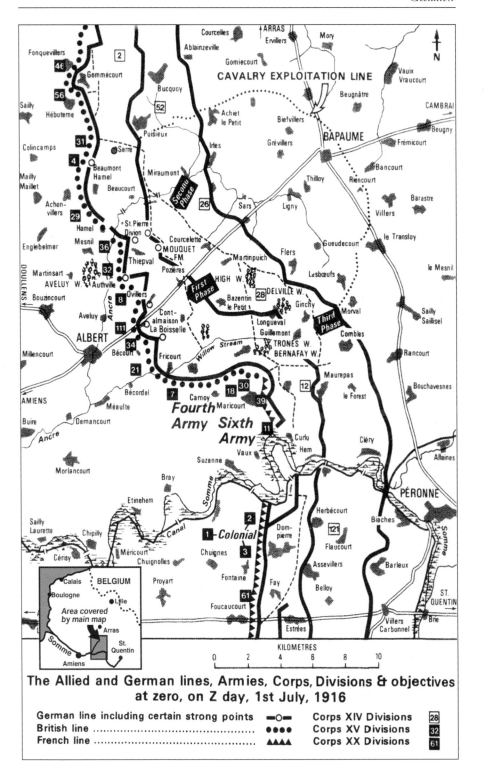

The Allied and German lines, Armies, Corps, Divisions & objectives at zero, on Z day, 1st July, 1916

German line including certain strong points ━○━	Corps XIV Divisions 28
British line .... ●●●●	Corps XV Divisions 32
French line .... ▲▲▲▲	Corps XX Divisions 61

with wired knife-rests and concertina rolls pegged down with iron pickets. North and south of Thiepval the enemy was very vigilant, reacting strongly with lights, artillery and machine-gun fire to raiders in the vicinity. Some battalions grew depressed by their inability to raid successfully. Further north, in the area of VIII Corps, the few optimistic patrol reports of 'some gaps' and 'very much damaged' were countered by 'not much damage', 'no sign of a gap anywhere', and the telling, unconscious humour of a sergeant of the 1st Inniskilling Fusiliers who remarked, 'I don't think they've been trying to cut the wire in this area.'

It was not an amusing prospect, however. The Inniskillings were in front of the Hawthorn Redoubt, by Beaumont Hamel. They were in VIII Corps. North again, in Third Army's sector, 46th Division of VII Corps faced Gommecourt, and here patrols had been searching in vain for several nights for a gap to pass through. Not only did they fail to find a gap of any size but, on the eve of the assault, one discovered a hollow, hitherto unnoticed in No Man's Land, filled with unmarked wire.

Weeks before – on 16 May – Haig's staff had issued one of the commander-in-chiefs many letters on Rawlinson's plan. The third paragraph began: '3. As regards artillery bombardment, it should be of the nature of a methodical bombardment and be continued until the officers commanding the attacking units are satisfied that the obstacles to their advance have been adequately destroyed...'[38]

The officers commanding many attacking units knew very well now that, on their own front, the wire had not been satisfactorily cut and was very much an obstacle to an advance. Brigade and divisional commanders knew it, and the photographs were available to commanders of the assault corps. Did they tell Rawlinson? It seems either they or his staff did not, except to give hints of the difficulties on the left flank. His diary on the night of 30 June contains the entry '...The artillery work during the bombardment, and the wire-cutting has been done well except in the VIII Corps, which is somewhat behindhand...'

Haig seems to have been in ignorance of the true picture:

Friday, June 30. The weather report is favourable for tomorrow. With God's help, I feel hopeful. The men are in splendid spirits. Several have said that they have never been so instructed and informed of the nature

[38] See *OH, 1916*, Vol. I, Appendix II.

of the operations before them. The wire has never been so well cut, nor the Artillery preparation so thorough. I have seen personally all the Corps Commanders and one and all are full of confidence. The only doubt I have is regarding VIII Corps (Hunter-Weston) which has had no experience in fighting in France and has not carried out one successful raid. It must be regretted that the commander-in-chief had not made searching enquiries into the reason for the failure of 'Hunter-Bunter's' command.

PART III

First Strike

ZERO

At the end of that week of uncertain weather the clouds started to disperse. The Saturday night was dark but with Sunday the stars began to appear. There was no moon. In the bivouacs and ruined billets those who had been to sleep were wakened early. Breakfast was produced. The best quarter-masters had produced porridge, bacon and beans, and hot tea with rum. Others had tea and sandwiches. Those in the trenches were wakened later. Their fare was cruder and liable to be lukewarm except where the experts in brewing had found a sheltered niche in which to boil water. Many men had had a wash and shave before last light and made do with this. A number rose early from their rest to complete a quick toilet in a mess tin. Kits were packed and checked; those in rear with packs and greatcoats dumped them with their quartermaster sergeant; men fell in and rolls were called. By companies and battalions they marched into the darkness.

The traffic arrangements were excellent. Route signs and guides were all in place. Bridges had been painted white to show up in the dim light, tapes had been laid along dark paths. Men who had been to the same trenches many times found sections of the route unrecognisable in the gloom, and were temporarily lost until they came upon some landmark, but the columns did not go astray. As the parties from the rear approached the forward positions, they were frequently led above ground, thus avoiding the wearisome trek through narrow and wet communication trenches. Few suffered by this exposure in the forward area; the German artillery fire was negligible. By 3 am all assault waves from rear bivouacs had joined those forward. When it was light, final roll call began; arms, ammunition and kit were rechecked.

All men were in 'fighting order', that is belt with bayonet, water-bottle, ammunition pouches, shoulder braces and, on the back, groundsheet and haversack – the latter filled with the mess-tin, a tinned and an iron ration plus 'the unexpired portion of the day's ration', toilet gear, 'housewife' of sewing kit, spare socks and bootlaces. All men had two gas helmets and goggles against tear gas, plus a field dressing and iodine.

Some had wirecutters, half, at least, of each company had digging tools, shovels being in the proportion of five to one of picks. These were an additional load to the entrenching tool generally carried. All riflemen had 220 rounds of .303 cartridges, half of which were stowed in the pouches, the balance in a cotton bandolier. Everyone was directed to carry two sand-bags and, in many units, either two Mills grenades or a Stokes mortar bomb. The Lewis gun teams were certainly no less laden. With his rifle charged with ammunition, weighing about 10-lb, no man carried less than 65-lb. Often additional grenades, bombs, small arms ammunition or perhaps a prepared charge[1] against obstacles, stretchers or telephone cable increased the load to 85 or 90-lb. With this gear the assault, support and reserve waves now sat waiting in the crowded trenches.

The sun rose into a clear sky. Along the valleys of the Ancre and the Somme a white mist clung to the marshes, spilling here and there into the rising re-entrants on either side. Mist, too, followed the lower course of the Willow Stream towards Fricourt, and those airmen observing the ridge saw that the woods on top were full of it. But the warm sunlight began to disperse these vapours. It was a perfect morning. Despite the din of shelling, birds could be heard singing amongst the nearby woods and out amongst the mustard in the pasture. Perhaps these morning songs would have been less audible if the intensity of the bombardment had been

---

[1] A prepared charge of explosive – usually the Bangalore torpedo, at this time an iron pipe filled with guncotton primers, used for cutting gaps in wire. This device was subsequently developed into a more powerful and manageable engine. See *History of the Corps of Royal Engineers*, Vol. V (Institution of Royal Engineers).

maintained; but it had not.

The programme shot on 'Y1' and 'Y2' was significantly lighter than that on 'U' to 'Y'. However, between 6.25 and 7am the final tasks of the preliminary programme were begun; the enemy positions were generally lost to view as almost every gun or howitzer began to shoot. The infantry more distant from the enemy trenches were seen by pilots and observers of the RFC, to emerge from their trenches and move out into No Man's Land to form up some way forward for the assault. Within the secrecy of the trenches, other parties moved down shallow galleries dug beneath or up to the enemy wire to avoid the most open or obstructed of the approaches. In deeper tunnels, miners of the Royal Engineers awaited the moment to explode the 11 mines dug beneath the enemy defences. The Stokes mortar men and the machine-gunners stood by their weapons. Zero hour approached on 'Z' day.

DIVERSION AT GOMMECOURT

While Rawlinson's Fourth Army were moving into their final assault positions, the commander of the German 2nd Guard Reserve Division reported that he was about to be attacked. This was no surprise to Below. Both he and Prince Rupprecht had expected that the salient, formed as a right angle by the village, wooded park and north-western approach would be a target of the British offensive. The manifest preparations in early June[2] had led him to reinforce the sector with 2nd Guard Reserve in the middle of the month, though he could ill-afford to commit another division to his extended line,

About 7.15 on the morning of the 1st, observation stations to the rear reported that a smoke screen was developing round the salient. However, though the bombardment had been intensified since 6.25, the fire trenches facing north-west were not being shelled. Several observers came up from the deep dugouts of the 91 Reserve Regiment, the local garrison, to see what was happening. To their front, the ground ran level to the British lines, 400-500 yards distant, and beyond to the edge of Fonquevillers village. A change in the wind blew gaps in the smoke, through which khaki figures were seen advancing. The alarm was sounded. Riflemen, machine-

2   As Third Army's attack on the Gommecourt salient was by nature of a diversion, these preparations were deliberately exposed by VII Corps. On 27 June, the corps commander told Haig: 'They know we're coming all right.'

gunners and bombers rushed up the steps to the trenches and took their places at the parapet. Rapid fire was ordered.

The Tommies 'advanced quietly as at manoeuvres'. Though the wire was extensively torn to the front it was indifferently gapped. Bunching to pass through these few openings or while halted to scan the fence for others, the German small-arms fire hit them with terrible effect. To those who took refuge in shell holes, the bombers paid attention with rifle grenades until the mortar-men and gunners brought down their fire.

The centre of 91 Reserve had not been as quick to ascend as the right, however. A little after 8 o'clock it became clear that fragments of the British assault companies had got into their trenches – some had even penetrated to the support line. While a strong force of machine-guns was left on the parapet, the intruders were hunted down. By the end of the morning the German trenches were clear apart from a few scattered survivors who, after hiding for some hours, returned to their own lines to say misguidedly that others were holding out. A last excursion was made to contact them in darkness by their friends, the Lincolns and Leicesters,[3] but it failed, like those earlier, on the wire.

Southward it was a different story. The smoke screen and bombardment continued to deny effective observation of the British trenches and the German wire. Through this white cloud the four assault battalions of the British 56th (London) Division were moving quickly, sometimes losing their way in the heavy smoke but rarely stopped by the well-gapped wire[4] or the German artillery which began to fire on No Man's Land and the British trenches. 55 Reserve Regiment who held Gommecourt village and park, were unconscious of the imminent danger, as were the elements of 170 Reserve on their left. The forward companies remained safely below ground as the London Riflemen[5] jumped into their wrecked fire trenches. Too late, they stumbled to the surface to be captured and to see other Tommies hastening on to the almost empty support line. Shortly there was a close-quarter battle with the hastily emerging garrison in the reserve. In two hours the 56th Division had taken almost every one of its objectives.

Briefly overwhelmed by their success, the regimental commander of 170

[3]   1/5th Leicesters and 1/5th Lincolns who had not been committed to the battle.
[4]   The division had made sure of having gaps by sending out parties with Bangalore torpedoes to the enemy wire on the previous night.
[5]   The London Rifle Brigade and Queen Victoria's Rifles were first across, the Rangers and 1/14th London Scottish, also assault battalions, having a greater distance to cover.

Reserve made preparations to counter-attack. The enemy had penetrated 2,000 yards deep into the trenches but the powerful Kern redoubt was holding firm and to some extent preventing expansion eastward. He arranged with 55 Reserve that they should attack with four companies from this area while he struck the Tommies on their right and centre. Seven of his own companies were collected while two others were obtained from 2nd Guard Reserve,[6] all of whom were completely fresh. In the early afternoon this strong manoeuvre began to force its way through the British barricades. The Londoners were now running short of men and were soon desperate for ammunition, particularly grenades. All day they had been signalling for reinforcement, both directly across No Man's Land and to contact aircraft of IV Brigade. Ground and air observers saw again and again the signalling lamps send 'SOS bombs!' Several attempts had been made to reach them but the enemy barrage, intensified when news of the incursion was broadcast, prevented movement forward. Little by little the tide turned for the Tommies; the khaki ebbed; the field grey flowed into the forward trenches until at last all were re-taken. The last survivors clung to shell holes in No Man's Land until darkness permitted their return to the start line of the day.

'My God!' cried an officer of the Queen Victoria's Rifles when he heard the news of the 46th Division's disaster on the left. 'Then did we all fail?'

They had not failed at all. Their task had not been to capture Gommecourt, perhaps the strongest position in the sector, but to divert upon themselves 'the fire of artillery and infantry which might otherwise be directed against the left flank of the main attack near Serre'.

They had certainly achieved this end. In view of the task of their comrades to the south, it was as well that they had.

BEAUMONT HAMEL

Four miles south of Gommecourt, VIII Corps began the offen-sive in the last mists of the morning. Their positions were cut into the southern extremity of the ridge on which Gommecourt stands, in an area where two main spur lines run down in rough parallel south-east towards the Ancre. Halfway up the re-entrant between the spurs is Beaumont Hamel.

[6] 56th Division's attack was on either side of a German divisional boundary. 170 Regiment was in 52nd Division, the remainder of Gommecourt salient in the 2nd Guard Reserve. The incident provides an excellent example of the Germans' flexibility and speed in grouping and re-grouping.

Of all the corps tasks undertaken that morning, General Hunter-Weston's was the most difficult; for whichever way he tackled it, the ground lay overwhelmingly in the enemy's favour. To facilitate and protect the main advance, he was to squeeze open Fourth Army's left flank by forcing the enemy northward through the ring contour of Serre village. To do so, he was obliged to capture both spurs on either side of Beaumont Hamel and the fortified village itself. A main attack along the northern spur would have carried him round in rear of Beaumont Hamel, isolating it, but his left flank would have been completely open to Serre. This was the left-hand approach open to him. A move down the centre would have taken his assault force directly into the re-entrant, concentrating it as a target for almost every heavy weapon the enemy possessed. On the right the approach would lead his battalions down a forward slope directly on to the village and the lower end of the re-entrant descending to the Ancre. None were attractive propositions. As a fourth method, he might have attacked Serre directly but this would hardly have yielded the quick result desired. In the circumstances he decided to make his main effort on both ridges simultaneously with a linking force on the re-entrant. To occupy the defenders of Serre and commence their eviction, he detailed one division, the 31st, to wheel left upon it as the advance progressed along the northern spur. With 4th Division left and 29th right in the main attack, he was able to dispose the 48th[7] in reserve.

The trenches were closer here than at Gommecourt: about 500 yards at the greatest interval – chiefly opposite Beaumont Hamel and to the south – from 150-250 in the north. Those of the Germans were deep and well revetted, their tops meshed with barbed wire against trench raiders. Few of the chalky parapets were visible to the British; the trench line lay for the most part on reverse slopes on either side of the spurs, except behind Beaumont Hamel and below Serre where the fire positions rose in terraces on the enemy's forward slopes.

Though they were scarcely visible from the British observation posts, the entire trench complex stood out on air photographs as a formidable barrier to an advance. Yet, strong as these were in disposition, they were vulnerable to heavy artillery fire. The protection lay, as ever, in the dugouts, deep and dry, constructed through the quiet months of late 1914 and the whole of

[7] Two of its battalions were in the line, however, holding the extreme left flank of the corps; two under command of 4th Division for the assault.

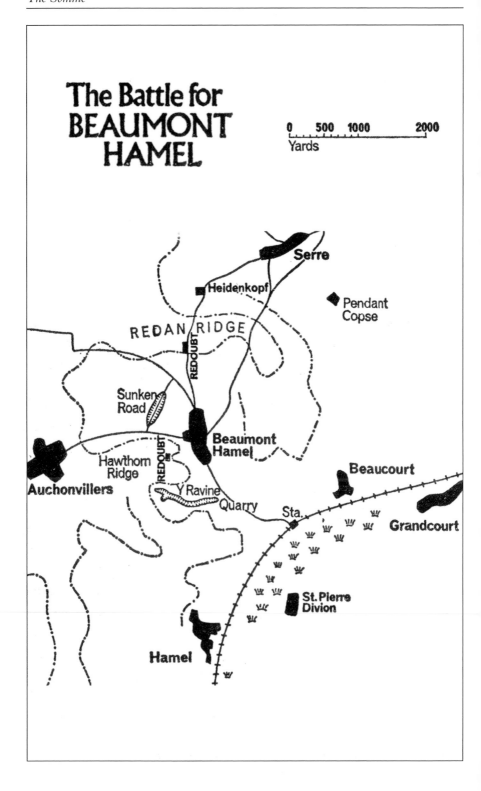

The Battle for BEAUMONT HAMEL

0   500   1000   2000
Yards

Serre

Heidenkopf

Pendant
Copse

REDAN RIDGE

REDOUBT

Sunken
Road

Beaumont
Hamel

REDOUBT

Hawthorn
Ridge

Beaucourt

Auchonvillers

Y Ravine

Quarry

Sta.

Grandcourt

St. Pierre
Divion

Hamel

1915; in the strengthened cellars and reinforced ground floor rooms of the villages; in such natural forts as the *Bergwerk,* an old chalk mine halfway back along the northern spur, a strong point linking Beaumont Hamel and Serre. Only one redoubt was reckoned vulnerable by the garrison: the *Heidenkopf,* a quadrilateral of reinforced and covered trenches in the firing line which barred the road to Serre. In the event of heavy artillery attack, it was not viable. The complex was mined accordingly by the Germans, to be blown as the enemy entered its upper works.

Opposite Serre, the 31st Division was facing 169 Regiment, divisional comrades of 170 at Gommecourt. But 4th Division and 29th faced the Wurttemburgers of the 121 Reserve and 119 Reserve.[8] Much careful thought had been given to breaking-in upon this foe.

To begin with, the artillery programme was designed to give as close support to the infantry as possible. At zero hour it would lift from the enemy fire trench and immediate supports in the usual way but thereafter it would 'creep'[9] back in the case of the field artillery, lifting 100 yards every two minutes, each 18-pounder firing six rounds per 100 yards step. The 4-5 howitzers were reserved to destroy machine-guns and other reinforced fire positions in the enemy first line, their high angle of fire being more suitable for this task in the constantly rising and falling ground.

Tunnels had been made forward in order to close with the enemy secretly: in 4th Division there were two. Cat and Rat; in 29th Division three, of which two were taken to within 30 yards of the enemy fire trench. On a grander scale, 252 Tunnelling Company of the Royal Engineers had mined under an enemy redoubt on Hawthorn Ridge at the top end of the southern spur. It contained 45,000 pounds of ammonal. The corps commander's plan was to blow this four hours before zero, that is, in the dark at 3.30 am. Such an event prior to the final bombardment would not only take out an important element of the enemy's foremost defence line but inevitably cause them to stand to, expecting an attack. After several hours of waiting, they would either stand down again or be caught in the trenches by the last hour of intense bombardment. There was considerable disappointment when it was heard that the commander-in-chief had

[8]   Regiments of 26th Reserve Division.
[9]   This was the first attempt at a creeping barrage, which was limited effectively to the 18-pounders only. The word 'creep' occurred as a description of the fire in XIII Corps orders for 1 July.

rejected the plan.[10] All other mines were to be blown at zero or zero minus eight minutes.

As a concession, it was agreed that the Hawthorn Redoubt should be blown at zero minus ten. This was a fatal error. The immediate consequence was that, in order to get men forward to occupy the crater, the field howitzer concentrations on the forward enemy machine-gun positions were to lift at the time of firing the mine – and for some reason which remains unexplained[11] the procedure was adopted for the entire line of the corps attack. This left the 18-pounders firing shrapnel from zero minus ten minutes to zero. The support was diminished further in 29th Division '...to avoid a pause at oooo, at minus three in each field battery, where one section will lift on to the support line...' So at the moment of infantry assault all that would be firing to occupy the enemy fire trenches would be half the division's 18-pounders. The mind boggles at this profound change in the concept of striking the enemy at zero hour; from a major blow in the area of Hawthorn redoubt it was to be changed to a light punch on the remainder of the, corps front and a tap by 29th Division. For this gross misjudgement or carelessness the corps and divisional commanders must be blamed. Yet these were not the only consequences of General Hunter-Weston's agreement to the new timing for his mine discharge.

The southern spur was called Hawthorn Ridge, the northern was known as Redan; and as on the Hawthorn so on the Redan there was a redoubt.

The 31st Division was the flanking formation earmarked to take Serre and then wheel left to protect the advance of 4th and 29th Divisions. They had tried tunnelling towards the enemy trenches but observers in Serre had seen them removing spoil. Both their efforts were traced on the ground, raided and demolished before the offensive began. Only a Russian sap – a thinly covered trench – remained intact on the morning of 1 July. At 7.20 the leading battalions climbed from the front trenches to make their way forward to the assault position while the preliminary bombardment was concluded. On the left of the divisional front, 94

[10] Haig was advised against a premature mine explosion by his inspector of mines, who offered his view entirely outside the tactical context. He said, with some reason, that the Germans were quicker than the British in occupying mine craters.

[11] It is probable that the operations staff made a mistake or the GOC corps artillery misunderstood the requirement. Unfortunately, no copy of the order issued to the artillery can be found.

Brigade was assaulting with two battalions, the 12th York and Lancaster with the 11th East Lancashire on their right. They were encouraged to see numerous gaps in the torn and tumbled wire ahead of them but dismayed, almost at once, to be swept by machine-guns in enfilade on the far left. These were fired by the northernmost company of 169 Regiment, most of whom were up from their dugouts to find that substantial portions of their trenches were intact. They were not, therefore, much troubled by the light shrapnel of the 18-pounders as there was overhead shelter in the heavily sandbagged posts from which they obtained a clear view of the Tommies across the knee-high grass.

The York and Lancasters had expected to be screened by smoke from this quarter but none had appeared. After a temporary pause, during which orders were shouted quickly down the ranks, those unhit in front dashed for the German trench, to be followed a little later by the survivors of the rear companies, crawling through the grass to avoid the sweeping machine-guns seeking them out. To their right one company of the East Lancashire also managed to get into the German trench, although the enemy were now manning the parapet and firing directly at them. A number of confused encounters began in the German fire and support trenches as parties from each unit made their way on towards Serre village. No one knows what happened to these men. Some fought on, besieged in the front and support trenches until darkness, but few ever came back. Some reached their objectives it seems; months later the graves of a dozen of the York and Lancaster men were found amongst the ruined houses and gardens of Serre. As they struggled forward, the German defensive artillery was falling on No Man's Land, on the British front and support trenches in a concentrated pattern. Above, the contact aircraft saw shells falling amongst the supporting battalions as they formed up. Below, survivors in the open sought shelter in the near end of the Russian sap. Of 93 Brigade there was no sign after the first 10 to 15 minutes. In the confusion of the carnage, it was afterwards learned that one small detachment of the 18th Durham Light Infantry had penetrated through the enemy line to reach its objective, Pendant Copse, 2,000 yards behind the line, to be swallowed by the enemy reserves. The three battalions of the West Yorkshire had become ineffective, the leading two, 18th and 16th, scarcely existing; In this early forenoon, the division had lost 3600 officers and men, of whom only eight were prisoners.

On Redan Ridge the first assault was the task of a single reinforced brigade, 11.[12] As they had feared, the leading battalions were immediately fired on by machine-guns in Ridge Redoubt as soon as they climbed from their trenches at 7.20 but they had not expected to meet aimed small-arms fire in almost equal volume from the supposedly masked enemy fire trenches on either side. Very quickly, however, two Lewis light machine-guns began to return the fire from the tunnel openings of Cat and Rat. But these became targets of machine-guns in the enemy support trenches and, after a few minutes, German bombers knocked out the crews and occupied their positions. The assault companies lay down in the grass while their Stokes mortars opened fire from behind, but the bombs did not disperse the enemy. Dashing and crawling alternately, 1st Battalion, the Rifle Brigade made through the enemy wire, followed shortly by 1st East Lancashire on the right and 1st/8th Royal Warwickshire on the left. The 18-pounders lifted on time as they passed the wire and the first British soldiers reached the enemy to find his dead and wounded among shell holes and smashed timbers. The fire trench as such had been totally broken-in by the long preliminary bombardment. The Württembergers pulled back to their tottering support trench pursued by the remnant of the East Lancashires' assault companies and the right half of the Rifle Brigade. Though they wrested part of the support trench from the defence, numbers were already mounting against them from the deep dugouts behind. From this point they disappeared without trace.

Behind, the support companies of each assaulting battalion had advanced directly into intense artillery fire. The contact aircraft spotted sixty-six German batteries firing into the VII Corps front.[13] This deadly rain of high explosives and shrapnel now forced the 1st Hampshires,[14] coming up as the right support battalion, into the shell holes amongst the rear of the East Lancashires. 'Ahead', said an officer, wounded at the time, 'the enemy wire was swept by the enfilade machine guns from Ridge Redoubt. Behind, the

[12] Six battalions, including two from 48th Division.
[13] Numerous German batteries in this area had orders to fire only against a general attack. In consequence they had not been spotted by air observers during the preparatory phase of the battle.
[14] While waiting to go forward, a number of short rounds from VIII corps artillery hit the battalion.

enemy guns were steadily smashing our trenches – or so we guessed; they were covered with smoke and dust from the bursting shells. It was just as if our own bombardment had gone into reverse.'

At one point, however, the run of luck had gone against the foe. In the *Heidenkopf* the machine-gun defending the German engineers jammed as they were preparing to blow their demolition. Through panic or confusion, the fuse was too short.

The explosion destroyed almost all the occupants and rained soil upon the adjacent dugout exits, closing them.

Near at hand were the survivors of the Rifle Brigade's left assault company and those of the 1st/8th Royal Warwickshires' right. They ran forward into the enemy fire trench and penetrated the support area to occupy 600 yards of its length. Soon they were reinforced by other detachments, similarly forced over to the left of Redan Ridge by the Redoubt's machine-gun fire; two companies of the 1st Somerset Light Infantry and elements of the 1/6th Warwickshire. The remainder of all these battalions, moving yet further to the left, was entirely killed or wounded by machine-guns from in front of Serre.

In rear, none knew what was happening. Flares of all kinds were being displayed – some friendly, some of the enemy, as it happened – each trying to signify a different idea. The rival artillery added to the confusion, though only for the assailants; the British guns had long since passed on to distant objectives. Since all the commanding officers were killed or wounded, their adjutants and company commanders in much the same condition, no messages had come back by runner, none were flashed to the aircraft or the ground stations. All that was known was the earliest information, sent back by two runners before 8 o'clock, concerning the heavy losses in the leading brigade, later confirmed by the contact aircraft. 4th Division commander realised that the action must be halted to discover the sources of resistance and, if necessary, make a new plan. While the aeroplanes of 15 Squadron were asked to make a close reconnaissance, instructions were sent off at 8.35 a.m. to halt the follow-up by 10th and 12th Brigades.

The two brigadiers of these formations had a joint observation station, 400 yards behind the fire trench. When the message came, they had both left to look for the approach of their battalions, forming-up further to the rear. At about 9.30 the leading units came up from their start line, widely dispersed as was customary against enemy artillery, and passed on towards the edge of No Man's Land. The orders to suspend the attack had reached the brigade commanders but they had then to send them on by runner to the commanding officer. The rear battalions were stopped but those ahead went unwarned; the runners killed or wounded en route to them. As before, on the left, survivors reached the quadrilateral of the *Heidenkoff*. There was a moment of tragic confusion as a leading platoon fired on the figures inside calling out to greet them – they did not know it had been captured – but they were soon reinforcing their predecessors. On the right substantial numbers gained the enemy support trench, which contained few Germans. From the air they were seen to press on for yards into Munich trench; and some khaki uniforms were identified a little later, 1,000 yards on again, north-east at Pendant Copse. But the aircraft reporting these movements had great difficulty in observing steadily. One pair came down to fifty feet, to be tossed crazily by the disturbed air of passing shells. Much later a few survivors crawled back to say that the force had been taken in rear by men coming down from the fire trenches in the north – where 31st Division had had such a disastrous day – and from the south, where 29th Division had attacked.

The Incomparable 29th Division – their own proud name from the days of Gallipoli[15] – began their attack, as they had always intended, in darkness. Several hours before dawn the end of each of the three tunnels under No Man's Land was opened successfully and secretly. Unheard by the Germans – though the morning's bombardment had not begun – Stokes mortars were erected and bombs brought forward. As on every day throughout the previous week, the nightly sounds of harassing fire were lost at 5.15 as the daylight shelling programme began. All ranks stood to. On the right, where the southern spur ran down to the Ancre, the assault companies climbed from their trenches at 7.20, some aghast to see the supporting artillery fire already lifting ahead of them.[16] From the left they heard a booming roar. The mine had gone up under Hawthorn Redoubt.

---

[15] 29th Division had taken part in the Gallipoli landings under General Hunter-Weston, where it had earned a high name. After the withdrawal its ranks were filled by reinforcements but many veterans of the Dardanelles remained. Haig was prejudiced against all who had joined in that campaign.

[16] The change in the fire support programme, due to the late firing of the Hawthorn Redoubt mine, had not been passed to many infantry units.

The German garrison, part of 9 Company, 119 Reserve Regiment, were caught by the –

...terrific explosion which for the moment drowned the thunder of artillery. A great cloud of smoke rose up from the trenches of 9 Company followed by a tremendous shower of stones, which seemed to fall from the sky all over our position. Three sections and more of 9 Company were blown into the air, and the neighbouring dugouts were broken-in and blocked. The ground all round was white with the chalk debris as if it had been snowing, and a gigantic crater, over fifty yards in diameter and some sixty feet deep, gaped like an open wound in the side of the hill. This explosion was a signal for the infantry attack, and everyone got ready and stood on the lower steps of the dugouts, rifles in hand, waiting for the bombardment to lift. In a few minutes, the shelling ceased and we rushed up the steps and out into the crater positions. Ahead of us, wave after wave of British troops were crawling out of their trenches, and coming towards us at a walk, their bayonets glistening in the sun.

Not all were walking. Two platoons of D Company, 2nd Royal Fusiliers, were running for the crater, behind them four Stokes mortars and four Vickers machine-guns. But they had the last slope to ascend and were heavily laden with kit and ammunition. Before they could occupy the crater, a detachment of Germans had reached the far lip and were mounting two machine-guns to hold them back. A fire battle began.

A little to the north 1st Lancashire Fusiliers came forward towards the sunken lane. In the darkness they had opened their tunnel, mounted their Stokes mortars and machine-guns in this scrap of No Man's Land and filtered forward almost half the battalion, including 100 bombers. At zero, as the remainder came forward above ground to join them, the *coup de main* force rushed forward, climbing the swell of ground to the east. If the enemy trench had been empty, they must have broken-in in force; but it was not. Alarmed by the firing of the mine near by, careless of the feeble final shellfire on their trenches, the resident company of Germans had come up to man their broken defences before 7.25. The greater number of the Lancashire soldiers were shot by small arms as their heads and shoulders rose up over the edge of the lane, the rest were caught in the next 20 yards.

Already the guns and howitzers below Serre and Puisieux were dropping their shells amongst the support companies of the Lancashire Fusiliers. At 8 o'clock the support battalions of the brigade attack followed on, the 16th Middlesex behind the Lancashire battalion, the 1st Royal Dublin Fusiliers behind the Royal Fusiliers. Each could see that the wire ahead was largely uncut and hung with bodies of their predecessors in assault, the few gaps piled with dead. Mercilessly shelled as they reached the northern edge of Hawthorn Ridge, the rear companies of the Middlesex were ordered back. The Dublin Fusiliers were engaged by machine-guns from the Bergvjerk behind Beaumont Hamel and could not advance down the forward slope. They inched back into cover to collect their own wounded and attended to some of the Royal Fusiliers, whose pattern of casualties extended up to and beyond the German wire. Beyond this obstacle, however, in which only seven or eight gaps existed, the numbers dwindled. In the German fire trench, or what remained of it, the trail ended with the men who had reached the enemy line. And they were dead.

All that was left of the Royal Fusiliers battalion was 120, and these finally gathered by Hawthorn Crater. Captain Goodliffe, coming forward after the assault to find his comrades, questioned the wounded to discover where they had gone. One man with a broken jaw mumbled insistently in anxiety to help, repeating a statement over and over. After a little, Goodliffe thought he caught the sense of it. 'Did you say, 'We're doing no good on the right?' ' The wounded fusilier nodded his head in agreement.

On the right 86 Brigade had attacked just above the morning mist in the Ancre valley, moving on Y Ravine to clear this two-armed declivity before crossing over the re-entrant south of Beaumont Hamel. Along the German wire the gaps were difficult to see, for none were decisive breaks; the general result of the bombardment had been only to loosen the fence. The 2nd South Wales Borderers came down the slight gradient at an easy pace, the far lip of the ravine just in their view. The rear ranks of the two assault companies were about thirty yards from their own trench when three machine-guns opened fire from Y Ravine. The right-hand company received the worst of the fire so that those on the left were free for a moment to run forward in an effort to cross the wire to close with the assailants. It was, of course, a piece of hopeless gallantry, they could not cover the distance in the time. A line of bodies fell just a hundred paces short of the German fire positions. The support companies in rear were unable to see this final tragedy of the assault, being immersed in the smoke, blast and splinters of the German barrage.

This had taken five minutes.

The right-hand battalion of the division was the 1st Royal Inniskilling Fusiliers. Leaving C Company in reserve in his assembly trenches, Lieutenant-Colonel R C Pierce assaulted with his remaining three rifle companies, each platoon being in single file. This formation had been adopted because of enemy strong points on the battalion right flank and was designed to offer the least target to machine-guns in enfilade. But it now served well to minimise casualties against the machine-guns on the left in Y Ravine and the nearest platoon of the Württemberg 9 Company south of Hawthorn Redoubt. Had the Inniskilling companies been in line, they would not have survived the approach to the wire. About two-thirds of those who had started were still on their feet – Colonel Pierce was not one; he was dead – but this number fell quickly because of the delay they suffered in finding places to cross the wire. Three or four detachments from two of the companies managed to pass through, however, carrying still the trench bridges they needed to span the deep German fire trenches. These were little damaged here and empty. They hurried on towards the support trench, seeking to cut round behind the enemy strong points on the right. A fire fight, bombing and counter-bombing began with the enemy supports. They had some cover amongst the shell holes and several detachments occupied the German communication trenches, but the total numbers were critically few in face of two German platoons forming up to counter-attack them from the eastern end of Y Ravine. Even before this force could deploy, the Inniskilling detachments were overcome. Almost a company of Württembergers swarmed up from the dugouts below the fire trench to occupy their own parados from which a hail of fire swept those lying in shell holes. While those above ground were shot, bombers crept down the communication trenches and took the Irish soldiers sheltering there in rear.

The first phase of the attack – and its awful consequences had been observed by the commanding officers of the support battalions, scheduled to cross the fire trenches from the rear at 8.50 am. Each of these officers, commanding the 1st Border and King's Own Scottish Borderers respectively, suggested to the brigade commander that there was a requirement for further bombardment. It was clear that the machine-guns on the flanks were most active, with signs of other hostile small-arms fire immediately to their front. Unfortunately, Brigadier-General C H T Lucas had seen white flares in the enemy positions and judged these to be the signal arranged with the assault battalions to signify their success. He had also had a brief report from a contact aircraft confirming the presence of British khaki close to the enemy support trench. These facts, combined with an easement in the enemy shellfire on No Man's Land, decided him not to delay matters. The Border and KOSB battalions continued their advance.

Though there was distant firing – the Inniskilling detachments were still fighting – the machine-guns had stopped when the leading companies crossed the British fire trenches by the bridges laid for them. But as soon as they stepped into the gaps in their own wire, the Germans opened a rapid volley with rifles which, almost at once, was joined by the flanking machine-guns and several to their front. When these gaps were choked with bodies, the advance stopped. A very few survivors lay intact beyond in shell holes. Rallied, they continued the advance from crater to crater, losing a few more at every step. At last the remaining handful were ordered to halt and take cover. It was about 8.13 in the morning.

The divisional commander, Major-General H de B de Lisle, received the aircraft report concerning the Inniskillings' entry on the right, the news of the white flares – actually lit by the Württembergers to call for supporting fire – and confirmation of the committal of the remaining battalions of 87 Brigade. Whilst he knew that the latter were 'temporarily held up by some machine-guns' – the reported assumption of a super-optimist in a dugout – he did not consider this enough to delay exploitation of the initial success. 88 Brigade was therefore told to despatch its two leading battalions – 1st Battalions, The Newfoundland Regiment and The Essex – supported by the concentrated fire of 88 Machine Gun Company. Left and right, the battalions were to move forward individually behind the two assault brigades. One, the Essex, could not reach No Man's Land; they were physically obstructed by the endless lines of wounded in every trench and deep shell holes where attempts were being made to succour them and, forward, by a profusion of dead bodies. The German guns had shelled this section of British fire, support and reserve trenches extensively at 7.35 with terrible success. Left, the Newfoundlanders were ordered to continue alone. They had advanced in the open to take cover in the forward shell craters until their zero hour. At 9.5 they rose and marched forward in open ranks, half-turned towards Y Ravine, lonely newcomers to the zone of destruction. Almost in unison, the machine-guns fired from Y Ravine, perhaps from the right also. The sustained effort appeared to be from the Ravine.

The long burst of a machine-gun does not kill a battalion; indeed, some men in a line will almost certainly pass through the run of bullets, in the gaps between them, so to speak. But if the line of men perseveres with a determined gallantry, over a long open approach, the end is certain. So it was before Y Ravine. The Newfoundland officers and men would not halt; they had orders to advance into the enemy line: they advanced. 710 men fell. Some minutes, later, three companies of the Essex emerged on their own front to fall, as gallantly but as forlornly just inside the enemy line,

Thus ended the assault of the 29th Division.

Less than three hours after zero General Hunter-Weston was faced with the bitter decisions of defeat. His staff – by no means all box wallahs – had received with eagerness the reports that the assault tunnels had been opened, the mine fired. Then there was a long pause. In war, as in peace, men tend to repeat what is hopeful, to overlook what is disagreeable. Thus the news concerning the capture of the *Heidenkopf* quadrilateral and the entry to Munich trench and Pendant Copse was given prominence. The sustained flow of wounded, the absence of prisoners was left unexplained. Every practicable means of communication had been thought of and established; but the media were inadequate to maintain the close contact needed by each of the senior commanders. Even the aeroplanes, over the centre of action and in crude radio contact, sometimes misled. The disasters of the morning were too profound to remain undiscovered, however. The accounts of survivors and wounded returning were consistent. The brigade commanders or their staffs went forward – Brigadier-General Prowse was wounded and died at this time – and came back themselves to report to division. Appalled, the divisional commanders sent their own messages to corps.

The thickset, heavily moustached, jovial 'Hunter-Bunter', who had seen no mean share of action, had a difficult choice. Discontinue the battle? He could not do that; the information indicated that British soldiers were still fighting in the enemy line. Abandoning all idea of reaching his deeper objectives he ordered the remaining reserves forward to capture and make good the Munich trench. The artillery was to begin a fresh bombardment. The reserve division, 48th, was brought up to within two miles of the front in case of need. Then the attack was postponed because of the confusion forward, made worse by the disruption of most of the deep telephone cables by heavy artillery. Major-General Lambton, commanding 4th Division, reported that he could not get ammunition forward to the *Heidenkoff*, even by small parties, owing to the shell and machine-gun fire. This apart, it would take hours to reorganise his front trenches in readiness for a second attack. The attack was abandoned. Throughout the afternoon, local efforts continued to reach the men in the enemy trenches – those of 31st Division were no longer effective – and after dark the *Heidenkopf* and Hawthorn craters were abandoned except for a reinforcing company from the 1st Royal Irish Fusiliers in the quadrilateral. This little party fought on through the night as the order to withdraw did not reach them, to return at noon next day, 2 July, with all their wounded and three prisoners.

All through this day and the next, stretcher parties were out, collecting wounded and, later, dead. The Germans acceded to a temporary informal truce in which they took in their own men from the original fire trench, removed many of the British dead from their wire – the British were warned off this zone with occasional shots – and made no secret of the Lewis guns they bore away with bodies on their stretchers. The infantry, gunners, sappers, Service Corps, dressers and bearers from the field ambulance came forward to keep the clearance work in progress without pause night and day.

It was a gigantic task. The corps had lost 14,000 officers and men.

THE BATTLE FOR THE RIDGE

As the battalions in VIII Corps prepared to make their bloody but futile assault on Redan, and Hawthorn Ridges, those in X and III made ready to attack the main objective. In the simplest terms, General Morland's corps, X, was to capture the summit features 2,000 yards beyond Pozières. Thus they shared responsibility for seizing the northern half of that high ground on which Haig's plan depended. If jointly they took out the enemy's two lines of defence, it would give him success. If only one broke through,[17]

---

[17] The III Corps plan did not include a breach of the second line in its objectives but the reserve division was to be prepared to pass through on to it.

the prospects would be bright.

General Morland was determined to get as close to the front as he could without becoming too involved in any one divisional battle. He chose an observation platform in a tree at Engelbelmer, some three miles from the German outposts, as his command post, from which a duplicated telephone cable ran to his exchange in rear. Near by was a heavy battery whose fire attracted enemy shells. General Pulteney came forward later in the day to the Tara-Usna Ridge astride the main road running from Albert directly through the German position to Bapaume. Many observing stations had been dug in here, both for commanders and gunners. Artillery was massed in action on the reverse slope. Forward, there was an excellent view across the valley to the German trenches in front of Ovillers and la Boiselle, and of the two village fortresses themselves on either side of the highway. General Morland's gunners had a similarly good view of Thiepval from a ridge in front of Engelbelmer – the Mesnil – but between these two areas of high ground, over a distance of two miles, there was none from which the battery observers could see the enemy outposts and wire except by trench periscope.

Unlike the positions to be attacked by VIII Corps north of the Ancre, those to the south lay on the forward slopes of the spurs running down to the river. The British fire trench was on inferior ground, not only in being under continuous obsertion from the high slopes of the spurs; it was also in enfilade to the German machine-guns tucked away in the re-entrants.

Fortunately, the leafy trees of Thiepval and Authuille[18] woods on the river bank in X Corps' sector, and Tara-Usna Ridge in III's gave a measure of cover to those coming forward by day.

Each corps had two divisions in the line, one in reserve.

On the left of X Corps, 36th (Ulster) Division was to attack with one brigade astride the Ancre, linking with VIII Corps' movement on Beaumont Hamel, while a second captured the high feature above Thiepval. 32nd Division – like the Ulstermen, a part of the 'New Armies' – had first to capture Thiepval village and the spur below, which ended in Liepzig Redoubt. This done, they would move on to take the Germans' second line.

[18] French ordnance survey maps do not show a Thiepval Wood.
The wood immediately west of the village is called '*Bois d'Authuille*', the one below '*Bois de la Haie*'. I have followed the British nomenclature.

Then came the III Corps sector. 8th Division, a skeleton of the Old Army revived by the vigorous recruits of the New, was to advance on a frontage of 1500 yards up the low spur of Ovillers, then onward to the high ground of Pozières. Both fortified villages were to be taken by the early afternoon. Below the Albert-Bapaume highway, 34th Division, which had arrived in France as recently as January, was directed on la Boisselle and Contalmaison. In attacking these positions, many of its infantry would be in action for the first time.

Well before zero, the majority of the battalions were tired by the heavy work of digging assembly trenches and carrying forward stores. In X Corps a group of men had been engaged in digging a Russian sap towards Leipzig Redoubt. But this was trifling in comparison with the tunnelling and mining to the south. 8th Division had cut two communication trenches, 14 feet below ground towards Ovillers, 34th Division one by la Boisselle. Much deeper, 179 Tunnelling Company had advanced over 300 yards to two positions on either side of la Boisselle: Y Sap and Lochnagar.[19] Fifty feet down, the sappers had placed 40,600 and 60,000 pounds of ammonal in position for zero.

As the time drew near, the natural apprehensions of the assault battalions were magnified as the result of their final raids and patrols. Despite the reassurances of staff officers and gunners, there were extensive areas south of Thiepval where the enemy's wire remained uncut. The worst of these was opposite the gap between the observation ridges. There were also numerous reports from those who had been up to and sometimes through the wire by night that enemy machine-guns were still active in spite of the bombardment. A company commander returning from a raid opposite Thiepval on 30 June wrote, '...and I am certain that the four machine guns firing on the wire here are in the same positions as they were eight days past.' The retort of one divisional staff was that battalions were 'windy': a temerarious reply telephoned from the secure comfort of a headquarters dugout.

'...the mist lay as wool over the valley of the Ancre. I went out about 5 am and found the men resting quietly with no visible signs of excitement. The bombardment has been constant during the night and has been vigorously replied to. For the past few days it has been quite impossible to maintain

[19] Two smaller mines were close by.

telephone communication with Brigade and we have had to rely entirely upon messengers...' So Colonel David Laidlaw, commanding officer of 16th Highland Light Infantry, wrote his impressions in his diary, in the last few hours before zero. With the 17th on his immediate right, he was to assault the Leipzig Redoubt.

Below the long, rounded southern spur of Thiepval, the Jocks of the two battalions massed in the assembly trenches forty minutes before zero. There was little room for anyone to sit down and, indeed, few wished to do so. No chatter ran among them. The faces of most were 'impassive, almost sullen: but little ill-temper was shown as groups jostled one another to let an officer or the sergeant-major pass along the narrow trench. An occasional message or order was shouted, to be repeated along the crowded lines against the roar of the field batteries and the Stokes mortars, and the continual thump, thump, crump of the shells bursting up the spur. Thus they stood quietly, patiently, fearfully, while the minutes dragged past 7 o'clock, 5 past, 10 past, 15, 20, under the blue sky and the ascending sun which dried the last of the dew from their chalk-streaked jackets.

Just after 20 past, the first four platoon commanders of the 17th HLI stepped up to the parapet and began to crawl forward to the close craters in No Man's Land. Before 7.30 the two leading companies had joined them in the variety of deep and shallow holes torn in the pastureland. They were now less than forty yards from the German trenches in Leipzig Redoubt.

Suddenly the tempo changed. The stow march up into the assembly trenches, the long pause there, the careful crawl forward, the last two minutes of waiting were past. It was zero hour. With a shout they sprang up as the guns lifted. Pipes skirled; men cheered. In a moment they were passing through the wire, gapped by the guns in a score of places. By 7.32 the foremost companies were leaping down into the circlet of trenches above the chalk quarry. Almost 300 Germans hurrying up from the deep dugouts below were instantly made prisoner.

The third and fourth companies now joined the first two in the chalk quarry. For five confused minutes the whole battalion crowded the outer defences of the enemy redoubt, shouting and talking excitedly, their prisoners scattered amongst them. It was 7.50 before the second wave was extricated and formed up to assault the inner lines, while the remainder began a systematic search of the dugouts. Yet all seemed well. 150 yards east, across an open stretch, no bobbing enemy helmets were to be seen; the inner defences seemed as empty as they had found the outer. Whistles blew; they ran up and over the trenches, the leading platoons of each company spreading hastily out into line. And almost at once – almost before they heard the sharp crackle of the concealed machine-guns – the first men began to fall. Before 8 o'clock, more than half were dead or wounded, while the remainder lay in the cratered ground, sheltered from the weapons to their front but often exposed to those firing in enfilade on their left. The assault had come to a standstill.

It is one thing to bring men to assault with zeal. They will form up obediently while the guns pound the objective. They will leap with ardour across the start line and fight with passion as they tangle with the enemy positions. But it is another thing to get them going again when the enemy has brought the first brave assault to a halt. An *ad hoc* plan must be made often by a man himself lying under heavy fire. His men must be reformed and the plan made known to them. A whole new process of fire and movement must begin.

This difficult task was now undertaken by a captain on the right and a subaltern on the left – the only two officers intact of the ten who had gone forward. Independently of one another they regained a measure of control over the scattered survivors about them and were on the point of doubling back under the hostile machine-guns when a rain of shells descended on the enemy. The brigadier, advised of their plight by his artillery commander, had switched two field batteries to their assistance – an act forbidden by corps order.[20]

Back once more in the Leipzig Redoubt, the remnant of the second assault wave, 17th HLI, found a few of the 16th who had entered the chalk quarry from the left. An angry, wounded man shouted, 'If you'd been in the right place, we wouldn't have caught it. Where are the rest of you?' A Jock of the 16th replied, 'On the wire.' And though this was no longer true – those alive and able to move had crawled back by this time – it was a fact that not one of the battalion had passed through the enemy wire. As they had reported, it remained virtually uncut.

At Thiepval village there had been similar disasters, though for different

[20] The order was that fire plans would not be altered during the assault.

reasons. Opposite the tumbled ruins 16th Northumberland Fusiliers had launched two companies behind a rugby football, drop-kicked in a high arc from the assembly trench. Untouched by the bombardment, in withdrawn, reinforced position, four machine-guns, trained and ranged on the gaps in their wire with deadly accuracy, fired belt after belt of ammunition into the eight platoons till all but eleven men had succumbed. On the Northumberlands' left, 15th Lancashire Fusiliers achieved a limited success while the village machine-guns concentrated on the flank units. One hundred of their men reached the enemy fire trench before the dugouts disgorged the defence. Believing that the support companies in rear would deal with this garrison, they hastened on towards the village, amongst whose shattered walls, on the surface, no enemy were to be found. But the enemy they had left behind in the dugouts now emerged in good time to catch the Lancashire support companies in No Man's Land. They were thrown back by intensive short-range fire. The line was sealed once more and the fusiliers in Thiepval cut off. An aeroplane of 4 Squadron reported that khaki figures were working their way along the northern edge.

The sum of the Flying Corps reports and those from brigades and gunner observers gave General Morland at 8.30 a picture of events up to 8 o'clock. He knew that 17th HLI were in Leipzig Redoubt; that 16th HLI, and the Northumberlands had been repulsed. He had been told that the Lancashire Fusiliers were in Thiepval, while attempts were being made to reopen communications to them by forcing again the enemy front trenches. On the left he had confirmation that the attack astride the Ancre had been a total failure involving heavy casualties. This meant that the hamlet of St Pierre Divion on the south bank remained in enemy hands. What had happened to the other Irish Brigade, 109, assaulting between river bank and Thiepval? Bugles had sounded in the trenches at 7.30; the men up by the wire had gone forward into dust and smoke, since when there had been no word. The support battalions had followed on just as the enemy barrage on No Man's Land increased, but survivors had been seen to cross the enemy outposts. Still there was no news.

At 8.32, 36th (Ulster) Division commander sent a message to General Morland asking whether he should commit his reserve brigade behind 109 or not. It was planned that they should pass through them to take the German second line but if they should go forward it would be through the shellfire on No Man's Land to an unknown situation on the battlefield beyond. The corps commander had now been told that VIII Corps had failed to break-in and III Corps were in difficulties. It seemed to him wiser to wait for more information. He might, for example, need the Ulster reserve, 107 Brigade, to reinforce a break-in to Thiepval village. At 9.10 he instructed 36th Division to hold them back.

It was too late. The three battalions, 8th, 9th and 10th Royal Irish Rifles,[21] were marching out of Thiepval Wood and running across No Man's Land. They, too, disappeared into the smoke of bursting German shells except for luckless men who fell in dozens of dead and wounded among the craters.

Meantime 109 Brigade had won a sensational success. Led by the loth Inniskillings on the left, the 9th on the right, they had made a good pace through the tumbled heaps of the enemy wire and on across the first trench. Two days before, their patrols stated that this was 'heavily damaged'. It was now unrecognisable amongst the craters, arid the garrison in the dug-outs below was entombed. The gunners had shot well from Mesnil Ridge. The two Inniskilling battalions were slowed but not checked by the devastation of earth and timber. They had rehearsed extensively amongst the quiet fields behind the line – '...we could have found our way over there blindfold.' The support battalions, 14th Irish Rifles and 11th Inniskillings, entered the crater field as the 9th and 10th scrambled on in rough lines to the support and reserve trenches.

They were well up behind their own barrage. The next two enemy positions were taken before the defence was properly established, the Germans below waiting just too long before coming up to man their parapet. The bag of prisoners swelled. After eight days of bombardment, the eyes of some had a set, remote focus; others, whose reason had gone in the prolonged attempts to mend defences and man the watches under the heavy shellfire, were brought up sweating and ashen, groaning or chuckling. In the second reserve position, a few machine-guns were mounted by the quick and doughty but the 10th Inniskillings stormed them, cheering. The 9th, coming up on their right, helped to assault the vast raised complex of

---

[21] The fourth battalion of the brigade had joined the attack astride the Ancre.

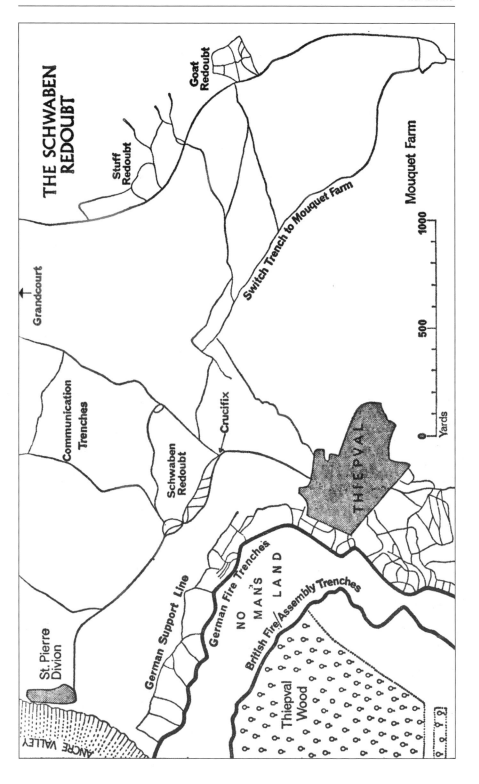

covered trenches, named the Schwaben Redoubt. A few bombers and riflemen were to be seen firing from the embrasures ready to check their progress when, to the surprise of both units, the 11th Irish Rifles appeared. This battalion had been forced south-east by fire from St Pierre Divion, where they had marched directly towards the redoubt, two companies now being astride its communications trenches to the rear. Surrounded by chance, surprised by the speed of the Irish, dazed by the last attention of the howitzers, the two companies surrendered. It was 8.30. They had advanced a mile in the hour. They were on top of the ridge.

If General Morland lacked news of this success, he was partly to blame. Either on his own initiative, or in approval of his divisional commanders', there was not a single commanding officer, second-in-command or adjutant present with the four battalions closing up to consolidate the captured enemy first line. There was no representative of brigade headquarters. All the officers concerned had been forbidden to leave their battle headquarters until their respective units had halted on the objectives. They expected that runners would come back with regular news of progress; and on this basis four battalions of infantry had been sent forward without a coordinator of any sort between themselves, the mortars, machine-gunners and two sections of Royal Engineers accompanying the force.

If the Germans had now mounted a quick counter-attack, 109 Brigade would have been in difficulties. They did not do so.

The British are apt to exult in their own military, mistakes and to extol the successes of their enemies. It is only fair to point out that the Germans, knocked off balance in this critical sector, almost lost it due to a series of mistakes.

Observers standing-to in Beaucourt Redoubt across the Ancre saw the Irish companies sweeping through the Schwaben Redoubt. Before this movement was complete, the information was passed back to headquarters of 26th Reserve Division in Courcelette. The commander, Major-General von Soden, at once committed his only reserve, II Battalion, 8th Bavarian Reserve Regiment,[22] with which he grouped a machine-gun company in the third defence line and an automatic rifle platoon at his headquarters. The telephones were set to work. But II Battalion had been moved to Irles at the head of the Ancre, where they arrived shortly after dawn. There was

[22] Of the other battalions one was in the line behind Beaumont Hamel with the Wiirttembergers; the other in the line by Thiepval to reinforce the defence garrison, depleted by British artillery fire.

no telephone line to them. When this became evident, a message was sent by an orderly NCO. He did not find the unit until 9 am.

Between regimental headquarters and division was an intermediate command: 51st Reserve Brigade.[23] Its commander had already instructed I and III Battalions of 8th Bavarian Reserve each to attach two companies to 180 Recruit Battalion[24] at Grandcourt for a quick counter-attack in a converging movement. Though the two companies of III Battalion were able to withdraw from their area, north of the river, they had a long and circuitous journey round to Goat Redoubt in front of Courcelette. The marching companies, often moving across open ground, were repeatedly seen by the Royal Flying Corps and shelled.

Meantime, the corps commander, Lieutenant-General von Stein,[25] had ordered forward two battalions of his reserve. But they were twenty miles from Courcelette. He repeated orders to the divisional commander to mount a counter-attack without delay. While the divisional staff awaited news of the brigade plan, Lieutenant-Colonel Bram, commander of 8th Bavarian Reserve, arrived at Courcelette. He was ordered to command the counter-attack. In the second line he found that he had scarcely any force to use: though the two companies of I Battalion were present, the order to attack from Grandcourt had not reached the Recruit Battalion; his II Battalion had started from Iries but was also being delayed by British shells; and there was no sign or report of his two companies from III Battalion. Colonel Bram was aware that speed was expected. He made a fire plan with the artillery and decided between 1 and 1.30 that he must act. The two companies were launched. Almost at once two companies of II Battalion appeared as reinforcements and there was news that 180 Recruit Battalion had started from Grandcourt with machine-gun support. Approximately 800 German infantry were now making their way towards the Irish position. It was close to 2 pm.

Much had happened to the Ulstermen since the height of their success at 8.30. The 9th Inniskillings had consolidated at an intersection of trenches called the Crucifix at the south-east point of Schwaben Redoubt. There they had been joined by the supporting 11th. But they were

[23] A formation not to be confused with the British brigade. The German brigade usually consisted of two regiments: that is, six battalions. Thus the German regiment corresponded most closely to the British brigade.
[24] Men completing their training in the line due to the shortage of troops.
[25] XIV Reserve corps commander at Bapaume.

battalions in name only; each had followed a course close to Thiepval and once out in the open beyond the mass of craters they had lost heavily to the village machine-guns. The assorted detachments of the 9th were commanded by the remaining officer, Second-Lieutenant McKinley; the 11th by Lieutenant Gallagher who was fortunate to find a warrant officer still active, Company Sergeant-Major Bulloch. Making a firm base at the Crucifix, McKinley patrolled down the empty trench towards Thiepval, Gallagher took a party back to repel a bombing raid – the first of many – from the Cemetery, and the sergeant-major set off to contact the 10th further forward. The sister battalion had penetrated the enemy's switch line leading north to Grandcourt and south to Pozières, where they had been reinforced by the arrival of the 14th Irish Rifles. Attempts were made to co-ordinate their defences.

Now the reserve brigade, 107, whom General Morland had failed to stop, arrived for the attack on the second line – still without an overall commander. But everyone knew their part They set off at a good pace across the grass, the 10th Inniskillings and the two Irish Rifles' battalions following for good measure. Across 600 yards of open ground scarcely broken by shells lay their destination, the Grandcourt line, marked by the high bunkers of Stuff and Goat Redoubts. Nothing appeared, neither men nor fire, to delay them as they closed quickly upon what seemed to be deserted trenches. And so they were. One hundred paces would bring the leaders unopposed possession.

From the rear the British guns and howitzers opened their barrage upon this very ground. The artillery were firing correctly to time; the infantry were early. In passing through the shells and machine-gun bullets striking Thiepval Wood and No Man's Land, 107 Brigade had understandably accelerated their rate of advance. Having no senior commander to control them, they arrived prematurely on the enemy second position by 10 minutes; and now on this day when so many barrages were to run away from the assault, they lay helplessly in the open, the only victims of their own artillery. Two-thirds of the Irish battalions were killed or wounded. Those nearest managed to run into the trench for cover. When the shelling ended, a few more joined them and soon they occupied Stuff Redoubt. But the main force was stricken and scattered. Undaunted, those who had occupied the German second line made ready to defend it. A small party of sappers blocked the approach from Grandcourt, while infantrymen dragged up sandbags to emplacements for the Vickers and Lewis guns.

Towards noon three of the battalion seconds-in-command came forward to see what was happening. Two returned to report the essential needs; ammunition, water and reinforcements. One, Major Peacocke of the Inniskillings, remained to coordinate the detachments at the Schwaben Redoubt, a key position now if they were to keep communications open past Thiepval. But the shellfire which had taken toll of 107 Brigade coming forward through No Man's Land and the machine-guns which had cut down the 9th and 11th Inniskillings effectively prevented movement forward. Thiepval Wood, the assembly area behind the British line, was repeatedly fired on; leaves and branches were stripped from the trees morning and afternoon by high explosive and the bullets crackling down and across the road to Hamel. Even so, Colonel Bram's counter-attack at 2 pm failed. Above the battlefield 4 Squadron reported that the German field batteries near by were continuing to fall back under the menace of the British presence.

Each side repeated its attacks through late afternoon and early evening: 32nd Division made piecemeal attacks on Thiepval; Colonel Bram's *ad hoc* force managed to reject the enemy in Stuff Redoubt but failed to advance numbers forward to the Schwaben. Bach suffered a mounting toll of casualties. In the mistaken belief, due to the confusion and paucity of communications, that a British company was lodged in Thiepval, General Morland did not mass his heavy artillery on the village to crush the machine-guns impeding movement across No Man's Land or commit his reserve division to exploit the Ulster success. Indeed, Thiepval remained largely free of artillery fire for many hours because the air had reported the presence of Lancashire Fusiliers in the village. Captain Hiatt of 7 Squadron flew specially to seek them in the afternoon but failed to make a positive identification. On his side of the line Colonel Bram could not discover the extent of the British detachments and twice permitted his infantry to expose themselves fatally above ground. At 5 pm General von Soden sent a message from his divisional headquarters: 'The Englishmen [*sic*] still sits in the Schwaben Redoubt. He must be driven out of it, out of our position. It is a point of honour for the division to recapture this important point today.

The artillery is to cooperate with all possible strength.'

Two attacks followed – one from Thiepval. In repelling these, the British machine-gun ammunition, became exhausted. The Lewis gun drums were already being filled from the rifle bandoliers. Now they had to fill the Vickers belts by hand from the same scource. Few grenades were left.

At 10 pm the two battalions of General von Stein's reserve reached the line. With this considerable reinforcement, three machine-gun companies augmenting the fire from Thiepval and the corps heavy artillery, a widespread counter-attack began. They had cleared Stuff Redoubt in daylight and now held the approaches to the Schwaben. Even so, the fresh battalions were stopped 200 yards from the bunkers by rapid fire. The flank companies were ordered to encircle the defences.

Inside the redoubt, where this latest action had exhausted the ammunition. Major Peacocke decided he must withdraw. Sending his walking wounded back, he arranged for detachments to retire in stages to the enemy's foremost support and reserve trenches. They had almost cleared the interior when a long line of men appeared – the first relief battalion of the West Yorkshires.[26]

But the time for reinforcement or relief had passed. Darkness was falling, their flanks were open, the enemy was already on three sides. Enemy shellfire was mounting. Creeping forward on either side of the Schwaben, the Germans saw '...thick lines moving westwards from the redoubt on a broad front towards the place where the enemy originally broke through. The doubt whether they were our own troops was resolved by flares sent up from Thiepval. The British steel helmets were recognised...'

Convinced at last that there were none of his men in Thiepval village. General Morland agreed to cancel attacks planned for the night hours. The initial success on the Leipzig Redoubt was maintained, though all the officers of 17th HLI, had long since fallen. 36th Division clung to the German front lines. It had been a calamitous day, yet so near success. There was little comfort in the news they had from VIII Corps, or from III.

If we are to judge heroism, sacrifice, endeavour in terms of wordage in an account of this sort, the part played by 8th Division on the left of III Corps front will be deemed negligible. Such a judgement would, of course,

[26] Three had been sent forward: 1/5th, 1/7th, and 1/8th Battalions, the latter two by companies.

General *Erich von Falkenhayn*

Generals Rawlinson and Haig

General Fayolle, Commander of the French Sixth Army during the Battle of the Somme

General Foch, French Northern Army Group commander during the Battle of the Somme

Field Marshal *von Hindenburg;* Emperor *William II;* General *von Ludendorff*

Men of a support battalion leave their trenches towards Morval just after zero, September 1916

The movement forward of a 60-pounder in October 1916. What remains of the wood of Bazentin-le-Petit is at top left; the village top centre.

A company of 1st Lancashire Fusiliers prepares to assault in the VIII Corps battle, July 1916.

The Vickers medium machine-gun, belt fed from right to left. The barrel is jacketed to permit cooling by water.

British 8-inch howitzers in action between Fricourt and Mametz, August 1916.

An Australian crew loads a 9.45-inch mortar behind Pozires, August 1916

The mine under Hawthorn Redoubt is fired, zero minus ten minutes, July 1, 1916.

A German heavy mortar in action

A British soldier keeps watch, surrounded by dead comrades.

The village of Beaumont Hamel after capture in November 1916.

Winter on the Somme: An ammunition limber on the road to Flers, November 1916.

The result of a British bombardment: a German machine-gun post smashed by fire at Guillemont, September 1916.

'The terrible road into Guillemont, straight, desolate, swept by fire...' The view from Waterlot Farm.

be fallacious. Yet there is little to say in detail which does not repeat the agonies of failure from Gommecourt southward on that 1 July.

The task given to Major-General Hudson was the direct ascent to the main ridge up Ovillers Spur while simultaneously capturing the village and Pozières, 2000 yards in rear. He protested that the frontage was excessive, particularly in view of the enfilade fire which must be suffered from Thiepval spur and la Boisselle in the south. He suggested that he should delay his assault until these enemy positions were themselves under attack. General Rawlinson, to whom the proposal was referred, denied it. The consequences were much as had been appreciated by the divisional commander and his staff, after prolonged personal reconnaissance along the line. The account of the assault is told by an eye-witness in the history of the 26th Reserve Division,[27] an officer of 180 Regiment facing the 8th Division.

The intense bombardment was realised by all to be the prelude to an infantry assault sooner or later. The men in the dugouts therefore waited ready, belts full of hand-grenades around them, gripping their rifles and listening for the bombardment to lift from the front defence zone on to the rear defences. It was of vital importance to lose not a second in taking up position in the open to meet the British infantry which would advance immediately behind the artillery barrage. Looking towards the British trenches through the long trench periscopes held up out of the dugout entrances there could be seen a mass of steel helmets above the parapet showing that the storm troops were ready for the assault. At 7.30 am the hurricane of shells ceased as suddenly as it had begun. Our men at once clambered up the steep shafts leading from the dugouts to daylight and ran singly or in groups to the nearest shell craters. The machine-guns were pulled out of the dugouts and hurriedly placed in position, their crews dragging the heavy ammunition boxes up the steps and out to the guns. A rough firing line was thus rapidly established. As soon as the men were in position, a series of extended lines of infantry were seen moving forward from the British trenches. The first line appeared to continue without end to right and left. It was quickly followed by a second, then a third and fourth. They came on at a steady easy pace as if expecting to find nothing alive in our front trenches... The

[27] M Gerster, *Die Schwaben an der Ancre* (Heilbron: Salzer).

front line, preceded by a thin line of skirmishers and bombers, was now halfway across No Man's Land. 'Get ready' was passed along our front from crater to crater, and heads appeared over the crater edges as final positions were taken up for the best view, and machine-guns mounted firmly in place. A few minutes later, when the leading British line was within a hundred yards, the rattle of machine-gun and rifle broke out along the whole line of shell holes. Some fired kneeling so as to get a better target over the broken ground, whilst others, in the excitement of the moment, stood up regardless of their own safety, to fire into the crowd of men in front of them. Red rockets sped up into the blue sky as a signal to the artillery, and immediately afterwards a mass of shells from the German batteries in rear tore through the air and burst among the advancing lines. Whole sections seemed to fall, and the rear formations, moving in close order, quickly scattered. The advance rapidly crumbled under this hail of shells and bullets. All along the line men could be seen throwing up their arms and collapsing, never to move again. Badly wounded rolled about in their agony, and others, less severely injured, crawled to the nearest shell hole for shelter. The British soldier, however, has no lack of courage, and once his hand is set to the plough, he is not easily turned from his purpose. The extended lines, though badly shaken and with many gaps, now came on all the faster. Instead of a leisurely walk they covered the ground in short rushes at the double. Within a few minutes the leading troops had advanced to within a stone's throw of our front trench, and while some of us continued to fire at point-blank range, others threw hand grenades among them. The British bombers answered back, whilst the infantry rushed forward with fixed bayonets. The noise of battle became indescribable. The shouting of orders and the shrill cheers as the British charged forward could be heard above the violent and intense fusillade of machine-guns and rifles and bursting bombs, and above the deep thunderings of the artillery and shell explosions. With all this were mingled the moans and groans of the wounded, the cries for help and the last screams of death. Again and again the extended lines of British infantry broke against the German defence like waves against a cliff, only to be beaten back.

The enemy lines were pentrated to a depth of 500 yards on the left; to about 100 yards on the right, but in such low strength that local counter-attacks evicted them quickly. The casualties testify to the effects amongst battalions whose posted strength numbered 27-30 officers and about 700 men.

		Officers	*Other Ranks*
70 Brigade	8th KOYLI	21	518
	8th York and Lancaster	21	576
	9th York and Lancaster	14	409
	11th Sherwood Foresters	17	420
25 Brigade	2nd Royal Berkshires	27	347
	2nd Lincolns	21	450
	1st Royal Irish Rifles	17	429
	2nd Rifle Brigade	4	115
23 Brigade	2nd Devons	17	433
	2nd West Yorkshire	8	421
	2nd Middlesex	22	601

It is not easy to discern the support from the assault battalions amongst these figures, for most of the former were caught upon the heels of the latter. Perhaps the most indicative are those of 2nd Rifle Brigade which, being in reserve, remained on its own side of No Man's Land. Most horrifying is the fact that, from the total of the division's losses, almost 2000[28] were killed outright. The clearance of the wounded became, as elsewhere, a major problem in the corps area. There was no less work for the stretcher-bearers in 34th Division, south of the highway.

Long before zero, before the battalions began to make their way out into the fire or assembly trenches, a German listening post nicknamed 'Moritz' picked up an interesting piece of new at 2.45 am on the 1st. The post was established just south of la Boisselle with an apparatus sensitive to telephone traffic, and the following was heard clearly: '...impress on all infantry units the supreme importance of helping one another and holding on tight to every yard of ground gained. The accurate and sustained fire of the artillery during the bombardment should greatly assist the infantry.'

They were listening to the tail end of Rawlinson's message to all ranks before the attack. The words were passed back via headquarters of 110

---

[28] The registered figure is 1927.

Reserve Regiment to 28th Reserve Division at Bazentin le Petit. A general alert was ordered against a morning assault. None were surprised in the dugouts of 110 Reserve, in consequence, when the British shellfire intensified at 6.30. Many of the German platoons were standing ready at the foot of the steps to their trench to face the 34th Division when the mines exploded at 7.28. The observers on Tara-Usna ridge saw '...a spout of black earth shoot up in the German line. I didn't actually see Y Sap go off as I was watching Lochnagar but the front of la Boisselle was hidden by smoke from it when I looked across a few minutes later.

The two or three little mines in front of the 'Glory Hole' [British outpost opposite la Boisselle] had also gone off with quite a crack. Patches of smoke drifted about for some time.'

These lingering patches of smoke were not left by the mine explosions; they were the remnants of a screen fired by the mortars to hide the assault on either side of the village. But the light wind blew perversely. The explosion, too, in Y Sap served little purpose as the enemy had evacuated the trenches above due to their devastation by bombardment. So the 20th and 23rd Northumberland Fusiliers had to advance up the 800 yards of Mash Valley without concealment of any sort. From Ovillers and la Boisselle the machine-guns fired in enfilade while the steady ranks of these Tyneside Scottish battalions grew thinner, ever more open as they approached the German trenches. Later, they followed the narrowing line of dead into the support line where, amongst the final handful of these tough and wiry men, mostly miners, lay the bodies of the two commanding officers.

There was no attack from the 'Glory Hole', the stretch of British outposts 100 yards from the nearest ruins of la Boisselle. The company there held firm while the mines detonated all around. The Lochnagar mine had now settled, forming a crater ninety yards across with a rim raised fifteen feet above the trenches. The explosion had filled at least nine dugout exits with spoil and frightened the occupants of several others into remaining below. The 22nd Northumberlands had been quick to follow their advantage. Though the right-hand companies were machine-gunned from Sausage Valley, the left half of the battalion was able to push through to the reserve trenches 500 yards on. The first group to arrive brought a Lewis gun, which drove the defenders under cover, but it jammed after a few moments. Without its aid the Northumberlands were too weak to hold their position but detachments from companies in the 22nd and 23rd Battalions were drawn to the firing and when Major Acklom of the 22nd came up, he took over command. Two or three dozen dead Germans were left where they lay. 'We took their stick grenades but left their rifles. Somehow the Jerry trenches were different to ours – better made in some ways. But I suppose we were always expecting to push on and they were expecting to stay.' They found one machine-gun but it was damaged. When the prisoners had gone, helping their wounded back to the British dressing station on Tara Hill, a runner came forward to report that the bombing party was moving up towards la Boisselle.

There had been two groups of bombers but one was dead in No Man's Land. The other had started out with thirty-two and was now down to ten, its officer, Lieutenant Rotherford, wounded. Leaving a 'block' of two men to guard their rear, Rotherford took the remainder up to the edge of the village, pursuing the last of the trench garrison. Near the fortress, resistance hardened and they were stormed with rifle grenades fired by unseen hands from sandbagged openings in an outpost redoubt.

After half an hour all that remained were Rotherford and Private Johnson, also wounded. They went back to join Major Acklom. Now all were pressed by German bombers working down the trench. There was no sign of the 11th Suffolks or 10th Lincolns who should have come up Sausage Valley on their right, so their flank was in the air. At 8 o'clock Major Acklom wisely took his force back to the enemy support trench where he was less exposed. The first of six counter-attacks upon them began at 8.45.

The Suffolks and Lincolns had started late because of the mine explosion. In their journey of 500 yards up Sausage Valley, they were shot at in enfilade from Heligoland Redoubt half right and directly from the Bloater trench ahead. The Suffolks were shelled with shrapnel as they left their lines. Some eighty men reached the Heligoland and tried to storm it but the first wave was burned to death by flamethrowers as they stepped up on to the sandbagged upper works.

The survivors of the Suffolks bore to their right to join in with the 15th and 16th Royal Scots, right-flank battalions of III Corps.

Both Scots battalions had been shelled and machine-gunned heavily as they advanced, one behind the other, the 16th losing almost half their number killed. But with the Suffolks and Lincolns assailing one side of the Heligoland, they forced through on the south, over the demolished German fire trench, through the support and on past the reserve to Peake Wood, 2000 yards in from their own line. Little detachments dropped off en route as 'blocks' to be joined by survivors from other units. Major Stocks, C Company Commander of the 15th, took command of the position, beat off two counter-attacks and got a message back to brigade headquarters giving his position. This was at 10 o'clock, and he was ahead of schedule.

His Jocks were within 500 yards of Contalmaison, the headquarters of the German 56th Reserve Brigade. From this direction and from the north, counter-attacks were mounted under fire from artillery and mortars. After an hour of close fighting with machine-guns and rifles towards Contalmaison and bombing sorties along the communication trenches to the north, the Scots party was pushed out of Peake Wood and partially encircled. Major Stocks gave the order to fall back. In the withdrawal he was wounded and fell behind, becoming a prisoner. Under command of Lieutenant Robson the remainder got back to Wood Alley to join a mixed force from every battalion in the brigade. From this area the enemy could not eject them, though they continued to try until dusk, when at last rifles and machine-guns lay idle.

The first day's battle for the ridge had ended. Darkness fell and brought an opportunity to the tired, sweat-stained men in the batteries to rest; to the grimed exhausted infantry to pause and cat-nap. In the north Major Peacocke brought his Ulster heroes back to the first German trenches. Thiepval fell silent except for the nervous discharge of a machine-gun occasionally until midnight. The mixture of regiments in Leipzig Redoubt took turns at sentry watch. Major Acklom's force fought off the last counter-attack and stood down on the enemy side of Lochnagar crater. A young Captain Bibby commanding a handful of the 25th Northumberlands who had found a way through to Contalmaison – which they had entered – joined friends of the Royal Scots, Lincolns and Suffolks in Wood Alley. The staff captain of 101 Brigade roamed No Man's Land with a supply party for the Jocks and failed to find them. Lieutenant Ash and twenty-seven sappers succeeded. The long tunnel under No Man's Land had been opened at last near the Lochnagar crater. Gunners, sappers, service and medical corps joined the infantry in finding the wounded among the craters to bear them back through Thiepval Wood and Authuille and Aveluy across the Ancre, or over Tara-Usna Ridge to Albert. Behind this battered town a 12-inch railway gun had found the range of General von Stein's corps headquarters in Bapaume, from which he had now been shelled. But otherwise, after the long bombardment, the front below the ridge grew relatively quiet. The shadow plans for pressing home the attack in the afternoon, at dusk, in darkness, had fallen away as the divisional and corps commanders had come to realise that the brigades and battalions they were directing to further combat were counting their men in tens, not hundreds. The turn of the reserve divisions must wait until the smoke had cleared, the movement ended and the little gains weighed.

Tomorrow they might try again. For those who had tried today, it was a prospect that needed sleeping on.

ABOVE THE SOMME

In those summer mornings, the aerodromes of the Royal Flying Corps became active well before dawn. The Moranes and Martinsydes, the BE2c's, DH2's, FE2b's and Bristol Scouts due for early sorties behind the line on reconnaissance or interdiction bombing, above the line for photography, infantry contact, counter-bombardment and fighter cover were brought out from the portable Borousseau or Martat hangars and checked over by fitters, riggers and armourers. Pilots and observers checked the latest news from brigade and intelligence – perhaps received new orders for an emergency task – and climbed into their open cockpits. The simple instrument panel and control system took little time to check. Ammunition belts were fed into the lock of those few machines with an interrupter gear permitting fire to pass safely by the wooden propeller; otherwise, the ammunition would be mounted in drums on the Lewis guns.[29] Maps would be checked, goggles lowered, silk scarves settled and the pilot would open his throttle when, there being no brakes to hold back the airframe, the machine would instantly respond, to taxi bumpily across the open French pasture towards the downwind point of take-off.

On 1 July the first reconnaissance sortie was over Bapaume at 5 am, watching the railway yards and approaches for movement and searching for General von Stein's corps headquarters. They bombed Bapaume later. Cambrai was reconnoitred and bombed, and St Quentin; loops, curves, bridges and cuttings along the railway between were watched. By later standards it was small-scale stuff; reconnaissance by a single Morane biplane under the escort of three Martinsydes: railway bombing by a formation of twelve, another of sixteen BE2c's escorted by Martinsydes, Moranes and FE2b's. The bombers carried two 112-pound bombs apiece, but had to do without their observer to appropriate the payload. It may have been primitive, but it was a very personal war they fought against the enemy's ground fire and his Rolands and Fokkers in the sky. Their losses manifest the dangers they braved.

Navigation depended almost entirely on reading map and ground, an easier job for the stationary balloonist than the moving airmen – except when the balloonist was under air attack. But the view of each was screened, as we have seen, by the morning mist until 7 o'clock when,

---

[29] A circular dismountable magazine. Both Vickers and Lewis guns fired .303 rimmed ammunition.

finally, the valleys began to emerge from the 'white cotton wool'. Now smoke from bursting shells, from mortar bombs and candles, and the rising dust obscured much of the battle line. The British and French trenches immediately above the Somme were noticeably spared returning German shellfire, however, and in many areas there was none.

Below, the attack of III Corps, so clearly marked for the air watch by the straight line of the Albert-Bapaume high road, troops could be seen forming up to attack the Fricourt salient and in 'the "ops" round the corner' against Mametz and Montauban, and the French targets of Bois Faviere and Curiu village on the northern marshy bank of the Somme. Behind each major formation could be seen the massed artillery, noticeably profuse in the French sector, supporting their assembling infantry: XV Corps round Fricourt and Mametz, XIII Corps towards Montauban and its approach spurs, the French XX Corps facing the reverse slopes of the Bois Faviere and the spur above Curlu. At 7.28, two of the balloonists reported the flash and eruption of mine explosions as the preliminary bombardment reached its climax.

Both the balloonists of I Kite Balloon Squadron and the pilots and observers of 3 and 9 Squadrons in their aeroplanes were about to see a carefully prepared and, in many instances, well-devised assault on this portion of the German defences most remote from the main ridge. South of the III Corps boundary – that is, south of Sausage Valley and the Heligoland Redoubt guarding its entrance – the line ran on down to the slender re-entrant of the Willow Stream to turn at right angles, opposite Fricourt village, continuing east past Mametz, on across the main spur descending from Montauban, past Maricourt – jointly in British and French hands – turning south again in a right angle just short of the Bois Favière.

At all levels of operations the two British corps assaults in this sector were inhibited by the tactical concept of the respective corps commanders. 'Sideshows' apart, this had become standard practice in France. There was little room for divisional initiative in manoeuvre or fire plan, none for brigades.

The major-generals trained their men in trench warfare, administered them in principle and acted as movement agencies in battle. Sometimes the divisional commanders were able to persuade their superiors of the unsoundness of a venture.

Sometimes they suggested a permutation or the exploitation of operations. But here above the Somme, as usual, the plans were corps plans down to battalion tasks.

Lieutenant-General Horne did not conceive a direct assault for XV Corps on his right-angled front. At Fricourt, on the corner, they would feint initially while encircling the village by an advance to the north – 21st Division's work – and from the south by an advance through Mametz – 7th Division's.

The line of the Willow Stream would be the boundary between the two formations, and when the two forces met upon it, 1500 yards behind the village, they would take that fortified ruin as a separate operation. Its most dangerous salients were mined meantime, while smaller mines were laid for the purposes of deception. A Russian sap was dug secretly to straighten the northern line of fire trenches, the head cover being removed during the last night of the bombardment. The artillery plan reflected enterprise: a concealed battery which would lie silent throughout the bombardment until the final hour; comprehensive allocation of howitzers to strongpoints; a barrage of 18-pounder shrapnel that would creep forward of the infantry; neat variations of percussion and time fuses. But in their brave, industrious, good-hearted, unimaginative way, those gunner generals lined all their guns up behind the infantry when the right-angle of the line offered a prime shoot in enfilade. Had the guns and howitzers of 21st Division shot for the infantry of the 7th and *vice versa*, or had the gun lines of each been reversed, they would have been shooting directly down the German trenches. Not only would all the 'unders' and 'overs' have landed amongst the enemy but the medium guns could have continued their fire up to the very last moment of the assault. This is surely not a matter of hindsight; Napoleon knew the tactic, and a host of master gunners through preceding centuries.

So the mines were fired at 7.28 – as at the 'Glory Hole', Y Sap and Lochnagar – now here in the German line immediately north-west of Fricourt village at the 'Tambour' to obliterate the machine-gun nests in two old German craters whose position enfiladed the British line of assault. Opposite Fricourt the holding battalion of 7th Green Howards watched with horror as, by some tragic error, A Company of their number followed the assault in which they had no part. A single machine-gun from the German Tambour craters slew all but 16 within 40 yards. And this same weapon, a survivor of the explosion, had already riddled the line of the 10th West Yorkshire on the left flank. From Fricourt four more cut into the leading companies of the 4th Middlesex and on up the line across the assault of the 8th Somerset, 9th and 10th KOYLI. There was almost no response from the German artillery; counter-bombardment had largely destroyed their capacity to shoot. But the British guns had failed, too, through no fault of the Royal Artillery. The target was littered with unexploded shells from which the fuses had dropped inert in flight or which had failed internally to fire.[30] Thus the methodical planning for the heavy howitzers was ineffective. Many of the strongpoints harbouring enemy small arms remained untouched in the final hours. And though the enemy own that 'the trenches and obstacles, the weaker dugouts and also the best observation posts were nearly completely destroyed...' by the preliminary bombardment of eight days, the presence of half-a-dozen machine-guns alone was sufficient to deny the swift success for which the 21st Division had practised and planned.

The concealed battery and three others specially placed out below Bécourt Wood were unable to reach the prime enemy of the assault with their light shrapnel.

On the front of the 7th Division the last hour of bombardment brought a limited return of German shellfire, augmented here and there by concentrations of enemy mortars when four subsidiary mines were exploded. This made the British fire and support trench a dangerous zone. The divisional commander had neatly appreciated the possibility, however, and all the infantry of his two assault brigades had been drawn back 400 yards. Three minutes before zero the assault battalions scrambled up the trench ladders, formed-up in their lines of companies and began to advance over their home ground while the Stokes mortars and Vickers poured an intense fire into the enemy line immediately ahead.

Not all the German wire was cut – the 2nd Gordon Highlanders had a costly delay negotiating a fence of it – and a profusion of dud shells had left enough machine-guns in action forward to cause casualties grievously. But the shellfire stopped, thanks to the air spotters, and by 7.50 there were enough men of assault and support battalions through the German foremost positions to confirm a successful entry. Too many of the enemy had been kept forward. A high proportion of prisoners here had been badly shaken by days of what they called 'drumfire'. Their relief by a fresh regiment had been much delayed by it, only one and a half companies

---

[30] See *OH, 1916*, Vol. I, pp. 355-356, 379.

getting in during the previous night. Perhaps it was these newcomers who fought back with grenades and automatic rifles amongst the mass of communication trenches; there were three or four teams prepared to die with their weapons in action. All the while, the mixture of city and country men, men from the north, Bordermen from Cumberland, Staffords and Manchesters, the Gordons' Jocks, Queen's men from Surrey, 8th and 9th Devons from the south-west, kept pressing steadily until they were under the walls of Mametz, into it, repulsed, consolidating on the south while others sought to outflank the smoking rubble, broken beams and crazily hanging slices of wall. Beneath, often protected by concrete faces and heavy armour plating, machine-gun posts drove off the masses; rifle grenadiers sniped the bold infiltrators from concealed shafts.

I do not know if General Horne came forward to see how his divisions were faring. He had no central tree platform but there were observation posts in plenty; his presence is generally reported at corps headquarters eight miles in rear, however, throughout the morning. At noon the information in his operations room was cheering. On his left III Corps had passed on aircraft reports that troops were entering Contalmaison – Captain Bibby and his isolated handful of Northumberlands – with others in force at Peake Wood – Major Stocks and his Jocks. On the right, XIII Corps '...has reached every objective on time and is still advancing'. The Royal Flying Corps confirmed that his own men were pushing forward north of Fricourt; they had seen the red contact flares everywhere in the first line of the enemy – news which offset the first reports of heavy loss in the assault. Mametz had been entered – he did not receive news of the repulse. An aeroplane had reported seeing guns withdrawing behind Pozières at 11.20. A kite balloon had observed a group of twenty Germans leaving Fricourt for the wood behind. It was enough for General Home. Anticipating the junction of his two divisions behind the village, he ordered the attack on Fricourt to begin with a barrage at 2 pm for assault at 2.30.[31]

These orders went out at 12.50. Before 1.30 pm there was news that indicated a less extensive gain which might have led General Home to postpone the operation. Captain Hawkins of 3 Kite Balloon Section had reported the ejection of 22nd Manchesters from Danzig Alley, which he was now arranging to shell with 78 Seige Battery. An observer of 9 Squadron

---

[31] By previous arrangement all attacks subsequent to zero would be preceded by thirty minutes of bombardment.

looked back as his pilot flew low in front of Mametz to see troops firing at the village from the Cemetery, clearly still south of the ruins. 21st Division confirmed that their '...progress is slow because of our losses reported previously. Very few battalions forward of Empress (German front) trench are believed to number more than one company in strength.' Brigadier-General Headlam, commander of 64 Brigade, had been leading a composite force of 200 in the foremost trenches north of Fricourt but returned to report when he found a commanding officer surviving. At 11 am he reached divisional headquarters to confirm explicitly that there was no foreseeable junction with 7th Division for hours. On receiving orders to attack Fricourt, Brigadier-General Glasgow of 50 Brigade pointed out that the 10th West Yorkshires had failed to retain even the enemy outposts because of their excessive casualties. If the 7th Green Howards now attacked, they must face in isolation the German Tambour and the enormously strong front of Fricourt. His headquarters had already passed back the news that the wire obstacle was largely untouched.

He was ordered to 'press home the attack as planned'.

There were three companies only to make the assault, due to A Company's premature assault at 7.45. At 2.30, after a manifestly inadequate barrage with a high proportion of unexploded shells, the Green Howards attacked obediently. There were now four small gaps in the enemy wire which they might negotiate while the 7th East Yorkshires gave covering fire from the north and four Lewis guns fired from posts dug in the light railway embankment on the south. But they did not need it. The battalion as such did not reach the German wire, for their ranks were emptied in three minutes. Fifteen officers and 336 men fell. Dutifully, those forward kept going, including walking wounded, to be killed in the enemy's fire trench. One or two men managed to hide in a cellar till night-fall. On the left of the Green Howards, the leading companies of the 7th East Yorkshires, hoping to exploit the enemy's divided attention, crossed into No Man's Land to lose three-quarters of their strength. The attack was stopped. One wonders why it began.

Fricourt was the low point of the XV Corps attack; Mametz the high.

During the early afternoon the persistence of the 1st South Staffords and the 21st Manchesters had brought them into the eastern half of the village.

When the Devons and Warwicks lined up to assault after bombardment, the bulk of the garrison remaining – some had been seen withdrawing behind Fricourt – came out with their hands up – 200 unshaven begrimed figures in field grey, some surprisingly wearing greatcoats on this fine day. Though there was much dangerous, unpleasant work to be done in clearing out the defences, 7th Division had played its part in breaking the enemy. For this is what had been achieved by the early evening.

XIII Corps' attack up the spurs to Montauban had worked perfectly. The exceptional care in every facet of training beforehand, the meticulous battle planning and preparations, the success of the counter battery programme, ground and air communications, all made for an overwhelming success. And the luck was with XIII Corps. There was good ground observation on the enemy's front defences. They had fortunately knocked out the German artillery command post with a heavy shell. In rear, the enemy had exposed his artillery to the air unnecessarily – '...the batteries had suffered severely...' The batteries in Caterpillar Valley (the head of the Willow Stream behind Mametz and Montauban) especially had lost numerous guns. When the British attacked, there were only ten field and thirteen heavy batteries in readiness and these had numerous unserviceable guns. And the majority of those serviceable were firing against the British at Ovillers. It is true that the enemy had at least fifty-four machine-guns to meet the attack by XIII Corps but the dugouts were less extensive in this sector and the greater part of the garrison was either concentrated in the deep shelters below the fire trench, where many of the exits were smashed, or in shallow protection in the supports and reserves which failed to withstand the bombardment. Much the same condition obtained on the front facing General Balfourier's corps, XX, above the north bank of the Somme. The concentration of French medium and heavy artillery was formidable. '...nearly all the deep dugouts in the first position were blown in, only a few specially deep ones were still partly serviceable. The garrison lay mainly in shell and mine craters.'

Without the least disrespect to the many county regiments which advanced towards some ugly skirmishing on the Montauban position, or to the twelve battalions of France which sped through the lingering river mists that morning, they had a simple infantry task compared to their colleagues in the north. They did it well.

By 11.30 the reserve brigade of 30th Division – on the right of XIII Corps – had passed through Montauban and was looking down into Caterpillar Valley and across the Bernafay Wood where the Willow Stream ends. By 12.30 they had a company of 20th King's in the Briqueterie at its southern end. The French were now upon all but two of their final objectives[32] and had pushed 1000 metres beyond in several places. They had not had to commit a single reserve formation towards this achievement. The one counter-attack of significance, a battalion of 62 Regiment advancing from Hardécourt towards the front of General Nourrisson's 39th Division, was broken up by fire before it reached the French line.

At first the impression of the enemy's defeat arose from his manifest losses in the area they had taken. The entire headquarters of 62 Regiment was captured and part of 6 Bavarian Reserve. The total of prisoners reached 1,882, mainly from the latter regiment which had come into the line to carry forward supplies and reinforce the decimated garrison as recently as the night 29/30 June. But the occupants who were left when the captives had been marched away, underlined the impression. The tumbled and torn bodies of the commander, staff and orderlies of headquarters 23 Regiment were found in Glatz Redoubt, the victims of a direct hit by a heavy shell. Above ground in Montauban there were neither living nor dead – save the red wisp of a fox that flashed across the street as the British entered – but, below, the cellars were full of dead, doubtless from the French 240-mm mortar battery which had pounded the buildings slowly day and night from the morning of 25 June until zero. Many had held a tangle of heads, limbs, torsos for at least a week. Beside these broken humans were the smashed weapons: '...mortars, machine-guns, several hundred rifles, two field guns dug in behind the north wall to enfilade Mametz and ammunition of all sorts in stacks and scattered about.' And there was booty. Silk shirts, the mild cigar dear to the German soldier, trinkets from dug-outs. The reserve rations had been eaten but an abundance of soda water was found in deep stores. The quick prisoners, the dead foe, the possession of his petty treasures, the sense of his recent presence all contributed to the impression that the enemy had been forced from his position, and that he was not apparently coming back. Indeed, those in the observation posts

---

[32] The exceptions being the northern and eastern edges of Boil Faviere on the enemy's reverse slope.

could see no movement; they were not fired upon. In Bernafay Wood, whose last occupants, a field battery, had been attacked by a BE2c at 10 o'clock, a patrol found only three weary infantry stragglers to bring back as their personal prisoners. They were Bavarians and did not know where their company had gone to, or even if they existed. They had seen no one in Bernafay Wood or in Trônes Alley, the trench connecting Bernafay to Trônes Wood, In this, at least, they seem to have been telling the truth, for an air spotter and a Manchesters' patrol confirmed that the Alley was empty all the way into the southern half of Trônes Wood. Across Caterpillar Valley, Marlboro' Wood was found to be empty, too.

All this was known at XIII Corps headquarters by 1.30 pm at the latest. General Balfourier, XX Corps commander, had already endorsed his divisional commanders' wish to continue the advance, at least until they made substantial contact. But they could not do so unless the British moved with them. General Congreve, XIII Corps commander, regretted that he could not. Despite Haig's clear orders to Rawlinson that his corps should exploit any opportunity to press in on the enemy towards a break-through, Rawlinson's own reservations had led him to stress the importance of gaining and consolidating their objectives.[33] And Congreve was a careful general; his care had helped his corps to success that morning, though it was now holding part of it back. XV Corps was not up on his left, he explained to Balfourier's liaison officer, and his own left-hand division was not completely on its final objectives. He wished to develop the defences of the ground he had won in case of a counter-attack. The French corps commander protested again in the later afternoon that they should move on but Congreve would not budge. A German medium gun near Thilloy fired occasionally into Montauban to interrupt an otherwise peaceful night.

[33] See Fourth Army Operation Order of 14 June 1916:
'5. The first day's operations will include the capture and consolidation of Montauban, , Pozières and Serre.

As soon as this line has been gained and consolidated, preparations will immediately be undertaken to commence the second phase of the operations.

The Army Commander wishes to impress on all commanders that the success of the operations as a whole largely depends on the consolidation of the definite objectives which have been allotted to each corps. Beyond these objectives no serious advance is to be made until preparations have been completed for entering on the next phase of the operation.'

BELOW THE SOMME

It had been General Foch's wish to delay his attack for some days after that of the British; a wish resisted by Haig, as we have seen. Nonetheless, he had his own way to a limited extent and gained an advantage for his soldiers thereby. For although Balfourier's XX Corps attacked at zero with the British XIII, the remainder of the French Sixth Army delayed a further two hours.

General Fayolle, the army commander, employed two corps in his assault below the Somme: 1 Colonial, advancing along the southern bank; XXXV on the right. General Duchêne's II Corps remained in reserve. Thirteen divisions was the total available, due to the demands of Verdun. Of these, two assaulted to the north, three to the south of the river on 1 July.

Yet the holocaust of Verdun gave the French here their second advantage, though one of which they were unaware. Falkenhayn's intelligence staff had counted the different French divisions through the months of fighting – for example, forty-two had taken their turn in the fortified zone between 21 February and 30 April as compared with thirty of the Germans. Quite wrongly, German Supreme Headquarters had assumed that the French were committed on the same basis as their own divisions – almost to exhaustion point. They believed therefore that they had worn out half the French Army by May. In fact, Joffre had restricted the period spent on either bank of the Meuse so that a division was not exhausted by the fighting; a draft of reinforcements, a turn in reserve and a spell in a quiet sector was adequate to refresh most of such formations.

The Sixth Army had therefore a double advantage in surprise on 1 July. The Germans did not believe they had sufficient strength to attack astride the river, and their attack did not begin until two hours after zero on the north side. By this time their bombardment, of overwhelming weight, had become intolerable. Eighty-five heavy batteries had been pounding for almost eight days on a frontage of 8000 yards. 'The front trenches had been totally obliterated; nothing could be picked out as a line of defence amongst the shell craters and the Germans had given up trying to link these with communication trenches to form an outpost line. The entrance to almost all the forward dugouts had been closed.' There were no forward wire obstacles to the assault and little remained of the heavy belt laid behind the supports to impede the assault up the shoulder above the long re-entrant of Fay. By contrast, the enemy artillery was silent. The eight heavy batteries and all but two of the field batteries were out of action.

For all these advantages, the *poilus* did not walk in upon their enemy's line unopposed. Machine-guns lying back covered the broken outposts and supports. On the bank of the Somme 2nd Colonial Division had a difficult approach along the water's edge to Frise village, a kilometre from their start-point. They had first to breach three lines of trenches and then pass on to take a switch line to Frise in rear, 700 metres distant. It was dusk before they had established themselves firmly in the cemetery in the south of the village, the remaining ruins being held by a company of 56 Reserve Regiment. 3rd Colonial Division had the task of clearing two adjacent villages, Dompierre and Becquincourt, one behind the other, whose cellars had withstood much of the high explosive. 61st Division, in XXXV Corps on the right of the attack, had to attack astride the extensive wooded re-entrant of Fay and to expose a developing flank to the fire from Estrées.

It was not easy; but the French were more used to the mass attack than their British allies. Many of their junior officers and NCO's had been in the great attacks at Arras and in the Champagne. Although they lined-up at the outset, they began to draw off into groups in crossing No Man's Land in which, loosely spaced, they would dash forward from crater to crater, point to point, while covered by the rifle and automatic fire of their comrades in other groups. Thus they denied the enemy the brave targets of Redan Ridge, Thiepval and la Boisselle. Once in the enemy trenches, blocking parties would bomb from the traverses while other groups crawled or dashed in bounds across the surface to cut off the enemy in rear. At 9.45 pm all objectives had been reached, except in the immediate area of Frise, while the entire central front had been pushed forward 800 metres beyond. They were within assaulting distance of the enemy second line, had taken over 3,000 prisoners and a great quantity of arms and equipment, including several field batteries. The eyes of the corps commanders were now fixed upon Péronne, four miles distant from the nearest French infantry soldier, and, more important, protected by only one complete defence line.

Thus the buoyant apprehensions of victory prevailed from Mametz to Fay, while the fearful memory of defeat encompassed the northern corps.

PART IV

The Long Agony

THE HIGHER COMMANDS

Upstream from the French Sixth Army's attack, headquarters of the German Second Army occupied St Quentin. It would not be excessive to say that General von Below, who spent 1 July there, had found the day very trying.

The town was bombed by three sets of British aircraft; and although they were aiming at the railway junction and marshalling yards, it was not comforting to know that the one was seriously damaged, the other partly destroyed. He received news during the forenoon that General von Stein, commanding XIV Reserve Corps, had been shelled out of Bapaume. This disruption of the corps communications added to the difficulties of obtaining news of the Allied offensive; for Stein's command ran from the Somme to Gommecourt. But it was clear by 1 pm that the enemy were breaking in; indeed, many of the afternoon reports suggested impending disaster.

The Allied preliminary bombardment had already killed or wounded many of those in the German defence line so that, before a French or British soldier attacked, it had been necessary to commit reserves piecemeal to man the trenches; the deployment of 8 Bavarian Reserve at

Thiepval and of 6 Bavarian Reserve between Mametz and Montauban had reduced the corp reserve by half. Day by day the artillery had also lost men and guns, particularly in the sectors immediately on either side of the Somme. The whole of 121 Division's artillery and six of eight heavy batteries had been destroyed south of the river by the French Sixth Army. North, 109 guns and howitzers were lost or out of action. Soon it was said that Bernafay and Trônes Woods were occupied by the British and that a general advance had begun towards the second line between Longueval and Guillemont. German divisional and brigade staffs in the area were forming up every available man to defend this line – batmen, orderlies, clerks, cooks, storemen.

There was no question of counter-attack; all local reserves had been committed and there were neither guns nor observers to provide fire support. 12th Reserve Division at Cambrai, part of the army reserve, were already on their way forward by rail but seemed unlikely to reach Longueval in time to prevent its capture. The 5th Division was entraining at St Quentin at 2 pm for the front of the French Sixth Army when it was hit by three BE2c's. The wagons containing the arms and equipment of one regiment were destroyed and the divisional move was delayed by eighteen hours, the regiment most affected being unable to move forward at all. When the army operations staff asked for details of the battle in the Somme sector, the reply was often that 'the situation is uncertain'.

During the afternoon elements of 12th Reserve Division, already in the third line, reached the second in the Longueval area. Even with this increment, numbers were insufficient to hold the fire trench and the supports and reserves were, of course, empty. Fortunately the British did not appear, though several patrols were seen investigating intermediate woods. At 1.30 General Stein issued orders to 12th Reserve Division to attack Montauban by night, and placed his last reserve regiment, 16 Bavarian Reserve, under command for the purpose. It was due to begin at last light but the division was still de-training. The order was postponed to 11.30 pm but the division was still marching towards the second line. At last, between 3 and 4 pm on 2 July, the four weary regiments of German infantry crossed the Willow Stream and began to ascend to Montauban Ridge, preceded by a weak bombardment which aroused the men of Congreve's and Balfourier's corps. British and French guns quickly fired a shrapnel barrage, killing and wounding numbers of the enemy who were closely packed for the assault. One regiment had already gone astray, joining in the attack along the Franco-British boundary. A small party managed to enter the Montauban ruins but they were shot or killed with grenades. There was no second attempt and the entire force drew off to the second line leaving dead and some of the wounded. They were pursued by shrapnel and small-arms fire in the dawn.

It did not help General Below that Falkenhayn persisted in the view that the main offensive might fall yet further to the north on the front of Crown Prince Rupprecht's army. However, the opening of the preliminary bombardment had been sufficient to convince him that an offensive was indeed beginning and orders had been sent on that day, 24 June, restricting the army at Verdun in its use of men and ammunition. After receiving reports on 1 July, the Supreme Command began to make withdrawals from the Verdun establishment. Below was promised sixteen heavy batteries, all but one of which would come from the fortress region. Three divisions and three flights of aircraft would be sent from the general reserve at once, but more could not be spared until the main front of attack was confirmed.

On the British front General Stein had decided to abandon Fricourt; it had been outflanked and must fall within a few hours of daylight. The majority of the garrison fell back to Contalmaison, where they were instructed to man a line from the rear of the village to Bazentin le Petit, an area which had been vulnerable to capture from the east. Throughout the night this voluntary withdrawal was not apparent in the reports sent on to Falkenhayn as it appeared to be a part of the British successes on 1 July. But on the 2nd General von Pannewitz, commanding the XVII Corps south of the Somme, asked permission to withdraw completely from the second defence line – the French had breached it at Herbécourt – in order to effect the relief of his depleted division on the south bank. General Grünert, the army chief of staff, acceded and that night the troops pulled back behind a screen of machine-guns.

Next day Falkenhayn came to St Quentin with Tappen, chief of the operations staff at the Supreme Command. He asked how such a voluntary abandonment of ground could have been permitted, remarking that 'the first principle of position warfare must be to yield not one foot of ground;

and if it be lost to retake it immediately by counter-attack, even to the last man.' As Grünert had sanctioned the withdrawal, he must take the responsibility.[1] General Below was told that he would be removed, to be replaced by Colonel von Lossberg.

This incident apart, 3 July brought an improvement in German fortunes. The second line opposite the British XV and XIII Corps was now completely manned – though the garrison comprised scattered detachments from many units. Trônes[2] Wood was re-garrisoned and plans made to occupy Mametz Wood and the Quadrangle to the south-west. The British still seemed content to rest on their successes of the 1st. By noon on the 3rd Bernafay Wood was still empty and a fighting patrol was pushed forward into it from Trônes Wood. Thirty-eight heavy batteries had now arrived as replacements with the likelihood of at least thirty more.[3] By the 5th, with the arrival of four fresh divisions imminent – two sent by Crown Prince Rupprecht – it was possible to reorganise the front. Falkenhayn reduced the Second Army responsibility to the line between the Somme and Gommecourt. A new corps headquarters, VI, came in under Lieutenant-General von Gosler to command from the north bank of the river to the Albert-Bapaume road.

General von Stein continued to command his remaining troops north to Gommecourt. Von Pannewitz, under a cloud for his withdrawal south of the river, was replaced by von Quast. The division delayed by bombing at St Quentin now took up its place to deny Péronne to General Fayolle.

Fayolle, who was later to become a Marshal of France, was one of the kindliest old gentlemen imaginable. He had retired before the war, what hair he had was white, and his high bald head was that of a savant. His mind did not belie his appearance, for he had a scholarly, gentle mentality and needed a stronger and younger man at his side. He provided wisdom, his Chief of Staff, the drive... This impeccable technician[4] had one fault, he lacked authority when dealing with

---

[1] In fact, Falkenhayn knew of the proposal to withdraw the division but made no effort to intervene (see *Der Weltkrieg, 1914 bis 1918*, Vol. X, p. 335). The Chief of the General Staff may have wished to use the occasion to demonstrate the inflexibility of his policy for defence. However, Crown Prince Rupprecht suggests that it was spite on Falkenhayn's part in having been proved wrong about the sector to be attacked (*Mein Kriegstagebuch*, 3 July, 1916).

[2] Trônes – this is a British misspelling of the French name ' Trôncs'. I have used Trônes as it is the name familiar to all who took part in the battle.

[3] By October Below's heavy artillery had been reinforced to 109 heavy batteries. The British had 107.

obstreperous corps commanders. Upon several occasions I had seen General Joffre step in with the weight and force of an 8-inch shell and re-establish instantaneous order amongst General Fayolle's argumentative but now dismayed subordinates.[5]

Colonel Duval was Fayolle's chief of staff and it was his custom to call a meeting each evening of the corps chiefs of staff to discuss the operations of the day, thereby exchanging information, and to consider those of the morrow and plans in more distant prospect. Such a meeting was held on the evening of 1 July in the village of Boves, at the western end of the Roman road into Amiens. The chief of staff to General Balfourier confirmed an aspect of the battle which had been the subject of several telephone conversations during the day: the British XIII Corps would not budge beyond their first objectives. The 39th division of his own corps was immediately next to the British 30th on the Montauban ridge. 39th division had not cleared the northern end of the Bois Favière as it lay in a gulley. This was unimportant. What the divisional commander wished to do was to push on to capture Hardécourt and the knoll above it. But a glance at the map would show this to be foolhardy if the British did not occupy Bernafay Wood, Trônes Wood and the ring contour immediately south of each. The Allied flanks would thus be secured. The divisional commander had asked his opposite number to proceed and the proposal had been referred to XIII Corps headquarters. But General Congreve would not move – they had asked him twice. 39th Division must therefore stand fast until the British reached at least the Guillemont position.

Next day, therefore, XX Corps remained in its positions while I Colonial and XXXV pressed on to and partially through the German second line south of the river. It was that evening, after they had depleted the number of the German 121st Division to the point of ineffectiveness, that General von Pannewitz asked permission to withdraw altogether from the second line of defence. With only a screen of machine-guns to resist them, the French exploited forward to Flaucourt and Belloy. The first was taken without serious opposition by a colonial battalion but Belloy resisted successfully a regimental attack – Pannewitz needed the Roman road immediately to the south to complete his evacuation; Estrées, astride the road to the west, continued to check XXXV Corps for the same reason.

---

[4]   He had been Professor of Artillery at the War College.

[5]   Brig.-Gen. (now Maj.-General) E L Spears, *'Prelude to Victory*, p. 127.

Fayolle did not press his advantage in ground on the north bank. The committal of a reserve division on this day, 3 July, would have swept him forward into the edge of Péronne; for his open flank rested on the river which would not easily be crossed by a massed German assault. But there was still no sign of activity by the British nearby and his instructions from Foch were simply to seize positions from which he might in due course turn south to advance along the Roman road. On the 4th he decided to advance along the northern bank where XX Corps completed the occupation of the Hem spur and village. South of the Somme he took Estrées and Belloy against hardening resistance. The German relief was almost completed. Local reserves were concentrating on his southern flank, now considerably exposed. On 5 July the enemy recaptured Estrées in a sharp battle preceded by a heavy barrage of artillery fire. His men fell back to the wood below Fay. At Belloy they were placed in defence; three German counter-attacks failed outside the village, many of whose houses were still standing. The opportunities for easy victories on Sixth Army front were now passing, as they had passed almost beyond reach of the British.

Rawlinson remained in his headquarters throughout 1 July; he would have been a perfect nuisance to the brigade and, divisional commanders if he had gone forward. The only advantage of doing so would have been the acquisition of first-hand experience of the conditions of the infantry battle.

He might, too, have given some immediate decisions either to save lives or exploit a local situation, but he had corps commanders to do this and had no reason to suppose that any of them were incompetent.

Much of the time he spent with Archie Montgomery, his chief of staff, not only to discuss the latest news – scarce for much of the day – but also to draw, in my opinion, on the innate stability of this quiet, handsome man whose height permitted him to stand eye to eye with his commander. Rawlinson had the subtler mind, a greater depth of imagination, but he was given to extremes of gaiety and gloom. Very properly, Montgomery dealt with the corps staff through the day; Rawlinson spoke directly to the corps commanders. They compared their news.

From time to time Gough came in; at first, hopeful of finding the prospect of a gap through which he might pass his Reserve Army. The afternoon news, which was passed for information to his headquarters at

Daours, three miles by direct road from Querrieu, quenched any precipitate thoughts of early cavalry action. Haig, too, drove from Montreuil to Querrieu, arriving after lunch. Considering the constant impairment of the communications in front of divisional headquarters, it is remarkable that Rawlinson had any information to give the commander-in-chief at all. 'We hold the Montauban-Mametz spur and the villages of those names', Haig wrote in his diary entry concerning the visit. 'The enemy are still in Fricourt, but we are round his flank on the north and close to Contalmaison. Ovillers and Thiepval villages have held our troops up, but our men are in the Schwaben redoubt which crowns the ridge north of the last named village. The enemy counter-attacked here but were driven back. He, however, is holding on to a position with a few men in the river (Ancre) valley.' The predominant optimism of the corps and army reports is evident here concerning Fricourt and Contalmaison. One does not know whether the diarist or a staff officer is responsible for the illusion concerning the overwhelming strength of the 'few men in the river valley' at St Pierre Divion and Beaumont Hamel station. I think it likely that this was Haig's own construction, for he goes on to say, 'North of the Ancre, the 8th Corps (Hunter-Weston) said they began well... I am inclined to believe from further reports, that few of the 8th Corps left their trenches.' It is extraordinary that this mean comment was not subsequently excised in shame by the author when the facts of the fighting on Redan and Hawthorn ridges, for Y Ravine and Beaumont Hamel became known. 'If 'few of the 8th Corps left their trenches', how did they suffer 14,000 casualties?

None of the losses were known accurately at that time – GHQ had no reliable figures before 3 July – and neither Haig's nor Rawlinson's headquarters knew why some assaults had succeeded while others had totally failed. Those who condemn Haig for ordering the continuance of the offensive on the 2nd – which he did to Rawlinson that afternoon – do less than justice to the men who had lost their lives on the 1st. Haig confirmed his wish to obtain a good position from which to attack the enemy second line. He did not tell Rawlinson how to do it but we shall see that he was understandably surprised to learn that Fourth Army commander had ordered the resumption of attack along the entire line under the arrangements of corps command '...as early as possible compatible with adequate previous artillery preparations'. The difficult task of coordinating renewed attacks by VIII and X Corps on Beaumont Hamel and Thiepval respectively was given to Gough. 'I have put Goughy in command of the two northern corps to coordinate their efforts and see if he cannot push them on again', Rawlinson entered in his diary against 10 pm. '...DH has placed the general reserve, that is the 38th and 23rd Division, at my disposal with a hint not to use them up too soon.'

These two formations came into Fourth Army to replace the army reserve sent forward by Rawlinson as reliefs for those with excessive casualties. 8th Division was thankfully drawn out of the line; it was believed that they had had the highest losses. The plight of the divisions at Thiepval was unnoticed, more so those of VIII Corps. Fortunately Gough made searching enquiries on his assumption of command. Just after midnight he telephoned Rawlinson to say that an assault on 2 July was out of the question, though they might do so on the 3rd. The response to Rawlinson's orders was confined, therefore, to two corps only: III, who would try again to take their first objectives; and XV who had yet to join up with XIII Corps behind Fricourt and take that heap of ruins.

Opposite Ovillers 12th Division had completed their relief of the 8th with instructions to assault over the same ground, but it was clear that the long drawn-out recovery of the wounded and the piecemeal hand-over by remnants of battalions would occupy the whole night 1/2 July. The divisional commander had also stressed the need for reconnaissance when ordered by General Pulteney to attack at dawn. In view of this, III Corps headquarters decided to bombard Ovillers and release smoke in front of it to deceive the defence, while pressing 34th Division into la Boisselle. A French NCO, Paul Maze, who was used by General Gough as a liaison officer with outstanding success, was sent to discover what was happening in this sector.

> Taking a short cut, I walked over the open across Usna Hill. Scattered in pits all over the place our field guns were firing. I was nearly shaken out of my life. Terrified, I ran down towards Mash Valley, dodging about over the rough ground as each sharp detonation displaced the air around me. I was indeed relieved to find a communication trench, into which I jumped.
>
> It led to a dug-out where, deep down in a tiny stuffy room, a

brigadier-general was writing out his orders. When I explained what I had come to do, he at once detailed a man to take me up to the front line. I stood watching my guide putting on his kit, squeezing his head into his steel helmet, grimacing as he tucked the strap under his chin. Picking up his rifle he slung it over his shoulder, and without a word started towards the front line. Along a monotonous, dazzling, chalky trench we walked, seeing a streak of blue sky above and the sandbags drifting past. As each corner of a traverse eclipsed my companion for a second or two, I had the illusion of following my own shadow. I screwed up my neck looking for la Boiselle: all I could see were more sand-bags over which smoke was drifting, following a succession of violent reports.

We walked on; I could hear shells whining past through the air, exploding ahead in a straight line towards the direction we were making for.

I wanted to wail, but my guide strode on. I could still follow the whistling rush of each shell bursting nearer and nearer, until one landed in the next traverse and made everything rock with the violence of its explosion. Covered in earth, my heart racing, I looked at my runner who, doubled up, had his chin between his knees as if he had been trying to squeeze the whole of his body under his steel helmet. I was relieved when he moved, unhurt. We moved on again.

The firing, without easing off, lifted over our heads and followed a perfect course down the trench we had come up. A few yards further on mutilated bodies were lying amidst fallen earth and tumbled sandbags, directly where the parapet had been blown in. In the next traverse stood a group of wounded men, white and shaken, with blood oozing out of their riddled tunics. We helped some of them into a dug-out where others had been already carried to safety. The enemy had the range of every trench, and they shelled them day and night. By the time I had reached the front line my interest in la Boisselle had nearly gone.

Through a gap between two sandbags I was shown the village, where smoke was drifting across skeletons of trees on a torn up mound. An uneven line of sandbags, stretching across piles of bricks and remnants of houses, faced our front trench. The enemy was there, a few yards away. His presence, so near and yet unseen, made upon me an uncanny impression.

The ground between our trench and the ruins beyond was merely a stretch of craters and burnt-out grass broken up by tangled wire, not unlike gorse-bushes. The dead were lying there in all conceivable attitudes, rotting in the sun. A veil of fumes from lachrymatory shells was rolling along the ground.

A small attack was to be made on the place that night. As I intended to see it, I went back to Brigade Headquarters to rest. The General was still busy with his plans.

Late that night I followed a company going up to the front line, making room all the way up for stretcher-bearers moving down with their casualties. The trench was narrow, and we had to squeeze past each man; in the darkness no one spoke.

I found the battalion preparing for the attack. A heavy dew had made the ground clammy and slippery. It grew cold...

Shells fired from Usna Hill were shrieking over our heads, crashing one after another a little way beyond in that mysterious gap. After an anxious wait the men began assembling round the scaling ladders and got ready to climb on to the high parapet.

Amongst much older men a young Tommy was awaiting his turn. He seemed weighed down by his kit and the loose belts of ammunition hanging from his shoulders; his small head was buried beneath his tin helmet. In a long nervous hand he held a rifle with fixed bayonet, and looked anything but anxious to use it. Heavy thoughts seemed to be in that boy's mind, and the lack of enthusiasm displayed by the rest filled me with misgivings as to the ultimate success of the attack. Vitality is low at that hour...

They were all moving slowly and in silence while the officers, apparently keyed up, were now gazing at their watches as the last seconds slipped away and guns from the valley were angrily spitting fire. The first men clambered up the steps, followed by the rest, who stumbled forward into the night after the barrage – black figures silhouetted against the flares, flooding the broken ground with brilliant light.

Machine-guns raked the open spaces, shells tore the air, bullets thumped against the parapet; wounded men were crawling back to safety, helped by a few terrified German prisoners. We waited – the waves hadn't got far. The few men who had survived the stretch of No Man's Land were scattered in shell holes on the edge of the village. Once again they had failed to reach an objective, which had already been obliterated.

When the day broke, fresh forms, lying ominously still, showed the cost of the few craters we had gained. A sense of new life was rising from the earth with the freshness of the morning.

I followed the wounded who were crawling down to the aid-posts. The stretcher-bearers, climbing over the earth in places where the trench had been blown in, were obliged to expose their burdens to the merciless sniping from la Boisselle.

At Brigade headquarters the general seemed rather disheartened with the result of the attack. When I left him to go back to the army, he said he was running a very tired brigade. I think he hoped I would mention it to them!

At length I came out of the communication trench and faced the iron crucifix standing at the cross-ways with its arms extended parallel to the Albert-Authuille road. Troops passing it going up and down to the line made its position very significant. It came to be well known by all those fighting in that area. It stood there uttering its message to thousands of men until almost the end of the war, when at last a shell shattered it.

Twisted bits of iron were all that remained on the road of a staff car which had been imprudent enough to drive up so far.

On the safe slope of a bank rising from the road an aid-post was receiving the wounded of the night. Further on a battalion in reserve was sheltering, as the enemy at the time were plastering with high explosives the village of Aveluy and the road leading to it. The men were casually watching the shells splash into the marshes down below and the shrapnel explode at the entrance to the village. A horse with a water-cart and no driver had bolted up the main street, whilst a party of men lay flat off the road waiting for a lull in the squall.

The French seventy-fives with us in this attack had also buried themselves under the bank and were shooting their gas-shells over the ridge at a terrific rate – the muzzles of their little blue guns, cocked up high, were recoiling with the smoothness of an engine.

I became anxious about my motor bike, left in a block of houses now being shelled. As soon as the shelling eased off I took the opportunity of getting it. I found it covered with dust, but otherwise intact. Riding up the hill through the shattered village, I looked down upon a well-known bicycle factory where machinery and hundreds of bicycle parts were twisted up as if in a paroxysm of agony. The traffic on the road further on was creating a fearful dust; some of the infantry passing looked as if they had been fighting in flour.

From the high ground of Hennécourt the view was very impressive. Down below the valley of the Somme made a graceful loop towards the town of Albert, with all its roofs open to the sky. The high tower of the damaged cathedral was squarely facing the rising ground which was striped by a maze of chalky trenches which the artillery on both sides were thoroughly pulverising. Still holding the infant Jesus in her outstretched arms, the statue of the Virgin Mary, in spite of many hits, still held on top of the spire as if by a miracle. The precarious angle at which she now leaned forward gave her a despairing gesture, as though she were throwing the child into the battle.

La Boiselle, where I had come from, was like a volcano in eruption. To my left, on a promontory, the remains of Pozières were bounding up and down with the bombardment.

At Fricourt, as we have seen, General von Stein decided to withdraw the majority of the garrison during the night. Though patrols brought back this information, the muddle of reliefs prevented the occupation of the village before noon on the 2nd. Eleven men, who had not received orders to leave, were found in the warren of fortified cellars. Dead horses, dead German bodies lay above ground; other bodies of soldiers were found in trenches and dugouts where the fuses of the heavy shells had not failed. Sunday 2 July was a clear sunny morning and close out of the west wind. Flies were settling on the rotting bodies. The stench of human decay pervaded the rubble.

Behind the village General Home's corps concentrated on joining up on the line of their original objectives for the 1st. There were a number of small actions against, enemy detachments, well-armed with machine-guns and automatic rifles, who had been left behind because they lacked telephone lines to the brigade headquarters in Contalmaison or simply because – many of the battalion and regimental headquarters having been destroyed – no one knew they were in position.

At 10.30 on the Sunday morning Haig came again to Querrieu. The reports he had had made it clear that the advance up the Albert-Bapaume road was fractional. He made it clear that he wanted the Fricourt position captured as quickly as possible in order to exploit their success. An advance from Fricourt-Montauban would take them forward to an assault line against the enemy's second defence positions. Moreover, an advance from this direction would take Contalmaison in rear. Gough's command should not attack again north of the Ancre, merely demonstrate, and the attack at Thiepval should be mounted only as a diversion, Rawlinson demurred. He not only wished to carry Thiepval, Ovillers and la Boisselle by direct assault but also to persevere with a frontal assault against Beaumont Hamel.[6] Congreve was worried about an advance from Montauban because the ground on either side of the Willow Stream was so open. Without explaining why he had neglected to occupy Trônes or even Bernafay Woods, Rawlinson added that many of their difficulties to XIII Corps area were due to congestion in the sector with the French. Haig promised to see Foch to discuss the development of offensive action jointly with XX Corps and left. But he was clearly unconvinced by Rawlinson's sterile policy. In the afternoon he sent a personal message directing that there should be no attack north of the Ancre, and the assault on Thiepval would be limited to two brigades. Kiggell, the chief of staff, telephoned Rawlinson about 10.30 pm to stress Haig's concern that they should exploit XIII Corps' position. Rawlinson replied that he was quite clear. He now mentioned that he was worried that there might not be enough ammunition for the heavy howitzers if they should meet opposition – he and the commander-in-chief had discussed ammunition expenditure that morning. The chief of staff assured him that any expenditure by the artillery was acceptable to gain a proper footing inside the German second line. Though Rawlinson was seeing Foch next morning, he would also ask GQG to urge an advance on the north bank.

It was not a good day for Rawlinson. Something – perhaps the first reckoning of the casualties, now to hand – had damped his spirits. All his worst forebodings about the operation had returned. Frequently, he walked about the garden of his headquarters, slashing at nothing with his stick, the round dome of his bald head bent forward.

---

[6] Compare this aim with the letter written to Major Clive Wigram for King George V next day (Maj.-Gen. Sir F Maurice, *Life of Lord Rawlinson of Trait* (Cassell), p. 162).

On Monday the 3rd, X and III Corps were to attack together, then: two brigades against Thiepval; two against Ovillers. An hour's bombardment would precede zero at 3.15 am. At 2.55 Gough rang III Corps to say that he had been unable to reorganise quickly enough for his attack; the two brigades to which he was now limited would not be ready before 6. Alone, therefore, two brigades of III Corps went forward to Ovillers, though with some artillery support on Thiepval spur. Five battalions passed through the enemy wire, now gapped. The total of infantry with small parties of gunners and sappers was 3,350. By 9 am almost 2,400 had fallen. Ovillers remained intact.

Thiepval remained intact at 6.15 am.

At 9 am XV Corps attacked to break the last resistance south of Contalmaison. Railway Copse and Bottom Wood were taken, the enemy surrendering or running back towards the well-developed Quadrangle Trench leading into Contalmaison. At 11.30 a contact aeroplane spotted a line of men coming back from the village, either to counter-attack or to reoccupy some of the ground abandoned. They turned towards the junction of III and XV corps. Though advised that fresh artillery support was being planned for him, Brigadier-General Rawling, commander of the left-hand brigade in the corps, decided not to wait. Going forward, he placed out his Stokes mortars and attacked with his reserve battalion, 13th Northumberlands, from a new direction, leaving the remainder of his brigade to press the enemy in Shelter Wood. By this move he captured 800 officers and men surviving of four different regiments, and while still gathering in this bag was able to throw back the counter-attack sent from Contalmaison. By 3 pm the action was over. A good six hours of daylight remained to reconnoitre Mametz Wood which covered the rear approach to Contalmaison and the enemy second line at Bazentin le Petit.

At 3 pm XV headquarters already had a piece of priceless information in their hands. An air observer had asserted that Mametz Wood was empty – and not only Mametz Wood, but also the Quadrangle trenches linking the south-west corner of the wood with Contalmaison. Asked a little later by his divisions whether they should patrol forward, General Horne replied that he could not 'engage in patrol action which might bring on an engagement before he was prepared to accept it'. Such a rejoinder reeks of the war games played before the war at Camberley. It bore no relationship to the needs of the moment and the force in his hand. But General Horne was a gunner, a very orthodox soldier, and one whose only knowledge of an infantry battalion's capabilities was by outside observation. He had only to telephone urgent orders to a divisional commander to infiltrate a battalion forward up the Willow Stream – whose valley was out of view both to Contalmaison and the enemy second line – as a preliminary to occupying the wood and Quadrangle trenches with a brigade.

What counter-attack did he fear? They had already repulsed a sortie from Contalmaison. His air spotters would remain overhead until darkness to warn him of any enemy force massing. The enemy guns were unable to threaten. His own were well forward and one division's artillery had already registered on the wood. General Horne rested on his arms.

At 3 pm, Haig noted in his diary on the 3rd, Generals Joffre and Foch were received (following the meeting between Rawlinson and Foch that morning).

> The object of the visit was to 'discuss future arrangements'. Joffre began by pointing out the importance of our getting Thiepval Hill. To this I said that, in view of the progress made on my right near Montauban, and the demoralised nature of the enemy's troops in that area, I was considering the desirability of pressing my attack on Longueval. I was therefore anxious to know whether in that event the French would attack at Guillemont. At this. General Joffre exploded in a fit of rage. 'He could not approve of it.' 'He *ordered* me to attack Thiepval and Pozières'. 'If I attacked Longueval, I would be beaten', etc., etc, I waited calmly till he had finished. His breast heaved and his face flushed!' The truth is the poor man cannot argue, nor can he easily read a map. But today 'I had a raised model of the ground before us... I quietly explained what my position is relatively to him as the '*Generalissimo*'. *I am solely responsible to the British Government for the action of the British Army*; and I had approved the plan, and must modify it to suit the changing situation as the fight progresses. I was most polite. Joffre saw he had made a mistake, and next tried to cajole me. ...I have gained an advantage through keeping calm. My views have been accepted by the French Staffs and Davidson[7] is to go to lunch with Foch

tomorrow... to discuss how they (the French) can cooperate in our operations (that is the capture of Longueval).

That night Generals Congreve and Horne acted decisively. XIII Corps assaulted Bernafay Wood after a 20-minute bombardment to capture the dispirited rear party of the previous night's counter-attack; seventeen prisoners of 12th Reserve Division, three abandoned field and three machine-guns. After dark 7th Division was permitted to occupy the southernmost strip and trenches of Mametz Wood.

The authority of army headquarters was obtained before these moves were made.

THE SECOND LINE

The thick, high cloud seen during 3 July shed heavy showers after darkness. The 4th was a cold, wet day, and dark. At first the trenches became slippery; any that were unrevetted crumbled. As the rain continued, craters filled with water, trenches with mud. 'Walking, let alone fighting became hellish...'

If the weather favoured either side, the balance lay with the Germans; attacks by the British were further delayed. The first desperate regrouping of Below's units between the Ancre and the Somme was completed by 11 pm on 3 July. From the 4th onwards it became possible to plan the relief of 28th Reserve Division by 3rd Guards, and then 26th Reserve at Thiepval by a mixture of battalions and detachments under Major-General Burkhardt. As far as possible, the reinforcements coming forward from holding battalions were fed to their parent regiments, but some men, as in the recruit battalions withdrawn from the line for drafting, found themselves amongst strangers. Time did not permit a nice discrimination in posting; the trenches were critically short of soldiers.

Three nights of aircraft strengthened Below's ability to oppose the supremacy of the Royal Flying Corps and provided a marginal capability to reconnoitre the British forward zone. The gradual accession throughout July of field, medium and heavy batteries from the rear, Verdun and Crown Prince Rupprecht's army restored a weapon of counter-attack, though ammunition did not permit indiscriminate shooting in defence. But this weakness was offset by the rapid replacement of all machine-guns lost on

7 Brigadier-General, General Staff (Operations).

1 July. From the 10th the weapons deployed in regimental and independent machine-gun companies exceeded those in position on 'Z' day.

The British attacks were resumed, as we have seen, chiefly on those positions best able to repulse them. Formation commanders were advised that they had attacked a total of fifteen German battalions in the first defence line, of which approximately eleven had been seriously depleted. As subsequent interrogation proved, this appreciation was premature; they had engaged thirty-three battalions, of which twelve were effectively destroyed.

The inaction of XV and XIII Corps permitted the Germans to survive their manning crisis. By the time Fourth Army was ready to advance against the second line, forty fresh or reinforced battalions were available to Below. In this same period of regrouping, Haig began to pull out his own badly mauled divisions and substituted them for others in First and Second Armies. Thus the Australians began to move down from Plumer's command in Flanders. As the gunner casualties had been relatively light, divisional artillery moved only when its infantry transferred to another army. There were few changes in the gun line otherwise, particularly amongst the heavy batteries. This continuity had advantages. Many of the New Army gunners had entered the line as novices – practice camps and a work-up in a quiet sector apart. The experiences of the preliminary bombardment and the many subsequent fire plans were developing expertise. The batteries became more accurate quicker to respond to a call, sensitive to the battle atmosphere. The forward observers were less likely to be tricked by light and shade, false crests and oblique slopes. Liaison with the air, which had started well, was prospering. Despite the German air reinforcement it became difficult for the enemy to move in the open immediately behind his line without attracting quickly a storm of shells directed by the Royal Flying Corps. General Below was compelled to reinforce his line by night.

Against these developments, the plans progressed at Fourth Army headquarters towards the breach of the enemy second line. But Rawlinson was reminded daily by Haig that a recrudescence of the offensive – as distinct from trench warfare – was impracticable unless close assembly positions and the flanks were secured beforehand. Essentially, Contalmaison, Mametz and Trônes Wood must be in British hands before zero. The possession of Pozières would be of the greatest value.

This insistence ended Rawlinson's dalliance with attacks in the north. On the night 4/5 July Gough's right boundary was brought south to include the Albert-Bapaume road. Henceforth, Fourth Army might concentrate towards breaching the enemy second line.

Hoping to reach Pozières, Gough now attacked at Ovillers. With terrible loss, five battalions managed to establish a lodgement just west of the village. At Thiepval the enemy reminded him that they were not a spent force. Storm battalions[8] ejected X Corps last holding on the ridge – the German support trenches retained by Major Peacocke when his Ulster men withdrew from the Schwaben. On Thiepval spur, the shallow position of the Leipzig Redoubt remained in British hands only after a bitter struggle.

South of the Albert-Bapaume road, first Horne, then Horne and Pulteney attempted to take Contalmaison and Mametz Wood between 4 and 12 July. There was no finesse; the methods were those of the battering ram, despite the protests of the divisional commanders. At great expense in lives, they succeeded, to earn the congratulations of the army commander. Contalmaison taken, the left flank was secure against Pozières; assembly positions were available in Mametz Wood and the ground was clear in front of the Willow Stream (Caterpillar Valley). All that remained as a preliminary was the capture of Trônes Wood which dominated the right flank of the proposed advance. On 12 July, 18th Division were told to take it '...at all costs'.

I have suggested that Rawlinson's sombre mood, his acceptance of passivity by XIII and, later, XV Corps immediately after 'Z' day was due to his dismay at the loss in his army. He took pains to question liaison and other officers as to the experiences of the battle line which, necessarily, he had missed. As the first week passed, it became increasingly clear that, whereas night assaults were not always successful, they gained their objectives more often than those launched in daylight.

I have seen nothing in official or personal papers to show who first conceived a night movement on the German second line.[9] Rawlinson and Montgomery had both wished to form up in darkness for the assault on 'Z' day, but the French believed it to be impracticable. Now, their own

---

8   Units specially organised, trained and armed for the assault.

architects. Fourth Army chose this method.

On the extreme left, the trenches east of Contalmaison and on the northern edge of Mametz Wood offered to III and part of XV Corps a convenient start line 400 yards from the German outposts. The Willow Stream – Caterpillar Valley – to the east, however, was 1500 yards back. It was satisfactory as an assembly area for the other divisions but too distant as a point from which to begin the assault. Here lay the advantage of darkness. Brigade staff officers and Royal Engineers would go forward into No Man's Land with white tape and field level to mark out the start lines on which companies must stand. Without fear of observation by the enemy, they might take these lines to within 500 yards of the enemy fire trenches. A screen of patrols was detailed to protect the taping parties – one brigade put out a platoon of Lewis guns and provided shelter for them on the open, rising slope by blowing 6-inch howitzer craters in a neat line at just the right distance from the enemy.

Rawlinson surely merits praise for insisting on adopting this audacious but imaginative plan, the more so as it was rejected initially by Haig and out of hand by the French, who thought him mad to try it. Foch was already vexed by the inability of XIII Corps to carry Trônes Wood, as promised, when Balfourier's left division advanced to Hardécourt on the 8th. Rawlinson asked him to join the army offensive by moving simultaneously on Guillemont village but he refused. It was openly said at his headquarters at Dury that Sixth Army should not take part in '...an attack organised for amateurs by amateurs'. Fayolle, in his reasonable way, offered to cover Rawlinson's right flank with a substantial artillery barrage.

The British were particularly grateful for this offer. The right flank worried Rawlinson more than the objections as to the risks he was taking. He knew the risks; they were mostly less than those of a daylight attack, when the enemy could see his targets from the first moment of exposure. In darkness he had the chance of getting into the enemy trenches by surprise. Fayolle's barrage would aid but could not replace a British garrison in Trônes Wood. And Trônes Wood, though partially captured on 11 July, was penetrated by the enemy once more on the 12th. General Congreve did not need Rawlinson to tell him the importance of the wood: the right flank of XIII Corps' assault would pass along its western edge. It

[9] But see Maurice, *op. cit.*, p. 164 and Fourth Army Papers, VoL VI, conference minutes for 8 July, 1916

was for this reason that Congreve relieved 30th Division from the area on the evening of the 12th and put in Major-General Maxse's 18th. He told Maxse that the army commander had ordered him to take the wood by midnight 13th/14th 'at all costs'. He added, 'even if it takes your whole division'. On 13 July, the eve of Bastille Day, the British liaison officer with the Sixth Army, Captain E L Spears, came over to Querrieu from XX Corps. General Balfourier wished him to reiterate the appeals telephoned during the day to abandon the night approach. Besides the inexperience of the officers and men, the artillery available was far too weak – both in batteries and shells[10] – to take on such a formidable defence as the German second line on a frontage of 6000 yards.

'Tell General Balfourier, with my compliments,' said General Montgomery, 'that if we're not on Longueval ridge by 8 o'clock tomorrow morning, I'll eat my hat.'

This confidence was not due to arrogance or optimism. All Rawlinson's capacity for observation and detail had been joined to Montgomery's practical sense. The operations chief, Pitt Taylor, had taken pains to see that everything corps staffs had asked for had been provided in good time. The artillery policy was changed for the better, thanks to a suggestion made by two of the divisional artillery commanders: the final stage of the bombardment should be changed from thirty to five minutes to deceive the enemy in his dugouts as to the moment of attack. And in order to bring the infantry as close to the barrage as possible, the field and medium batteries in close support would fire no shrapnel but high explosive with delay fuses.

The German aeroplanes were denied access to the Fourth Army zone. Some of the field and medium batteries moved up behind XV and XIII Corps were spotted by counter-battery aircraft but the British air patrols rarely left the Germans unmolested long enough to correct ranging shots. Meantime, Vivian, head of army intelligence, arranged for the aerial photography of every German trench and redoubt, repeating sorties when prints were not clear or in focus. He knew of the telephone leak at la Boisselle early on 1 July and arranged to feed false messages forward. In 62 Brigade, where it was known that a listening post was monitoring all telephone traffic, the word was passed on 13 July at 9 pm '...operations postponed'.

---

[10] The allocation of heavy howitzer shells was considerably less than that for 'Z'. For each day of the 2-day bombardment it was: twenty-five per 13-inch; fifty per 9.2 inch; 110 per 8-inch; 250 per 6-inch.

At that hour the marker parties were waiting in Caterpillar Valley, Mametz and Bernafay Woods for darkness. The British bombardment, which had been in progress since 11 July,[11] continued to fall on the German positions all along the Fourth and Reserve Army fronts, the French adding their weighty contribution. Behind and amongst the marker parties, 22,000 men of six assault brigades awaited the signal to move forward.

At the headquarters, 18th Division, General Maxse waited also. At 7 pm he had launched 5 Brigade in Trônes Wood. 7th Queen's, 280 strong, with a company of 7th Buffs to augment them, advanced from Bernafay Wood to seize the northern tip of Trônes, from which the enemy might escape to Longueval. The remainder of 7th Buffs moved up along Maltz Horn Trench from the south, bombing towards a strongpoint holding the south-east corner of the wood. A message was sent back to say that they had attacked and taken the strongpoint, but while the messenger was en route, a counter-attack ejected them. 7th Royal West Kents disappeared into the southern edge of the wood, aiming to clear through to the north.

As the British bombardment ended at 7 pm, a German barrage began. The British troops were lost to view in the welter of smoke, earth showers and tree fragments. At 10.30 pm the Buffs reported their inability to move on beyond the strongpoint, this second message coming back with a considerable number of wounded men. At about eleven the Queen's returned, having left a small party under Lieutenant B C Haggard in a trench near the northern exit from the wood.

The battalion had eighty men left, the Buffs company were a platoon strong. No one knew what had happened to the West Kents but all hoped to see a runner with news of success.

Nothing came back. Could they have seen into the mesh of trees and undergrowth, all officers would have been discovered as casualties, the men scattered. Shells, grenades and sudden bursts of small arms fire discharged at random into the night prevented their union.

At midnight. General Maxse telephoned XIII Corps headquarters and gave the commander his news. 'What do you mean to do about it?' asked General Congreve. 'I have 54th Brigade ready, sir,' he said. 'I shall put them

[11] On the evening of the 11th, after the first day of bombardment, General Horne said that his wire would not be cut before the evening of the 13th. The offensive was postponed twenty-four hours to permit completion of this work. Additional ammunition was found to sustain fire.

in, in place of the 55th, and shall hope to get possession by the time the main attack begins.' 'We all hope so,' rejoined Congreve, 'considering the main attack begins in three hours.' 'I should like to guarantee it', said Maxse.

At 12.25 he telephoned Brigadier-General Shoubridge, ordering him to capture Trônes Wood. 'Can we wait until daylight to make a reconnaissance?' asked Shoubridge. 'None of my people have seen it.' General Maxse said there was no time to spare. The only consolation was that it would be dawn before they entered the trees. 'I agree, sir. I don't think they can get there before 4.30. We had better arrange the bombardment to begin then.'

Maxse knew that 6th Northamptons and 12th Middlesex were close by and 54 Brigade headquarters confirmed that these two units would assemble in the sunken road, east of Montauban briqueterie, as soon as possible. Lieutenant-Colonel Frank Maxwell of the Middlesex would take overall command. Maxwell was a remarkable man, courageous in physical danger, fearless of his fellow men. He had won the – Victoria Cross in South Africa and had been noted, as Kitchener's *aide-de-camp*, for his amiable impudence to the great man. Much of his life had been spent in challenging difficulties but no task could have been more difficult than the operation awaiting him as he came forward to the sunken road with his orders. It was still dark. He called for the company commanders from amongst the mass of men on either side of the road and discovered that only one company of his own battalion had arrived. It had been planned that they should lead but now he told 6th Northamptons to lead on as quickly as possible, once the orders had been distributed. By the time they were ready, the sun was up. The cannonade of the main attack close by deafened them, though no one had much to say as they covered the open ground and entered the wood. Inside, Colonel Maxwell established his headquarters at a junction of shallow trenches, where he hoped to receive reports from the Northamptons and his own companies, all of which had caught up the force. The Germans were bombarding them with medium and heavy shells. He heard cries and firing in the distance but the spread of trees made it difficult to determine, their source. Two messages came back from the foremost company of Northamptons to say that they had successfully taken a strongpoint in the centre of the wood and needed

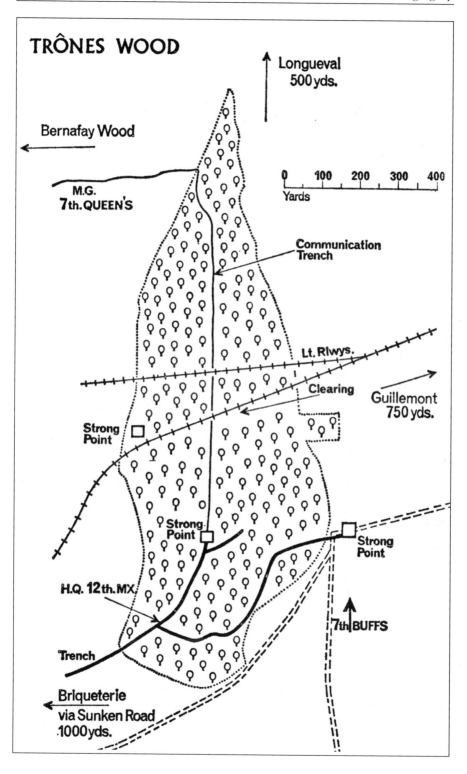

TRÔNES WOOD

Longueval
500 yds.

Bernafay Wood

M.G.
7th. QUEEN'S

0   100   200   300   400
Yards

Communication
Trench

Lt. Riwys.

Clearing

Guillemont
750 yds.

Strong
Point

Strong
Point

Strong
Point

H.Q. 12th. MX.

7th BUFFS

Trench

Briqueterie
via Sunken Road
1000 yds.

161

more grenades. No other news came in. Occasionally, little groups of soldiers would be seen wandering about in the distance, firing into the briars, peering under fallen trunks – men from several regiments. Buffs, West Kents, Northamptons. A pale slight doctor appeared and stumbled over Colonel Maxwell, dozing against a tree trunk. 'What the hell are you doing?' asked the colonel. 'I'm looking for the Middlesex headquarters.'

'I *am* the Middlesex headquarters', said Maxwell. But it was becoming apparent that he was a headquarters without a command, except for his last two companies waiting in reserve near by. It was 8 o'clock and they had been in the wood for three hours. He resolved to end the operation. Going along the trench leading north-east, he came upon two groups of mixed detachments; West Kents and a few Middlesex. Two of his platoons he sent off with orders to find 7th Buffs and capture with them the south-east strongpoint. All remaining soldiers, irrespective of regiment, were then extended in a single line from east to west across the wood. The officers checked their compasses and everyone faced north. They fixed bayonets and began to beat towards the enemy.

Snipers and grenadiers opposed them in random group. The line backed and filled as it was hit. Concerned that they were breaking-up, Maxwell shouted instructions to riflemen that they should fire into the undergrowth every ten to fifteen paces, selected men were to fire into trees still carrying enough foliage to conceal snipers. The orders echoed on to the flanks and were acknowledged. Faced by this wave of men and scattering of bullets, the broadcast enemy broke away individually to the north. After 600 yards, Maxwell's line reached a lane, through which passed a light railway. A strongpoint covered the clearing. They attacked, killed the occupants and captured their machine-gun. Forming line again, they went slowly on.

After beating through 1000 yards in this way, the sides of the wood began to narrow towards the northern tip. The withdrawing German parties could not escape to Longueval because it was under attack. These chose to run towards Guillemont, bursting out of the trees to the east. But the Buffs and Middlesex platoons had now secured the south-eastern strongpoint, from which Lewis guns fired into the fleeing enemy; Those behind remained under cover amongst the trees, to be shot or taken by some of Maxwell's men sent to comb out the apex. Captain Podmore came back to report that he had counted 600 dead Germans including those who had just perished.[12] There were hundreds more in the undergrowth behind, bodies of both sides, dead and wounded. Some of the latter had been lying alone, untended, hoping for succour for seven days. Some lay on to die, undiscovered till the war had passed.

Before this little sideshow began, the six assault brigades had formed up in silence on their tapes. A few enemy patrols came forward, one was captured, the others returned after short sorties to report all quiet. An occasional shell burst in No Man's Land, killing or wounding a luckless individual amongst the many thousands standing out on the open slopes. When the guides had led their companies on to the last tape, and the men had turned to face the enemy line, their anxiety to move forward out of No Man's Land was manifest. Rows of men began inching forward towards the band of flashing shells bursting on the enemy defences. Though most of the battalions had received heavy reinforcements – some en route for the line – there was still a substantial number who had fought or watched on 1 July. In their ranks there was a suppressed excitement, almost as if they were seeing the successful conclusion of a stupendous practical joke on the enemy. 'All the time I was saying to myself "You're there. You're there, boy. Right in the middle of No Man's Land and no one else can see you, no one's firing. You're going to get away with it – right up under the barrage into Jerry's trenches before he knows it." Smiling away to myself as if I was daft, and I was trembling. I felt it. We really might get away with it. We all felt it.'

Row upon row, they shuffled up the gentle slopes abreast of Contalmaison towards the Villa; to the wood and village of Bazentin le Petit; from Flatiron Copse to Bazentin le Grand Wood; from the tapes across the spurs to Bazentin le Grand village and to Longueval with its orchards and the spread of Delville Wood. The sky paled; men began to see each other's features clearly. At 3.20 am a gigantic roar swelled suddenly from the rear. A brilliant orange light flared above the dark line of Montauban ridge, lit the foul gloom of Mametz and Trônes Woods, flickered across the khaki host ascending from Caterpillar Valley. For five minutes the many batteries which had fallen silent during these last hours fired at a rapid rate – guns, howitzers, mortars – drowning the tack-tack-

[12] Interrogation of prisoners disclosed that 350 Germans had been active in the wood when Colonel Maxwell began to sweep it.

tack of the Vickers guns.

It was now more difficult to restrain the battalions. Many were less than 200 yards from the enemy trenches and they were anxious not to be caught on the wire. Some discovered the wire had vanished; one battalion was able to wriggle men through. Uncut wire was snipped apart by the cutters and dragged away by picks. As soon as the barrage lifted at 3.25, those who could do so sprang to the parapets to enter the enemy trenches.

The bitter lessons of 'Z' day were not forgotten in the tumult. Companies did not pass over the dugouts, leaving them to be dealt with by supports coming on behind; the first wave bombed the depths with grenades, and hurled down prepared charges brought forward by sapper sections dogging the assault. Few of the shelters were as deep or spacious as those in the first line; the enemy who did not come up to fight lay dead below or surfaced to surrender. In several sections the Germans reached the fire steps before their foe[13] but, where the defensive wire remained uncut, those who had gained the trench on either side bombed inwards, providing at least a diversion. So quickly and thoroughly was the work done that the supporting units, coming up to consolidate, found the enemy crushed or captive and all but two of the assault battalions ready to go for the second trench before the British barrage had lifted from it.

The leading waves began to filter across the parados, numbers running forward to positions of advantage, heedless of the short rounds of fire from their guns. Immediately the barrage moved on, assault parties rushed the second trench. The complex was secured an hour after zero when bombers, riflemen and Lewis-gun teams amongst the Bazentins turned to pursue those of Below's men who had not waited to be flushed from the rear areas. But the marksmanship of the British infantry did not match their ardour; running for Martinpuich or High Wood on the ridge, many of the reserve garrison escaped. To the victors it seemed a trifle to their achievement of the morning – a perfect approach out of the night and the breaching of the enemy second line by a salient 2000 yards across and 1000 yards deep. Indeed, the second line had been breached over a distance of 6000 yards, for the trench system had been taken all the way from Bazentin le Petit Wood to Longueval. Even in this latter zone, striking at once a fortified village adjacent to a dense wood, the Royal Scots forced their way in to the central

---

13 A sentry at Bazentin le Grand heard the British approach and gave the alarm. See p. 171.

crossroads and lined the southern edge of Delville Wood. Only Waterlot Farm, the little mound of bricks between Trônes and Delville Woods, remained untaken and unoccupied while the German artillery pounded and pounded it as if determined to crush the remains to dust.

Good news travels fast. By 6.30 Rawlinson was assured that all three corps were in occupation of their first objectives in the enemy second line. By 7 am he had a clear picture of the extent of the Bazentin salient. Amidst a jubilant headquarters the French liaison officer, Captain Serot, telephoned XX Corps. He announced himself; they asked eagerly for his news. '*Ils ont osé,*' he said. '*Ils ont reussi.*' '*Alors,*' was the rejoinder, '*le général Montgomery ne mange pas son chapeau.*'

For some time the information coming back sustained the atmosphere of success. Despite low clouds, aeroplanes confirmed every situation report made by III, XV or XIII Corps headquarters. The first columns of prisoners – 42 officers and 1400 men had been taken before the wounded were counted were seen marching back towards Caterpillar Valley. At 7.40, urged on by Rawlinson, Congreve ordered 2nd Indian Cavalry Division to advance in exploitation to High Wood. He and Horne began to move forward field batteries behind the newly won ground.

Horne was also looking ahead. III Corps had advanced the 1st Division to protect his left flank, but their holding in the second line was minimal. His own 21st Division in Bazentin le Petit Wood and village must push on north and west behind the enemy opposing the 1st, and thereby bring the right of III Corps into the salient. His own 7th Division, holding Bazentin le Grand, was in good order with a completely fresh reserve. Once the Indian cavalry had taken High Wood, he would relieve them with this brigade as a first step to occupying the entire ridge with the division. Behind the ridge, he knew, ran a shallow switch trench connecting the Pozières defences to Flers. 7th Division would cut this completely.

At 10 there were several reports of reverses. At Longueval German counter-attacks had thrown back the Scots detachments north of the central crossroads. In Delville Wood the southern edge was held only after several hours of fighting off a counter-attack in which both sides met head on with rifles, machine-guns and grenades at about thirty yards range. The Germans were well supported by artillery fire here, had received a strong reinforcement and were in possession of deep, well-sited defences. They were clearly determined to repulse the British infantry. The two brigades of Jocks in the 9th (Scottish) Division had now lost appreciable numbers. The reserve brigade, South Africans, was committed about 1.30. In the Bazentins salient, two weak counter-attacks were made between 8.20 and 9.05 but lacking the supporting bombardment or the force of the riposte at Longueval, they were soon dispersed. The ground temporarily lost was recovered, save for a machine-gun position – four guns – manned by determined crews at the north-west corner of le Petit Wood.

Just as the reports of these actions were reaching corps headquarters, all other opposition in the salient ended. After several hours of intermittent fighting there was silence. The battalions, their forward observing parties from the batteries, and the sappers had now a chance to look about them.

The crossroads at the northern end of Bazentin le Petit village stands at 151 metres above sea-level. Due north, from a mined house, the southern end of Martinpuich could be seen, but the bulk of the dwellings lay out of view on the northern slope of the ridge. Half right, across a wide re-entrant, lay High Wood on the road from Bazentin to Flers. The southern point of the wood is marked as 152 metres; the northern corner at 145 was just out of sight beyond the crest. A British force in this area would be able to see over the main Thiepval-Pozières-Ginchy ridge. The British guns might deny by day all movement along the main road south-west from Bapaume towards Pozières; the northern exits of Martinpuich would be under observation and, with Flers, in range to harassing machine-guns. But most important at this critical moment of the struggle, the northern end of Longueval and the northern edge of Delville Wood – centres of enemy reinforcement – would be vulnerable to closely observed artillery fire and in enfilade to mortars and machine-guns.

The countryside behind the enemy's second line contrasted strangely with the lower slopes, spoiled during the past three weeks. Here on the ridge wheat and barley ripened from the seed unreaped last year. Leaves grew abundantly upon the High Wood trees. The grass and clover, uncropped by pastured sheep, lay thickly around, smelt fresh, looked green and reassuring. The two brigade commanders in the Bazentin villages agreed on patrols, and had them despatched to the wood by 11.30. Everything was quiet. One brigade commander, Brigadier-General Potter, strolled forward into the open from Bazentin le Grand to show the ground to the commander of 3rd Division's engineers. Walking halfway to High Wood, they saw and heard nothing of the enemy.

Meanwhile, 3rd Division's commander had already suggested that he should push on his 76 Brigade, in reserve, to seize the wood. General Watts, commanding 7th Division on his left, had used only four battalions in the main attack and had placed his 91 Brigade in rear under warning to exploit to High Wood at 11 am. Both these suggestions were declined, the cavalry were on their way. Army headquarters approved this restraint.

They were living in a fool's paradise.

There must be no suspicion that the cavalry were deliberately lagging; they had been longing to take part for days. But in their own way the horsemen were restricted to a marching pace like the infantry. They had some twelve miles to travel from bivouac to front line and much of this lay over broken and pitted ground – some of it very soft. Progress was therefore mostly at a walking pace. There was scant opportunity for trotting; and no question, in any case, of galloping – they would have been little use on arrival, blown and in a muck sweat. The fact was, the cavalry were too far back to be used for exploitation. For once, the careful Congreve had omitted to have a study made of the movement plans, and the cavalry division headquarters had failed to think of the matter themselves.

When there was no report of the leading brigade – the Secunderabad – by noon, Rawlinson and Montgomery grew uneasy. Over four hours had passed since XIII Corps, under whose command the Indian cavalry were to operate, had ordered them forward. Now that he was so fiercely opposed at Longueval on his right and lacked a mobile exploitation force, it seemed that General Congreve was less capable of capturing High Wood than Horne. Like Congreve, Horne was aware of the importance of the feature;[14] and it was known that 7th Division in XV Corps had fresh troops which the divisional commander was anxious to push forward. At 12.15 army headquarters suggested to General Horne that they should be despatched.

By way of response Horne took the most astonishing decision. Longueval was not secured, he understood, so it was unsafe for the 7th to advance. Apprised of this curious view, Congreve conformed. When the Secunderabad brigade arrived below Montauban at 12.40, it was ordered to

---

[14] See Fourth Army memo of 13 July, 1916, 'Action of cavalry', para. 4, issued to all corps.

stand fast so long as Longueval remained in enemy hands. It did not occur to either corps commander that the capture of High Wood should materially improve the prospect of Longueval's reduction.

The events of the afternoon contrasted sadly with those of the early morning. At 1.30, 21st Division's attack to advance Pulteney's corps was postponed because two of the German machine-guns remained active in the north-west corner of le Petit Wood. It was reckoned that an hour and a half would be required to destroy them. But it was to be longer than this.

At 3 pm two battalions of enemy infantry, well supported by guns and mortars, came forward from Martinpuich to take Bazentin le Petit Wood and village. They would not have reached their targets if High Wood had been held in strength by 7th Division. As it was, without fear of enfilade fire, they advanced boldly. Between 3 and 5.30 pm, then, the salient was threatened: a valid tactical objection to advancing on High Wood. It was just at this time that Horne decided to do so.

He received a message from XIII Corps at 3.10 to say that Longueval had been taken – the message was erroneous. He replied to Congreve almost immediately that 7th Division would move to High Wood at 5.15; would the cavalry cover its right flank? Yes.

All agreement in principle was completed by 3.40 pm. We now know that no orders of any sort reached the cavalry brigade commander – in direct contact with XIII Corps headquarters – before 5.40. In XV Corps the order to advance the reserve brigade of 7th Division did not reach the brigade commander until about 5.20. No preliminary warning of any sort had been given; no opportunity made to permit the various commanders to go forward to make a reconnaissance while the artillery plan was being prepared. Indeed, neither of the brigade commanders was consulted in any particular about the fire plan though each had a telephone in use. But this was so often the custom of the time. It is only in retrospect that it seems ludicrous. Perhaps the most striking feature of the command and staff aspects of the morning and afternoon events is the absence of any sense of urgency.

The staff of XV Corps, producing the detailed arrangements for the plan, made one other prime error. They calculated that Brigadier Minshull-Ford's infantry brigade, moving forward from an assembly area just east of Mametz Wood, should travel at the same pace as the cavalry. The bombardment of High Wood was timed to end at 6.15 pm when, even by making a hot pace, the leading battalions, 1st South Staffords and 2nd Queen's, arrived in the southern end of Bazentin le Petit at 6.45. A brigade of 33rd Division was expected to be ready on Brigadier Minshull-Ford's left to cover his flank as the Staffords and Queen's advanced from the village. It had not arrived. Since the two cavalry regiments were in position on the right flank, the brigadier accepted the risk and gave the word to move. Behind a mounted screen – one squadron from each 7th Dragoon Guards and 20th Deccan Horse – the Staffords and Queen's began to cross the spur and re-entrant to High Wood, 1000 yards distant across the corn. It was 7 o'clock; nine hours had passed since the commanders of 3rd and 7th Divisions had asked permission to go forward.

After a day of low clouds and rain showers, the evening sky was clearing. Above the advance Captain Miller and 2nd Lieutenant Short descended in their Morane monoplane to search for the enemy. Between 3.30 and 4 pm other aircraft of the squadron had reconnoitred the wood and its rear approaches without finding an enemy soldier. Making a low run from east to west across the wood. Miller the pilot and Short the observer saw plenty; approximately a company occupied shell scrapes on the east, watching the approach from Longueval; perhaps another company – difficult to count amongst the crops where they hid – waited in front of the wood on the south west.

The two British battalions with the 7th DG and 20th Deccan Horse on their right were advancing quietly behind the cavalry a screen. Miller decided that the best way to warn them of the enemy's presence was to draw fire from the Germans in ambush. He began to fly to and fro above them and, this being unsuccessful. Short opened fire with his Lewis gun. To their delight a hot fire was returned. For several minutes the exchanges continued until a machine-gun opened from the bottom corner of the wood. The Morane shuddered under the impact of numerous bullets. They turned in from a different angle, the Lewis gun in action on the new target. Then, with strips of canvas hanging from his machine. Miller drew off. Short made a quick sketch of the enemy's locations relative to High Wood and they came down for a final run, dropping the information in a bag to the cavalry. Looking back, Short saw the regiments wheeling to a new line. 7th DG went into the crops with their lances; the Deccan Horse ran down the Germans in the shell scrapes. The infantry and part of the cavalry screen cooperated in flushing out dispirited riflemen but a number of the original ambush had crawled away through the crops. Two field guns were found in the re-entrant as the Staffords and Queen's marched the last 300 yards up the far side into the wood.

Nothing opposed their entry but the undergrowth. It was altogether thinner than Trônes Wood and the rides dividing timber sections were more numerous. But the leaves – despite the recent bombardment – trapped the shadows, and a host of saplings fortified the resistance of bramble, thorn and creeper. Halfway through, German snipers shot accurately into the leading ranks as the battalions cleared steadily towards the crest and, just beyond it, the switch trench. It was almost dark. Halted temporarily, they were swept by rifle and machine-gun fire from the switch trench, and mortar bombs began to drop along an open ride.

The light had completely gone. Neither side could see to engage the other and it was clear to the British commanding officers that they must gather in their widespread companies and prepare a defensive position. On the other side of the ridge the Germans were bringing forward wire, timber and sandbags to strengthen the switch trench, into which reinforcements were flowing. Two months were now to pass before High Wood and the switch were in British possession.

'AT ALL COSTS'

By 11 July Falkenhayn was clear in his own mind that all forms of general offensive must come at least temporarily to an end. Brussilov's success in Galicia necessitated a continuing reinforcement of divisions[15] to rally the defeated Austrians. On the western front, the Anglo-French offensive was absorbing infantry, guns and ammunition beyond the capacity of his reserve to replace it without drawing substantially on other sectors. On the afternoon of the 11th Falkenhayn visited the Crown Prince at Stenay-sur-Meuse to discuss the limited offensive which he had permitted to run on since 24 June when the Allied guns opened their bombardment on the Somme. Operations at Verdun had consumed some 200,000 men and 200,000,000 shells since February. Schmidt von Knobelsdorf reiterated his view that the Fifth Army could continue to sustain the attack using its own resources – at that very moment, they were about to capture Fort Belleville,

[15] Fifteen divisions were withdrawn from the western for the eastern front between 4 June and 15 September, those in the latter period being used against Rumania.

which overlooked the city of Verdun.[16] But Falkenhayn could not afford to keep these resources in being. The offensive in the fortified region must now come, finally, to an end. 'Henceforth', he told the Crown Prince, 'adopt a defensive attitude.'

During the 12th Falkenhayn dicussed with Below the policy for resistance on the Somme. He intended to bring General von Gallwitz up from Verdun to command an army group comprising the Second Army south of the river, First Army to the north. General von Below would command the newly created First Army, Colonel von Lossberg remaining as his chief of staff. As Gallwitz was junior to Below, the change may have been, incidentally, a final settlement of Falkenhayn's displeasure concerning premature withdrawals.

In effect, Below's command was greater in manpower and resources, if smaller geographically. His original force north of the river on 1 July had totalled four and a half divisions; it had grown to nine, while his reserves had grown proportionately. In discussing what total of formations he might expect to maintain, Falkenhayn spoke of the possibility of a major counter-attack.

In this connexion, the short line of the Hardécourt feature – Trônes Wood-Longueval was important; for it offered a prospect of assaulting the Allied flank. While accepting this Below pointed out that he would need five divisions – in addition to his reserve – for such a blow. They had not got them. It would be better to counter-attack south of the river, where the artillery could concentrate its fire on a considerable front. On the north their aim should be sustained defence and, in view of the enemy numbers, the need was for more machine-gun companies. He begged Falkenhayn to send him as many as possible.

Before learning of his supersession Below had completed arrangements for the long-term reorganisation of the front north of the Somme. He did not wish to change these. Lieutenant-General von Stein would take over a sector from Monchy-au-bois (four miles north of Gommecourt, facing the British Third Army) to the Ancre. Sixt von Arnim, commander of IV Corps, would form 'Group Arnim' with Burkhardt's, 183rd and 3rd Guard divisions from the south bank of the Ancre to Longueval. Von Gossler would command a 'Group' exclusive from Longueval down to the

[16] Only a handful of Germans reached the fort, from which they were quickly cleared.

Somme. All changes and reliefs were to be complete by 9 am on 14 July, a date unrelated to British intentions.

The Fourth Army secret had been well kept. None knew of their approach until a sentry at Bazentin le Grand grew suspicious at 2 o'clock in the morning of the 14th. He fired two flares and caught a glimpse of the eager Tommies on the lower slopes. His battalion stood to and warned its neighbours. Those in Longueval sent out patrols,[17] the others did not believe that the British could attack until well after dawn and remained at rest, except for those handing over their trenches in the plan of relief. Thus Rawlinson's renewed offensive caught Below both by surprise and at a critical moment of reorganisation. The 16th Bavarian Regiment, holding much of the line, lost 2,300 officers and men. When Sixt von Arnim assumed command at 9 am, he was told that beside serious losses of field artillery, the second line had been breached completely. He found '...no rear positions, no (developed) switches, no communication trenches'; he gave orders that every unit should stand fast where it was 7th Division of his own corps was already coming forward from Bapaume to take over the Pozières-Bazentin le Petit sector. Whatever was immediately to hand would have to reinforce Longueval. High Wood and the switch trench through it was empty except for a handful of survivors from the garrisons in the Bazentins, who lacked machine-guns. It remained empty through the afternoon and early evening; for Arnim chose to use the remaining two battalions for the counter-attack on Bazentin le Petit at 3 pm. It was after 6 when two companies and a machine-gun company moved up the switch trench into the wood, where some were put out in front as a screen while pioneers began to deepen the trench and the machine-gunners developed emplacements for their weapons. So close were the timings that the advance of 91 Brigade and the cavalry, aided by the Morane above, brought wild reports to Arnim and Below that 'the British have broken through northwards between Longueval and Pozières.' By 8.40 pm they were said to have taken the line Martinpuich-High Wood-Flers, and to be advancing still. At St Quentin, Below placed every element of reserve – four divisions – under Arnim's command with orders that the British must be contained. By morning, calmer, truer news came through on the telephone. Two of the divisions were returning to general reserve. Their soldiers had spent a

---

[17] Four went out. One ran into the infantry forming up near Bernafay Wood, to be killed or captured. The remainder cannot have patrolled much beyond their wire because they returned to report all clear.

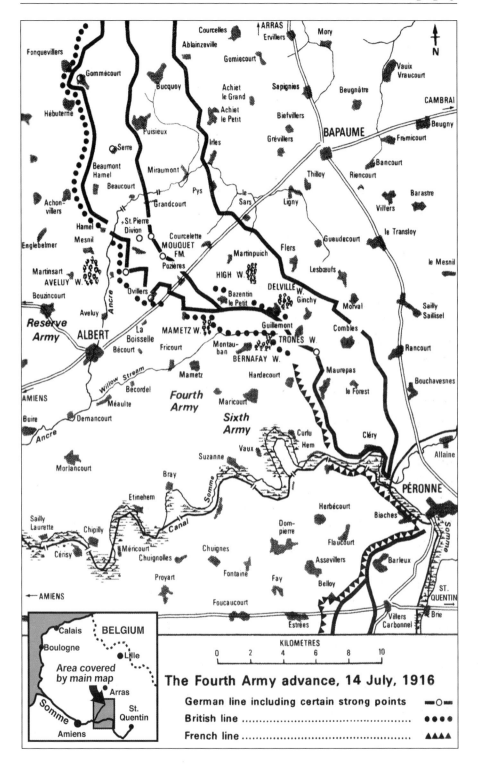

vexing night marching to and from railway stations.

The second half of July became a bloody slogging match. The changeable weather favoured neither side; for each was as much on the attack as in defence. 'At all costs' – the phrase came too readily to the lips of the higher commanders. Foch used it to invigorate Sixth Army in the rebuffs it suffered as the corps closed up painfully towards Péronne on either side of the river. Sixt von Arnim used it at Longueval where he believed he had the strength to push the foe back across Caterpillar Valley. And Congreve used it as Delville Wood became truly an inferno, the trees burning fiercely after days of bombardment, despite a drenching rainstorm. The South Africans earned the ungrudging praise of their comrades and their enemies in holding and counter-attacking this awful corner of the ridge, in the crumbling Longueval streets, in the ravaged orchards and wood whose defences drew in six divisions before acknowledging defeat. Horne decided that High Wood must be taken 'at all costs' but the cost was too great for the number of men he had to expend. At Pozières Gough ordered the capture of the village by 1st Australian Division without waiting for the remainder of the Anzac Corps but he mercifully used the fatal phrase only for the capture of a stretch of trench.

The remaining Australians of Birdwood's corps were soon to join the other Diggers in their attempts on the smashed village, which once had lain within the first day's line of objectives. But before their translation from the Flanders front, 5th Australian Division was committed with the British 61st in a venture ill-devised by Haig to tap the enemy front to see whether, owing to the reinforcement demands on Prince Rupprecht's army for the Somme, it was hollow. General Sir Charles Monro believed that the best way to do this was a frontal attack in full daylight with singular lack of coordination between either of the attacking infantry forces or their artillery. He had the opportunity, as the weather was bad, to cancel the operation – Haig left the decision in his hands. But he lacked the moral courage to do so. Australian and English battalions advanced to their doom across the waterlogged ground.

Falkenhayn, learning of the venture on 19 July, telephoned Prince Rupprecht's headquarters, expecting to discover that the offensive he had so long forecast in the area was beginning. On this occasion, with the needs of the

Somme pressing upon him, he needed little reassurance that he was wrong.

By 31 July, at a cost of approximately 90,000 casualties on either side of the line, Pozières, Longueval and Delville Wood were in British hands – but not High Wood. The French positions north of the Somme were little advanced above Hardécourt and not at all beyond Hem. Below the river they had reached the bank opposite Péronne. By 31 August, after losing about the same figure, the British had advanced 500 yards on two-thirds of their active front – discounting the static line north of Nab Valley – but had yet to take High Wood, Ginchy or Guillemont. The French had captured a new line from 200 metres forward of Hardécourt to 2000 metres forward of Hem.

The Allied commanders were learning to use the phrase 'at all costs' somewhat less. The German Supreme Command had seen a change of a different nature.

THE NEW BROOMS

General von Lyncker received us on our arrival in Pless, about 10 o'clock in the morning of August 29th [recounts General Ludendorff[18]]. He informed me that Field Marshal von Hindenberg had been appointed Chief of the General Staff of the Field Army, and that I was to be Second Chief. The title 'First Quartermaster-General' seemed to me more appropriate. In my opinion there could be only one Chief of the General Staff; but, in any case, I had been expressly assured that I should have joint responsibility in all decisions and measures that might be taken... With bowed head I prayed God the All-Knowing to give me strength in my new office.

The circumstances in which the Field Marshal and I had been summoned to take Supreme command were extremely critical. Whereas we had hitherto been able to conduct our great war of defence by that best means of waging war – the offensive – we were now reduced to a policy of pure defence.

The Entente had gathered up all their strength for a mighty and, as they thought, the last blow, thrown us on the defensive and brought Rumania into the field.

It was this last event which had brought about Falkenhayn's dismissal. For some months, his prestige had been waning. Unfavourable comparisons had been made throughout 1915 between operations on the western front

---

[18] Gen. E von Ludendorff, *My War Memoirs, 1914-18* (Hutchinson). Vol. I, pp. 239 *et seq.*

– where Falkenhayn exercised a direct day-to-day control – and those on the eastern, where Hindenburg and his deputy had an almost unbroken record of success against the Russians. However, the plan for the Verdun offensive had raised hopes of Emperor and Cabinet for a significant success, if not a decisive victory in the west. As late as 3 July there was a prospect of the Emperor reviewing his troops in the city of Verdun – a band had actually been brought forward for the ceremony – but the continuing pressure on the Somme closed the offensive entirely, as we have seen. Falkenhayn's plan to bleed white the French Army had failed. The entry of Rumania into the Allied camp six weeks later was believed to be a direct consequence of the decline in Germany's position. Dissatisfied with Falkenhayn's single-handed control of operational policy, the Emperor called Hindenburg and Ludendorff to a conference at Pless concerning future plans. '...General von Falkenhayn had to reply that he could only regard this summoning of a subordinate commander, without previous reference to him, for a consultation on a question the solution of which lay in his province alone, as a breach of his authority that he could not accept and as a sign that he no longer possessed the absolute confidence of the Supreme War Lord which was necessary for the continuance of his duties. He therefore begged to be relieved of his appointment.... His request to be relieved of his office was granted in the early morning of August 29th.'[19] Almost at once, he set off to command an army in Transylvania against the Rumanians, whom he had the satisfaction of overthrowing.

The new brooms had no illusions about their difficulties. Their own fortune in the east had frequently been jeopardised by the wanton and corrupt leadership of the Austro-Hungarian armies, whose failing in Galicia had influenced Rumania to join the opposing camp. But each admits he had not fully understood the nature of the war in the west. Against the Russian masses it had been possible to employ the old tactical concepts and doctrines. On the western front, where their numbers more nearly approached those of the enemy, the practised leadership and organisation of the Germans was offset by the professional expertise of the French and the ardour and intelligence of the British New Armies. The struggle in this theatre had therefore been more intense, more precisely balanced than that in the east, where it was nothing to advance 20 miles

[19] Falkenhayn, *op. cit.*, pp. 284-285.

after a successful assault, or to withdraw the same distance without losing the campaign.

On the 5th September, the Field-Marshal and I paid our first visit to the West. We travelled via Charleville, where Supreme Headquarters had been established hitherto,[20] to Cambrai, the headquarters of Crown Prince Rupprecht of Bavaria....

The conference in Cambrai took place on the morning of the 7th, while a violent struggle was proceeding on the Somme.

We were all obsessed by thoughts of that terrible conflict. The western front was not at this time at all well organised. The constitution of the armies into army groups had not yet been carried far enough. The Army Group of Crown Prince Rupprecht had been created as a result of the Somme fighting in August.[21] It included Sixth Army before Arras... and the other two armies, also engaged, the First and Second, under General Fritz von Below and von Gallwitz...

The Chief of Staff of the Fourth Army, General Ilse, and Generals von Kuhl and von Luttwitz,[22] the chiefs of staff to Crown Prince Rupprecht and the German Crown Prince's army groups gave us a summary of events on their sectors. Colonel von Lossberg in his serious way, and Colonel Bronsart von Schellendorf with his usual vivacity, supplemented General Kuhl's report of the battle of the Somme with more detailed and intimate descriptions of events. The loss of ground up to date appeared to me of little importance in itself. We could stand that; but the question how this, and the progressive falling-off of our fighting power of which it was symptomatic, was to be prevented, was of immense importance.... My mental picture of the fighting at Verdun and on the Somme had to be painted a shade darker in view of what I had just heard....

The most pressing demands of our officers were for an increase of artillery, ammunition, aircraft and balloons, as well as larger and more punctual allotments of fresh divisions and other troops to make possible a better system of reliefs...

I attached great significance to what I had learned about our infantry

[20] It was now moved to Pless, in the east.

[21] On the 28th.

[22] Schmidt von Knobelsdorf had been sent to command a corps in Russia after attempts to continue the attack at Verdun against the Crown Prince's wishes. Appealed to by his son, the Emperor took the unusual course of agreeing with him, when von Luttwiz was appointed to the vacant position in Fifth Army.

at Cambrai, about their tactics and preparation. Without doubt they fought too doggedly, clinging too resolutely to the mere holding of ground, with the results that the losses were heavy. The deep dugouts and cellars often became fatal mantraps. The use of the rifle was being forgotten, hand grenades had become the chief weapon,[23] and the equipment of the infantry with machine-guns and similar weapons had fallen far behind the enemy.[24] The Field Marshal and I could for the moment only ask that the front line should be held more lightly, the deep underground works be destroyed, and all trenches and posts be given up if the retention of them were unnecessary to the maintenance of the position as a whole, and likely to be the cause of heavy tosses.

In the case of the hostile infantry, the strength of the men had been greatly increased by their war machine; we, on the other hand, had still to rely chiefly on our men. We had every reason to be sparing of them...'

So had the French; and so had the British every reason to be sparing.

On 29 July General Robertson, Chief of the Imperial General Staff in London, had written to Haig:

The Powers that be are beginning to get a little uneasy in regard to the situation. The casualties are mounting up and they were wondering whether we are likely to get a proper return for them. I do my best to keep the general situation to the front, and to explain what may be the effect of our efforts – more especially having regard to our allies. I also try to make them think in German of the present situation. But they will persist in asking whether *I* think a loss of say 300,000 men will lead to really great results, because if not we ought to be content with something less than what we are now doing, and they constantly enquire why we are fighting and the French are not. They argue it is mainly a question of numbers and big guns. The latter we have not yet in sufficient numbers, and the former is affected by whether we are losing more than the Germans. I am sorry to worry you in this way but it is necessary you should know what is passing. I really know very little as to your present appreciation of the situation, and think it necessary you

---

[23] The same weakness was increasingly prevalent in the British Army. See *OH 1916*, Vol. II, p. 292, for example.

[24] The facts now available do not support this statement. For example, the cumulative total of Vickers machine-guns delivered to France by 20 June, 1916, was 20,000 complete equipments. At this time the Germans had almost 63,000 on the western front. A useful background to British production may be seen in D Lloyd George, *op. cit.*. Vol. II, p. 610.

should send me another secret statement of your views. It is probable that you will be sent for in the course of a week or so, if matters continue much as in the last fortnight, in order to tell the War Committee what you think. In general, what is bothering them is the probability that we may soon have to face a bill of 2-300,000 casualties with no very great gains additional to the present. It is thought that the primary object – relief of pressure on Verdun – has to some extent been achieved.

After reading this through, Haig added a minute, or perhaps, in view of its tone, a personal memo: 'Not exactly the letter of a CIGS. He ought to take responsibility also. I have no intention of going before the War Committee while this battle is going on.'

This was less than fair. Robertson could not he expected to take responsibility for Haig's plans, though he was known always to be ready to represent them to the Cabinet War Committee in the most favourable way. Haig was well aware that Robertson had had difficulty since the beginning of the year in convincing ministers that an offensive was necessary;[25] and a 'new broom' in the War Office, Lloyd George,[26] was an activist in the political discontent with the news coming from France.[27] His experience as Minister of Munitions had led Lloyd George to mistrust the competence, imagination and organisation ability of senior military officers. He had not changed this view on becoming Secretary of State for War; and being concerned to sweep away muddle and mismanagement wherever he found it, he became suspicious of the direction in France when he equated casualties to results.

There was no misunderstanding between politicians and senior general officers concerning responsibilities and authority in their respective fields. Haig, for example, was expected to produce results; how he did so was his affair. But the men he needed to produce these results were provided by the politicians. If they felt that manpower was being squandered, they might cut off the supply – and this would not have been diffcult to do in the second half of 1916 because there were genuine manpower difficulties. By 8 June the conscriptive Second Military Service Act had been brought into force, not without considerable political difficulties for the Prime

---

25 See pp. 26-27

26 Lloyd George became Secretary of State for War in place of Kitchener, who was drowned on 5 June, 1916. For Ll G's own account of his transfer from Munitions to War, see *op. cit.*, Vol. II, Chap. XXVI.

27 So was Winston Churchill. See *The World Crisis* (Thornton Butterworth), Part I, pp. 117-192.

Minister.[28] The long-standing fears in Asquith's Cabinet of a blood bath combined with strong sectional interests in Parliament opposing compulsory military service might yet combine to impose a policy of defence in France.

Whether primarily for this reason, or because he knew Robertson to be a shrewd counsellor, or – less likely – because he recognised that he had a duty to keep the Government informed of events for which they, ultimately, were responsible to the nation, the commander-in-chief gave an account of his stewardship next day. His letter (AOD 90 of 1 August) is summarised in his diary entry for the 3rd.

(a) Pressure on Verdun relieved. Not less than six enemy Divns. besides heavy guns have been withdrawn.

(b) Successes achieved by Russia last month would certainly have been prevented had enemy been free to transfer troops from here to the Eastern Theatre.[29]

(c) Proof given to world that Allies are capable of making and maintaining a vigorous offensive and of driving enemy's best troops from the strongest positions has shaken faith of Germans, of their friends, of doubting neutrals in the invincibility of Germany. Also impressed on the world, England's strength and determination, and the fighting power of the British race.

(d) We have inflicted very heavy losses on the enemy. In one month, thirty of his Divns. have been used up, as against 35 at Verdun in 5 months. In another 6 weeks, the enemy should be hard put to it to find men.

(e) The maintenance of a steady offensive pressure will result eventually in his complete overthrow.

Principle on which we should act. *Maintain our offensive.* Our losses in July's fighting totalled about 120,000 more than they would have been had we not attacked. They cannot be regarded as sufficient to justify any anxiety as to our ability to continue the offensive. It is my intention:

(a) To maintain a steady pressure on Somme battle.

(b) To push my attack strongly whenever and wherever the state of my preparations and the general situation make success sufficiently

[28] For example, see Lord Hankey, *The Supreme Command* (Alien and Unwin), Vol. II, Chap. XLV.

[29] This was not, of course, correct, though Haig was unaware at the time of the flow of divisions eastward.

probable to justify me in doing so, but not otherwise.

(c) To secure against counter-attack each advantage gained and prepare thoroughly for each fresh advance.

Proceeding thus, I expect to be able to maintain the offensive well into the Autumn.

It would not be justifiable to calculate on the enemy'a resistance being completely broken without another campaign next year.

At a distance, this sounds pessimistic; and indeed some critics, in quoting the words, conclude that Haig had already lost confidence in his ability to break-out. The facts do not support this view.

Haig had modified his early optimism but had not abandoned his aim to break-out on the Somme, or elsewhere through the success of a double blow. It will be recalled that he had thought – and stocked – for a seven-week battle originally. After failing to exploit the High Wood opening on Bazentin Ridge, the army commanders had been warned that they must undertake a 'wearing down fight' once again to secure tactically sound positions from which to begin a third major offensive.

When he replied to Robertson, approximately a fortnight had passed since two divisions had been squandered in the sounding operations in Flanders – a failure which brought him no return. He could not make up his mind whether the result was due to ineptitude on the part of First Army, the strength of the German position or lack of skill in the assaulting infantry – the mean and unworthy excuse of individuals on General Monro's staff. The battle intelligence of Fourth Army inclined him to believe that they had not yet drawn off sufficient numbers from Flanders and Artois. But four to six weeks hence, their 'steady pressure' should have weakened the enemy sectors north of the Somme sufficiently to try again, and in strength, the effect of a major blow above the river with a second one to the north of Arras.

Ammunition supplies had improved; they should not be inhibited by shortages. The flow of reinforcements was adequate – though no more – to replace losses in the ranks. What concerned him greatly was the shortage of regimental leaders and trained staff officers.

Records and personal accounts of the time show that this shortage was becoming critical. For example, a diarist in an infantry battalion in Fourth

Army notes the departure of the, commanding officer to be a brigadier on 8 June. On the 14th the new CO, a captain, appears from another battalion of the regiment. Later in the month, '...S has gone to command a battalion of Cheshires: an achievement for one who was company sergeant-major only twenty months ago.'

It was difficult enough to find able and experienced men to be commanding officers, so many were killed or wounded as the casualty returns relate. For the same reasons it was even more difficult to find officers to command brigades. The requirement here was not only to plan and control operations while offering a close leadership of the raw battalions, but also to supervise the detailed staff work; for the shortage of trained and experienced staff officers was acute. Where this was unfulfilled, the consequences were felt by the infantry as the following unfortunate experiences of a battalion of the London Regiment relates. Their commanding officer tells the story from his diary and personal papers.

The battalion left Millencourt at about 4 am on 3 September and marched to St Riquier where it entrained for Corbie. We reached Corbie during the morning and proceeded to march to Daours where we were to have been billeted.

When we got halfway there, however, we were overtaken by an officer of the divisional staff who told us that there had been a mistake and that we were to go to Sailly-le-Sec. We therefore turned about and marched back through Corbie, arriving at Sailly-le-Sec in the afternoon. The transport which had left Millencourt on the previous afternoon arrived shortly after the battalion.

The battalion at this time was fairly up to strength as far as NCO's and men were concerned. A large proportion of the men, however, had only been with the battalion for two or three weeks and had very little training. As regards officers, it was considerably below strength. The actual trench strength was not more than twenty-three. A large proportion were only attached and like the men had only been with the battalion for two or three weeks.

About midday on the 5th, orders were received that the battalion was to be lent to the 15th Brigade and was to move up into the line that evening. We moved off (from bivouacs) at about 3 pm and arrived at the 15th Brigade HQ in Chimpanzee Trench between Maricourt and

Trônes Wood just as it was getting dark. Here we drew grenades, rockets, etc., which took a little time.

I found that the brigadier was at advanced HQ. I therefore went on, leaving the battalion to follow. Advanced HQ was a trench north west of Hardécourt (near the south-east corner of Trônes Wood). I reported myself to the brigadier who handed me my orders and then left me with the brigade major to obtain what information I could.

The orders were written, as follows:

SECRET   A.2
15th Inf Bde Operation Order No. 60. 6th September 1916

The Kensington Regiment will relieve the 7th Irish Fusiliers in the line tonight. As far as can be understood we are holding the line established by the 16th R. Warwickshire Regt this morning – viz – from a line due south from the southern corner of Leuze Wood – two companies in that line and two coys in the line we got back last night from Point 48, Falfemont Farm, east of Wedge Wood to T.26 C.7.6. [trench map reference]. On relief the 7th Irish Fusiliers will withdraw and form a local reserve in the new trench south of Angle Wood.

In addition to the troops holding the line from Point 48 to T.26 C.7.6. there are 300 men of the 15th Brigade under command of Major Deakin. The OC Kensington Regt will endeavour to extend his line from the south corner of Leuze Wood in an easterly direction and dig himself in as close as possible to the enemy's trench running through T.27 a & d. This trench is heavily wired.

The right of the 95th Brigade is at T.27.5.8.

The French state that they have met with great success to the south of Combles and as the 95th Brigade have got their objective, it is quite possible that the trench through T.27 a, b & d may be found unoccupied. Active patrolling must take place to ascertain whether the line is held or not.

If the OC Kensington Regt considers he can get the line with infantry only he will take it and push out patrols into Combles. (The French are doing this tonight.)

Acknowledge.

The brigade major supplemented this order with the news that the enemy were in full retreat and ready to evacuate Combles at any moment, if they had not already done so. The Kensington patrols were warned to look out for the French, however, as their patrols were entering the village and the flanking French battalion was practically on the south side of the village.

This was nonsense. Subsequent questioning made it clear that the brigade major had never been forward of headquarters and had no personal knowledge of conditions at all.

By the time I had received my instructions the leading company of the battalion had arrived, and we then proceeded, on towards the front line.

There had been a good deal of rain and the ground was very slippery, there was no road and the men had to march in single file and were carrying heavy loads. In addition to this the guides, who belonged to the 7th R. Irish Fusiliers, had only arrived in this part of the line on the previous day and were not at all certain of the way. Consequently it was beginning to get light when we arrived at Falfemont Farm.

I found the CO of the 7th Irish Fusiliers sitting in a hole near the ruins of the farm. He gave me the following information;

His battalion had arrived in the line early on the previous day having been lent to the 15th Brigade in the same way that mine had been. He had been ordered to attack the trench in front of Combles, and was given to understand that it was not strongly held. They had advanced (about 500 yards) towards the trench until they came upon strong uncut wire entanglement which was hidden by standing corn and weeds. Very heavy rifle and machine-gun fire was then opened on them from the trench and from the direction of Bouleaux Wood (300 yards north). About 350 men were killed and wounded. The survivors had fallen back and taken up a position in shell holes.

I subsequently saw an officer of the brigade machine-gun company who confirmed what the CO of the Irish Fusiliers told me.

I ordered two of my companies to take over the front line and to get the shell holes connected by a trench. The remaining two I kept in support in the old German second trench line.

I sent out a patrol under an officer to obtain information with regard to the trench in front, and also sent over to get in touch with the French regiment on my right.

On their return, the patrol reported that the trench appeared to be strongly held and that it was protected by strong uncut wire through which they could find no gaps. They had had one man killed.

The colonel of the French regiment sent me a plan showing the position of his line. From this it appeared that the French line was not nearly so far advanced as I had been given to understand. I could get no confirmation to the story that a French patrol had been into Combles. I at once sent the plan back to brigade HQ.

...I did not consider it advisable to send troops over in daylight, as any attempt to do so would probably have warned the enemy that an attack of some sort was being contemplated, and would almost certainly have resulted in them being heavily shelled.

My idea was to take the trench first, and if I found that I was unable to do this, to push my line forward as close to it as possible.

At about 3 pm, the French made an attack in the direction of Combles. The attack was not successful and they withdrew to their original line.

As the Kensingtons moved out to their attack after dark, enemy reinforcements came into the trenches in the opposite direction. A German barrage fell shortly on the advanced British companies and the trenches from which they had started. When this had fallen away, another company was sent forward but the Germans were now thoroughly roused and too strong to be dislodged from their positions. The commanding officer kept one company forward in Leuze Wood when it became light and decided to try again after darkness that evening.

About 11 am the next morning, after his night attack, he received the following message.

169th Brigade:

To Kensingtons

1. 7th RFC (aeroplanes) report that the trench in T. 27 a, b, etc., is still unoccupied.
2. You had orders to occupy this trench last night and an explanation is required as to why it was not done.
3. You will push patrols along it at once, approaching it through Leuze Wood and will strengthen these patrols by further parties until the

trench is properly held.

4. Frequent reports on the situation must be sent to Brigade. I have had practically no reports from your Btn.

(sgn) E S Coke, Brig Gen.

Now the two remarkable things about this message are, firstly, that it came from 169 Brigade and not from 15, to whom the CO had reported on arrival; and secondly, that it states he had been ordered to take the enemy trench, which was not at all the sense of the 15 Brigade Operation Order.

The previous brigade headquarters, 15, had been relieved by 169 without proper discussion of what units were doing, and without notifying the forward battalions that command had changed. No member of either headquarters had been forward to see what was happening, to offer guidance or help to any of the commanding officers.

Not unreasonably, the Kensingtons replied by pointing out that a series of reports had been sent back, but doubtless they had gone astray, being addressed to 15 Brigade.

Though the majority of brigades were better run than this, the general standard of staff duties was falling because numerous young officers, like some of the old, had not lived in the trenches and could not visualise the difficulties under which regimental officers worked, where the leadership and welfare of their semi-trained men was the prime task. In one brigade, for example, reports and returns were required from companies through their respective, battalion headquarters at the following times as a matter of routine, in addition to incident reports: 3.30 am, 8.30 am, 11.30 am, 3 pm, 3.30 pm, 7 pm (three), 10 pm (two indents).

The indifferent brigadier, brigade major and staff captain – though fortunately in a minority – might spend their entire time in the line in the headquarters dugouts two to three miles behind the rear battalion trenches – perhaps five behind the fire trench – when their brigade frontage might be no more than 1000 yards. From this point they would plan operations by map, irrespective of tactical considerations: a callous and craven *modus operandi*, developing a bitter cynicism amongst regimental officers and NCO'S of experience and a demoralising attitude of *laisser faire*. An officer in a Welsh battalion which had seen a good deal of fighting on the Somme wrote in his diary on 20 August:

Since our division has not yet made any progress this tour [in the line] the GOC is pressing, and the brigadier very pressing, to 'do something'. D Company is for it tonight. All arrangements have been made behind by some person or persons unkown to us. Sketchy is not the word for the order.

There is no word one dare utter of the prospects. I went with the CO to see some 4.5s register [targets]. We thought their observer uncommonly easily satisfied. At zero his battery fired without attracting much attention from those interested, and no one heard anything of the trench mortar fire. It was possible that the sounds were drowned by the clatter of arms and equipment in tremulous hands, which someone likened to a 'runaway tinker's cart'! Anyhow, the senseless scheme of an attack in a thicket after dark by tyros was a washout from the start; the men didn't follow their officers out of the trench.

Whether Haig[30] or Rawlinson or Gough appreciated that this is what was happening incipiently in the second month of the offensive, they were clear that the results of sector operations by corps were not making the sort of progress for which they had hoped. Frequently Haig investigated trench actions which had resulted in heavy casualties and called to task those who for 'want of thorough preparations' had launched men precariously or exposed them needlessly. From these enquiries he was aware that all too often the soldiers were led by men without understanding of fire and movement, whose only advanced training would be gained in the trenches – if they survived. But he was no less aware that at least a nucleus of trained and experienced officers must remain with the staff. Contrary to popular caricature, a high proportion of regular officers from infantry, artillery and engineers were not enamoured of a soft billet at corps, army or general headquarters. Many were denied promotion by being held back, while numbers genuinely thought it their duty to serve with the men of their parent regiment or corps in battle and repeatedly asked to be released. In one of his rare moments of confidence, Haig remarked to his *aide-de-camp* on 20 August. 'I expect you know C asked me again today if he might go back to command a battery. I am sure many of you find it frustrating being here amongst maps and papers but we must have a few people who can be trusted to do really reliable work without skimping details.'

[30] Hankey, *op. cit*, p. 163.

With a third great battle close at hand, Haig's reluctance to lose trusted men is understandable. By 12 August essential calculations concerning the allocation of fresh divisions, their battle training and prospective movement forward to the line were complete – and were, incidentally, shown to the King, visiting the BEF at this time. On the 18th a memorandum was issued to enable armies to prepare plans for the offensive, which should begin sometime in mid-September. The factors of infantry, artillery and ammunition – and of the enemy's depleted order of battle – were not alone responsible for this tentative date. Haig hoped that, by then, he would have some new brooms of his own to sweep open a corridor: the 'tanks'.

MOTHER'S CHILDREN

It is one of the curious facts of human development that revolutionary ideas, in the mechanical sciences at least, spring to the minds of inventive men in widely separated areas at much the same time. Hence – Marxist arrogance and chauvinism apart – the Russians' claim to have conceived so many of the discoveries attributed to Western Europe.

No one can be sure who first thought of an armoured, self-propelled vehicle to advance on caterpillar tracks across the broken ground of the battlefield.[31] The British were a little ahead of the French in production, perhaps, because of the good fortune of the former in finding an imaginative officer of the Royal Marines as secretary to the Cabinet War Committee, Hankey. On 11 November 1914 he received a letter from a military colleague, Major E D Swinton, at GHQ in France, saying; 'Re Caterpillar. I put your idea before Fowler, the Chief Engineer on 22.10. He wrote to the War Office (Directorate of Fortifications and Works). Whether it is the result of this or the original information given by me (from Marriot) before the war, Marriot tells me that several have been ordered. This may be for purely tractive purposes, or for bursting in against positions as suggested by you.'[32]

Even so, the conservative outlook prevailing in the War Office would probably have stifled the suggestion had not other energetic imaginations been caught, amongst them that of Winston Churchill who had the

---

[31] For origins, see: B H Liddell Hart, *The Tanks – The History of the Royal Tank Regiment* (Cassell); Maj.-Gen. J F C Fuller, *Tanks in the Great War* (John Murray); *OH, 1916*, VoL II, pp. 245 *et seq.*

advantage of being alternately a Cabinet minister and a battalion commander in the trenches.

By 26 January, 1916, such an armoured fighting vehicle had been made at Lincoln, and by February it was performing across ditches and other obstacles in the most satisfactory way during trials at Hatfield Park. Though rejected by Kitchener as 'a pretty mechanical toy but of very limited military value', the enthusiasts persevered. Haig, who had first heard of the project when he assumed command in the previous December, pressed for a supply of the caterpillars to France. A unit began to form up at Bisley, training centre of the (motor) Machine Gun Corps – to whom the vehicle was disposed – and when production models became available a unit began to form up in Thetford in June, 'Mother',[33] the very first tank, now had some children: 'males' carrying two six-pounder guns and four Hotchkiss machine-guns; 'females' with one Hotchkiss and four Vickers. The order for an assortment of 100 was increased to 150.

In preparing for one of his early conferences with his corps commanders – that of 16 April – Rawlinson had written in his notes a heading 'The Tanks', then 'Tanks, speak to corps commander alone'. But he did not mention the subject; the words were almost obliterated in green and red pencil before the meeting. The title would have meant little to an enemy agent; it was a nickname, suggested by the appearance of the metal boxes suspended between tracks, but the subject it covered was most secret. Unfortunately, it could not after all be mentioned because the vehicles would not be ready for the opening of the offensive on 'Z' day. It would take some time to train crews for the tanks; first, technically, in driving them and keeping engines, tracks and suspension as a working entity; next, tactically. Tactics, indeed, would have to be devised; the only point which had general agreement amongst the inceptors was that the tanks must be used en masse to exploit both surprise and shock action to the maximum. It was appreciated that a number would break down or be knocked out by artillery to the extent that, used singly or in small groups, the secret weapon might never reach the enemy wire but lie out in No Man's Land for convenient inspection by German raiders.

At one time Haig had hoped to postpone 'Z' day until 15 August, not only because of the time needed to train the New Army divisions but because of

[32] Hankey, *op. cit.*. Vol. I, p. 228.
[33] Manufactured as a prototype by Wm. Poster & Co.

the possibility of having tanks in the first assault. We have seen that this strained Joffre's blood pressure dangerously,[34] not least because of the situation reported from Verdun. With the third great battle in view Haig understandably asked urgently for the first fifty machines. 'Even if I do not get so many as I hope,' he wrote to Robertson, 'I shall use what I have got, as I cannot wait any longer for them, and it would be folly not to use any means at my disposal in what is likely to be our crowning effort for this year.'

Winter was approaching. The summer weather they had chosen would be passing into autumn when the third offensive of the campaign was mounted. It is all very well, with our present knowledge of what the tanks could do to say, why ever didn't he wait until next year, when training and trials would have been advanced to a proper operational fitness? Time does not press upon us critics, nor the burden of casualties. It has become popular to suppose that Haig cared nothing for the bodies rotting in the crater fields or the maimed passing through the dressing stations. He may have been an enclosed man, self-righteous and at times self-satisfied but he was not a heartless one. It was not in his nature to weep or mope publicly but almost all his personal dealings with people indicate humanity. It was for this reason that he reduced – eventually stopped altogether – his visits to the centres where the dying and wounded were coming in.

In a letter to Haig on 29 August Robertson wrote: 'I hope the Tanks prove successful. It is rather a desperate innovation.'

At Thetford, Mother's children were organised into a family. It was called the Heavy Section, Machine Gun Corps,[35] and was to consist of six companies, A to F, each company being twenty-five tanks – four sections, each of six tanks, half 'male', half 'female', with one spare machine. Supply and workshop backing was provided for each two companies.

Amongst the pine trees, across the rough heaths and certain selected areas of plough, the crews began to get the feel of the tanks – trying their manoeuvrability, their armament; learning to stow the many items of gear – ammunition, fuel, lubricants, tools, rations; learning how best to avoid being scorched by the massive engine amidships and to live with its fumes which filled the interior, despite extensive exhaust conduits. Their

---

[34] See p. 58/59

[35] In July 1917 the tanks broke away from the direct association with armoured cars and machine-guns on being given the designation 'The Tank Corps' – a corps in their own right.

exercises were often interrupted by visitors from London, but in one task or another they covered many miles of ground. They had just completed the first elementary working-up when orders came for France. Between 13 and 30 August C and D Companies, with their quartermaster and workshop entrained for the coast. After a brief concentration at Yvrench, near Abbeville, their port of disembarkation, the tanks were loaded on railway cars on 7, 8 and 9 September. Above Bray they disembarked in the railway Loop, two miles from the Somme's bank. Now they were in that desolate area of ruins and shell craters, and all about them the guns rumbled in the savage tunes of war.

THIRD TIME...

Haig waxed optimistic once more.

He had been 'disturbed' by XIII Corps' failure to exploit its swift capture of the Montauban ridge on 'Z' day, and 'deeply concerned' when he discerned the opportunity similarly missed at High Wood. He blamed Congreve for both omissions, unaware of Horne's pedestrian caution while Mametz Wood stood empty and, later, on the Bazentin ridge, when 7th Division chafed to advance. Now Congreve and his headquarters had gone, relieved[36] due to the general's failing health, and XIV Corps had taken command of the right flank under Lord Cavan. Horne, faithful apostle of the Commander-in-chief, remained as neighbour, mutually admired as a strong man who produced results, for which reason, perhaps, the tally of his casualties was overlooked.

On this matter of killed and wounded, Haig felt more hopeful. So many of his losses sustained on 1 July had been due, he believed, to the ineptitude of inexperience. So much had now been learned of the weaknesses at all levels in the offensive, so much was being done to remedy them. Corps commanders and their staffs now appreciated, for example, that six hours would elapse between the issue of an order at their level until its reception in the fire trenches. In future they would issue preliminary warning instructions during periods of waiting to permit reconnaissance. The fresh divisions were receiving training in the lessons of the early assault – next time the first wave would not lag behind the barrage, or be surprised by the enemy emerging from dugouts passed over. The shortage

[36] The corps headquarters relief took place on 14/15 August.

of experienced leaders and staff made this sort of instruction necessary, but they were meeting the need. For those who could not leave the forward areas, the new GHQ pamphlets should prove a useful guide.

And there were the tanks.

About the time that C Company was loading its armoured caterpillars on trains at Thetford, GHQ was giving formal notice[37] of their arrival in France and participation in the forthcoming offensive. Army and corps commanders were instructed to visit the tank training area at Yvrench, to study the potential of the secret weapon and to arrange for the training of their infantry in cooperation.

In the same period, and much in the context of tank employment, Gough and Rawlinson received their planning directive for the battle. The Reserve Army was to force the enemy off the northern end of the main ridge away from Fourth Army. Rawlinson was ordered to breach the enemy's third and last main line of defence, through which the massed horsemen of five cavalry divisions would move – east in defence, north in attack against the enemy rear – the first phase of the break-out, Gough's plan, conceived as a purely infantry attack, was independent of the small force of tanks he might expect. Any effect they might have must be a bonus 'until I know more of their possibilities'. Rawlinson, obedient as ever to the Chiefs wishes, yet understandably inclined to repeat his triumph of 14 July, proposed three successive night attacks with his tanks and infantry under a full moon.[38]

Accepting Gough's operation in principle, Haig rejected Rawlinson's, and this time he would not be won over to the Fourth Army view. It was a deliberate plan, attempting a slow, stage-by-stage destruction of the enemy defences. Haig wanted boldness he had complained that his instructions for bold initiative at all levels on 1 and 14 July were disregarded. The use made of the tanks and the cover of night were not sufficient to compensate for a want of boldness now, when the last main enemy line lay between them and a break-out. He saw Rawlinson privately before issuing a detailed directive next day, 31 August, which allowed of no doubt as to the requirement.

Rawlinson commented in his diary:

[37] See *OH, 1916*, Vol. II, Appendix 15.
[38] He proposed to start on the first night of the full moon, 11 September.

August 30. The Chief is anxious to have a gamble with all the available troops about September 15, with the object of breaking down German resistance and getting through to Bapaume. The general plan will be the same as before. We are to establish a flank from Morval to Bapaume, facing east, and attack with all the troops available. We shall have no resources in hand save tired troops, but success at this time would have a great effect throughout the world, and might bring the Boche to terms. If we fail, we shall have all the winter in which to recuperate, and there will be no counter-attack left in the enemy. It is worth the risk.

Now came September.

M Poincaré, President of France, had warned the British commander-in-chief that the equinox was approaching; from 25 September the weather was usually unsettled for several weeks. They must not delay their attacks. He referred, of course, to the great offensive that was coming; both French and British armies were on the eve of a widespread effort to secure advantageous positions beforehand; 'the offensive before the offensive' as a gunner staff officer remarked. By the Ancre, this began on 3 September with another frontal attack towards the Schwaben Redoubt, which failed as dismally as its predecessors, and less gloriously, for many of the infantry were raw, many of the veterans dispirited. 'They went up the line and half of them went over and half went through the motions', a Yorkshire sergeant related. 'And half of those that went over knew nowt and walked straight into our barrage. No spirit and no sense,' South of Thiepval, crumbled, unrecognisable, but still a bastion of German defence, the Australians spent their last full day in this sector fighting characteristically with rifle, bayonet, bomb and fist for Mouquet Farm, and the deadly trench, Fabeck Graben. When the Canadian Corps relieved them next day the Diggers had done all of their share for weeks in the intransigent sector around Pozières, from whose subliminal dust, fittingly, they took a fragment to endow their war memorial. They had had enough of Gough's constant pressure with demands for energetic action by a staff believed to spend its own energy in boar hunting. The daily reinforcement of failure, with no apparent reason for the sacrifice, made them long to return to Flanders and the paternal presence of Second Army commander. They took to singing 'Take me back to Daddy Plumer's Army' in the background when visited by senior commanders and staff.

High Wood, shorn long since of its leaves, remained a wilderness in the centre, hiding a German garrison. And Delville Wood, though largely British, was still contested. Here Rawlinson determined to be rid of enemy encroachment before the offensive began; as he determined also to close towards the enemy third line on the east by the capture of Ginchy and Guillemont.

An attack at noon on High Wood was thrown back at 3 pm by a counter-attack from the Switch trench. This was on 3 September. On the 8th, the 2nd Welch and 1st Gloucesters tried again at 6 pm and forced their way in amongst the tree trunks. But the enemy artillery and machine-gun fire left them isolated; none could get forward to support or supply them and they were forced to withdraw after darkness. Due to continuous trench warfare, the Gloucesters were reduced to three officers and nineteen-six men, losing their commanding officer, Lieutenant-Colonel A W Pagan, in the last action. Distressed at being evacuated to hospital at a time when the battalion needed him, he stole out from the ward in pyjamas and dressing gown, bluffed a military policeman who asked for his papers and rejoined his men.

At Delville Wood, infantry of the 24th and 55th Divisions slowly forced back the German line through the northern edge between the 3rd and the 8th. On the 9th an ardent Irish attack carried Ginchy and pursued the Bavarians through the village, where three kilted pipers, who had survived the crushing German barrage, stopped to play amongst the cratered foundations.

The eastern, right flank of Fourth Army was now almost upon the far objectives given to it for a break-out on 1 July. For Guillemont had fallen on 3 September after repeated attacks in August. The 'terrible road into Guillemont, straight, desolate, swept by fire,' was now made safe. The 59th Brigade, before whose determined assault the village had fallen, discovered beneath the torn surface – no longer to be judged an area of human settlement – an intricate network of tunnels radiating to strongpoints and connected to the village wells. Along the track to the south, the extreme right of the British Army had edged its way forward towards Combles, the flank unit reaching Falfemont Farm, where the Kensingtons took over from the Inniskillings and lacked sadly the support or interest of those in rear.

This seemingly trivial capture of a farm that no longer existed and perhaps an acre of broken cornfield beyond opened new opportunities for Fayolle's army. For some time his main effort had been extending to the north bank of the river, his place astride the Roman road having been taken by the Tenth Army under Micheler. He now had I Colonial Corps on the British left flank, VII Corps along the northern bank, with XXXIII on the south, and hoped that the latter would soon also cross over in the overall effort to breach the enemy's rear-most line.

His army attacked on 3 September and made spectacular progress immediately on either side of the river. Onuniecourt, a finger of land round which the river looped south to Péronne was taken by XXXIII and Cléry, opposite, by VII Corps. Parallel with VII, the Colonials captured le Forest village. The problem was the left flank, lying back south-west of Combles; for until the British right advanced, the French had to line the lower edge of the Combles ravine against German sorties from the far side. The Falfemont Farm positions commanded the ravine, however; poor and shallow as they were. With this in Allied hands on 6 September, the French regiment on the extreme left flank attempted to push through the southern outskirts of Combles and failed but was urged to keep clear of the ruins thereafter as Foch and Haig had agreed to encircle them. On this understanding the divisional commander decided that he could break through the defences running south, since the advance eastward from le Forest would permit him to capture them from the rear. Three days of heavy fighting along the Sixth Army front and the scudding rainstorms brought about a halt before he could do so.

Almost a week passed while the infantry regiments completed their reliefs through wet and slippery trenches. Fayolle, notably strict in the expenditure of artillery ammunition, was dismayed to discover that the condition of the ground had retarded the dumping of shells in the corps area. He resumed the attack on the 12th with some doubts, but in the knowledge that Haig was depending on him to enter the third enemy line before the 15th. After a difficult struggle amongst the front trenches in the forenoon, the right-hand Colonial brigade routed the greater part of a battalion holding the high feature south-east of le Forest and exploited its success across the top of the Bois Mameres. At once, the line gave way to the north and the left flank of 1 Corps advanced round Combles until the south and east of the town were cut off. Pressing simultaneously with repeated infantry assaults, VII Corps reached the main road from Bapaume to Péronne at Bouchavesnes where, after a successful flanking movement by the 27th Chasseurs, the village – by no means a total ruin – was taken. With a substantial part of the German third line in their hands, Foch urged Sixth Army on: I Colonial Corps to Frégicourt and Rancourt; VII Corps on Moislains; XXXIII across the river to Mont St Quentin.

They were demands outside the strength of the infantry, now weak in numbers and spent after the ferocity of their assaults. I Corps managed to capture Priez Farm on the 14th; they were now less than a kilometre from Rancourt. XXXIII were caught in the mud on the bank of the river before they reached the Mont St Quenun defences. Struggling to free themselves, two battalions were hacked down by shrapnel.

The operations had been remarkably successful, a significant overture to the British offensive. Regretting that he would not be ready to join the assault at zero, owing to the need to reorganise, General Fayolle promised Rawlinson that his heavy artillery would not rest to give every support.

Haig's appreciation of achievements and prospects in France had been read to the Cabinet by Robertson on 5 August. Warmly received, even by Lloyd George apparently, it elicited a message of support from the Prime Minister and his colleagues. A month later Asquith arranged to visit the BEF and to see the Somme battlefield for himself. Amongst others in a small party he brought the secretary to the War Committee, Colonel Sir Maurice Hankey, who noted the following impressions:

> *September 6th...* we motored out to Fricourt. It was a glorious hot day. As we approached the battle of the Somme the roar of the guns, which had been continuous and loud even at Beauval, became tremendous. We stopped a few minutes at Albert. The cathedral is an extraordinary sight. At the top of a tower was a gigantic gilt figure of a Virgin and Child, which has been hit by a shell and is actually hanging horizontally over the road, face downward, a most pathetic sight. The French say that the day it falls the war will come to an end.... After leaving Albert we came out on to bare rolling country with low hills. As far as we could see in every direction was an extraordinary collection of booths, dug-outs, horse lines, 'sausage' balloons, waggons, supply and ammunition

dumps, field hospitals, tents and all the paraphernalia and impedimenta of a huge army, intersected with field railways. The roads were 'chock-block' with huge columns of motor lorries, ambulances, water carts, guns and troops. They were changing divisions up at the front, which made it particularly crowded on that day, and we were constantly held up for long periods. The roads were frightfully cut up, and the weather had been heavy, so the movements of troops were mainly confined to the roads.

...One could appreciate the advantages of the mastery of the air, for all this medley... was within easy artillery range, but could not be seen by the enemy owing to the intervening ridges...

Near Pricourt, we met Raymond Asquith, the Prime Minister's eldest son, who was waiting at a cross roads, having ridden over on horseback to meet us. As we jolted up the broken, shell-smitten road to Pricourt, which lay close to a shell-blasted wood, I heard the curious whizz of a large howitzer shell – sounding, as they always do, as though it rotated eccentrically and not on its axis. By this time we were in the middle of our own guns, and some long 6-inch were firing over our heads, cocked-up at extreme ranges. I noticed they were in wire cages, camouflaged to conceal them from aircraft observation. As we came through the 'street' at Pricourt – as a matter of fact there was literally not one stone left on another – another shell came and burst not more than a hundred yards away. We got out of our cars and hurried to a 'dug-out'...

[Next day, the 7th.]... we drove on to see the 'caterpillars' of which we found about sixty-two, painted in grotesque colours. While we were there a German aeroplane, flying at a great height, came overhead and the whole of the tanks took cover under trees etc., or were covered with tarpaulins painted to resemble haystacks.

In the evening at dinner, I tackled both the chief of staff, Kiggell, and Butler, the sub-chief, about the 'caterpillars'. My thesis is that it is a mistake to put them into the battle of the Somme. They were built for the purpose of breaking an ordinary trench system with a normal artillery fire only, whereas on the Somme they will have to penetrate a terrific artillery barrage, and will have to operate in a broken country full of shell-craters, where they will be able to see very little. They were not very receptive, but

Butler gave me a hint that they might be used to open up a new front as well, and next day I met Frank Lyon, the Brigadier-General on the Staff, VII Corps, and he told me he was to have the next twenty 'caterpillars' and to use them in the region of Gommecourt on September 20th, whereas the big attack on the Somme is to be on the 15th.[39]

It was true that there were other plans afoot; but whereas, in the days before 1 July, Haig appears to have had serious intentions of switching his main effort, none of the enterprises fore-shadowed in September developed beyond cooperative or diversionary operations. First and Second Armies were told to be ready to assault Vimy Ridge and the Messines-Mont Sorrel areas respectively. Third Army was to be ready to attack north-east from Gommecourt on a front of 8000 yards. Smoke and gas were to be released, raids to be made, bombardments to fall. Once more, the idea of a coastal landing was discussed with the Royal Navy[40] but only as a measure in the long term. Immediately, the Dover Patrol was asked to assist in a deception plan, in which troops would be seen to embark in full equipment with artillery support on two successive days at Dunkirk. Every project was subordinated to a break-out between the Somme and the Ancre; to this end, despite acceptance of the principle that they should be launched as an entity,[41] the tanks were scattered amongst the divisions whose sectors were believed to contain the most difficult defences to overcome.

12 September, the day Fayolle's Colonial Corps pushed round Combles, was fine and warm, though cloudy. The British bombardment began at 6 am. Imagine now that you are an infantry soldier in a rifle platoon, in one of those divisions which Hankey and the Prime Minister saw going up into the line past Fricourt; or a Canadian who has been in the line since the Australians were drawn out. You are in the trenches with your comrades. If you are one of those men who has so far escaped even a scratch you will be beginning to wonder how long your luck will last. Probably, you have had between two and five platoon officers in the past six months – subalterns do not last long; they are killed, wounded or promoted. Almost certainly, your commanding officer will have been away wounded for a

[39] Hankey, *op. cit*, Vol. II, pp. 512 *et seq.*
[40] See *OH, 1916*, Vol. II, p. 244 and footnote I; Adm. Sir R Bacon, *The Dover Patrol* (Hutchinson), Chaps. VIII and IX.
[41] See *OH, 1916*, Vol. II, Appendix 15, para 4.

time, unless you are in one of those battalions where each incumbent has been killed in every major attack. If you are in the reserve trenches, you will be carrying forward trench stores, ammunition or supplies each night, unless you are patrolling or raiding, or digging assembly trenches for the next operation. By now you will have got used to that itching under the arms or in the crutch which, on examination of its persistence, discloses the greyish bodies of lice, your personal parasites. You will pick them off and crush them expertly between your thumb nails, powder your body, the seams of your clothing, expecting that, with luck, you will keep the little fellows down to manageable numbers. You will not, of course. If you sleep next to a lazy man without a sense of personal pride. But you are long past caring about the packed conditions of rest in a dugout, often you will catch up on a lost night's sleep lying in the open trench on some stretch of the earth which has dried out.

It is said that there is to be another 'big push'; a series of rumours have come from battalion headquarters, or from the administrative echelon in rear, where the quartermaster's or the transport officer's staffs are experts at picking up information. From the front trench, standing between walls of drooping sandbags, or in a patched-up shell crater, you look over the parapet with a periscope. No noteworthy feature catches your eye unless you happen to be close to one of the great woods, where the stripped and splintered boles challenge penetration.

A sea of craters, so called because the raised lips of each resembles waves, the hollow troughs on an ocean may restrict your view, but beyond these you will see lines of wire appearing and disappearing as they bend and stretch along the enemy trenches. You are looking at his wire through your own; but his is wider and thicker; he expects to stay where he is, your superiors are always expecting you to go forward. You may wonder what sort of a man Jerry is. You know he smells differently; his dugouts have a sour taint when you enter them, no doubt due to the bread he eats which is sometimes found, dark and brick hard a day or two after being delivered. Perhaps he finds the smell of your dugouts strange – sweat, urine, lamp oil and fumes all mixed together in a familiar and now rarely noticed odour.

You will leave all this behind soon. You will put on all your kit, fill up pouches, haversack, pockets with ammunition and other necessaries. You will fix bayonets. You may get a last word on the plan, which means 'over the top', across No Man's Land, through the gaps in the enemy wire – hope they'll be there – into Jerry's trench, bomb the dugouts, bomb down the communication trenches; get ready for the barrage to lift again; over the top once more and into the reserve trenches, or perhaps only into his supports if they happen to lie some way back from the outposts. It may have been explained to you with the trench map or the air photograph but you won't have had much time to look at these; there aren't enough to go round for a long personal scrutiny. Meantime, got to reply to a letter from home. 'Somewhere in France. Dear Mum and Dad and one and all at home, writing this today as tomorrow's the thirteenth – don't want to try my luck, ha, ha...'

13 September: low clouds, scattered showers, a cooler day than the 12th. The sun totally obscured, dusk came early. The tanks began to move out from the Loop to corps assembly areas. Due to the fact that fitters from the Army Service Corps had worked on each vehicle since its arrival in the battle areas, one only had been set aside as unfit for the road. Forty-nine went forward to dumps of petrol, oil, ammunition and supplies dumps established in many cases by hand of the infantry who were not necessarily gratified to serve the new arm of the battlefield in this way.

14 September. The French attacks came to a halt except for Priez Farm but I Corps and some army artillery were preparing to fire for the English next day. It was fine and warm; the white clouds reflected dazzling sunshine. Most of the assault and support battalions received their orders during the day but some were still busy carrying forward ammunition and supplies and so had to wait until nightfall. Guns and howitzers continued to bombard. Late that night, tanks were coming forward, some helped by guides with masked torches or luminous patches, themselves guided by white tape. Some tank commanders had to rely on the maps and air photographs painstakingly marked up by the staff with local information several days before. These were of little value in darkness in the featureless landscape. thirty-three tanks had reached the corps assembly areas. The balance were strewn along the approach roads in rear; broken down or ditched.

15 September. Zero was fixed for 6.20 am, forty minutes after dawn. In the last hour of firing there was no change in the tempo or intensity of the bombardment so as to avoid warning the enemy of the approaching assault. twenty-four tanks were able to begin at the correct hour. Aeroplanes flying

low overhead had been sent to deceive the enemy as to the source of this unusual din.

One hour before the main attack General Horne sought to clear finally the pocket of enemy clinging to the south-east corner of Delville Wood. Three tanks were due to help but two failed to arrive. The other, under Lieutenant H W Mortimore, became the first to operate in the history of the war.

His 'male' Mark I, tank number 1 of D Company, joined two rifle companies of the 6th King's Own Yorkshire Light Infantry in the capture of Ale and Hop Alley trenches. The armoured caterpillar lumbered into action from the Ginchy road, firing in the general direction of the enemy. Soon it was astride Hop Alley from which a number of Germans, astounded by the phenomenon, came out to surrender. The KOYLI hurried on towards Ale Alley to complete their task but, before they could reach it, machine-guns firing from crater outposts near by caught them in enfilade. All the officers being killed or wounded, the surviving sergeants took command, bombed the crater emplacements, cleared Ale Alley and had their men ready to join the principal assault at zero. On his way to rendezvous for this same hour Lieutenant Mortimore's tank received two direct hits and the crew jumped clear, leaving two dead inside.

This first experience of armoured assault thus ended before the offensive began. Elsewhere, comrades in C and D Companies were waiting and eager to try their hand.

On the extreme left the seven tanks allotted to the Reserve Army had been passed to the 2nd Canadian Division. In two groups of three[42] they were to precede the infantry on either side of the main road to Bapaume to capture the Sugar Factory 800 yards behind the enemy fire trench. In darkness, with roaring engines, they moved forward to take station, encountering almost at once a slowly searching German bombardment. It was feared naturally that the tanks had been discovered, though the crews themselves were so inexperienced; that they paid little heed to the shells. In fact, this fire was the prelude to several enemy bombing raids between 3 and 4.30 am, believed to be seeking prisoners. The Canadians threw back the last party at dawn and hastened to make ready for the assault.

Six battalions thrust north-east in a movement directed ultimately towards

[42] One was kept in reserve.

the capture of Courcelette. The artillery's preparatory work had been well done with the result that the leading companies had no difficulty in keeping up behind the barrage after clearing out each trench. By 7 am the Sugar Factory had been taken with 145 prisoners, entirely without assistance from the tanks which had been unable to match the infantry pace. Of the six in position, one had broken down. One was kept in reserve behind the lines, one had bogged just astride the first German trench and two others were stuck in the enemy support area near the Sugar Factory. The remaining two followed their routes of advance faithfully, even though in rear of the infantry, and were, by the Canadians' report, instrumental in encouraging many Germans to surrender from strongpoints and dugouts as resistance to the advance area grew more determined. An officer taken prisoner told his interrogator that the use of tanks was '...not war but bloody butchery'. Fresh and elated, the Canadians were ready for the advance to Courcelette village.

Some days previously Haig had warned Rawlinson that Courcelette could not be taken until Martinpuich, south of the main road, was in the hands of his own flanking units. It had been agreed that the Reserve and Fourth Armies should aim at their capture on the first day. Four battalions of the 15th (Scottish) Division scrambled from their trenches at 6.20, hoping to take Martinpuich amongst their first objectives, even though two deep trenches lay in front, an intermediate defence to the strongpoints and bunkers amongst the ruins. The enhanced skill of the gunners, the energy and enthusiasm of the Scots battalions new to the Somme fighting combined for a joyous success. Hurrying forward, they ran at first into the rear of their own creeping barrage yet, as so often on the ridge, benefited from their eagerness by finding the enemy quite unprepared to receive them. Their boldness and resource would have delighted Haig's heart; for almost without a pause, once they had cleared the German shelters, the leading companies not only progressed to the southern half of the little town but on beyond to the far end. Behind them came one tank – its mate had been hit by shellfire in the moment of starting which did excellent work during the period of clearing out adjoining trenches. Scots and Canadians joined hands.

On the right of 15th (Scottish) Division was the 50th (Northumbrian) and, below High Wood, the 47th (London). Because of its critical position on the ridge, possession of the wood enabled the Germans to deny an advance between it and Martinpuich; its early loss would open to capture the trenches 800 yards in rear. The left flank of 50th Division – three Yorkshire battalions amongst the Geordies – advanced as quickly as the Scots, preceded by two tanks which rapidly overran the German defences on the eastern face of Martinpuich. But elsewhere, eastward along the crest, machine-guns lying back behind High Wood fired into the advancing rifle companies from enfilade. By 10.30 am so little progress had been made that Pulteney curtailed the corps' effort for the day and ordered the 50th and 47th Divisions to aim only for the second of their three objectives.

In making his plan General Pulteney had not helped the assailants of High Wood by directing that the four tanks disposed to help them must pass through the wood itself. 47th Division commander had been advised against this by the tank officers who felt that the tree stumps were too close for the caterpillars. He had passed this view on, giving it his support. But the brigadier of the corps artillery objected that he could not provide a proper bombardment of the enemy fire positions because they were so close to the British after weeks of attack and counter. This was sustained by Pulteney, even though it was common practice to pull back temporarily one's own forward troops by night in such circumstances. At 6.20, therefore, three tanks – the fourth was ditched at the start point—advanced with the infantry, bumping and rolling and scraping through the timber. The leader crossed the first German trench which it at once began to rake with its machine-guns, but after a few minutes a medium shell set it on fire. The other two in the group, unable to find a way forward, worked eastward looking for an open passage. In the confusion they lost their bearings and came out amongst their own lines. One bogged in a shell hole, one ditched beyond and, seeing soldiers manning the trendies nearby, opened fire, killing and wounding men of the London Regiment waiting to move into the wood.

During these tragic setbacks the infantry attempted to get forward but met as ever in the past the deadly fire of enemy machine-guns and automatic rifles from the widespread cover. The assault of 141 Brigade, attempting to clear through from south to north, fell away as the four battalions' losses mounted.

By 10 am they had made no material progress. On their right, 140 had pushed elements along the eastern face of the wood, but this gave no advantage. The brigadier of 140 proposed that they should try a bombardment of mortar fire to dislodge the enemy. About 11 o'clock his trench mortars were concentrated as a battery to open rapid fire at 11.40. In seven minutes they fired 750 bombs.

Once more the Londoners came forward, forcing their way into the close cover with grenades, not sanguine of a light reception. They were surprised when, at first in groups and then *en masse*, stained, filthy Bavarian soldiers stood up in their trenches with raised hands, spent beyond the limit of their resistance. Two months and one day had passed since the patrols of Horne's corps had found the green wood empty of defences.

The run of the battle had removed Horne from this situation, however. The centre of XV Corps was Delville Wood, on the north side of which his 41st Division was directed on to Fiers village and then to the Gird trenches north-east of Gueudecourt. On the left, next to the High Wood position, the New Zealand Division was to secure the spur north-west of Fleis against counter-attack. 14th Division, on the right, had to advance through a series of intermediate trenches to capture Gueudecourt village itself. Eigteen tanks had been allocated by Rawlinson for the corps operations, a measure of the importance he placed on their work for the day. While the hazardous curtain-raiser was played out by the KOYLI companies and Mortimore's tank at the south-east corner of Deiville Wood, the remaining armour made ready with the assaulting brigades to breach the enemy line.

Seven out of ten tanks reached their starting points for 41st Division in the centre of the corps. They began to move forward along the line of the road from Longueval to Flers, in rear of the infantry advancing from their trenches. The vision of the drivers was very restricted; in the final minutes of the bombardment neither they nor the commander could be sure of their bearings. The leading rifle companies were already disappearing into the smoke of the barrage while the support came up from the trenches to disperse in artillery formation.

All three divisions – New Zealand, 41st and 14th – pressed closely under their own creeping shellfire, many taking the view that this was preferable to waiting behind to be hit by one of the German shells falling spasmodically on the British line. All lost killed, and wounded in this way. Amongst the supports, eighty to ninety of the New Zealanders on the left flank fell to the

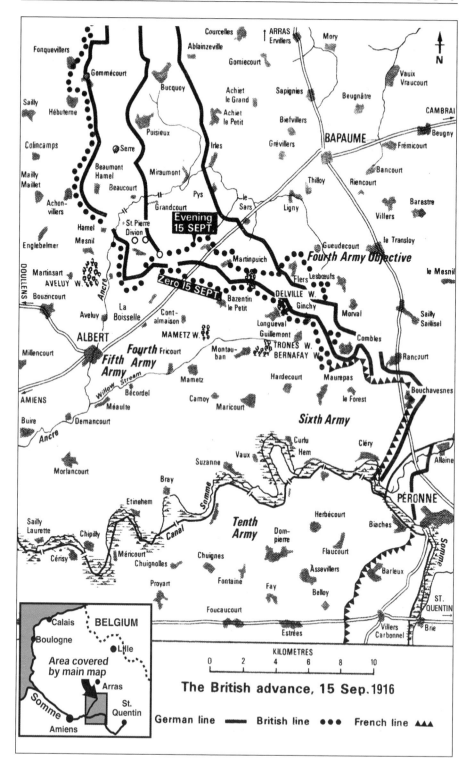

The British advance, 15 Sep. 1916

German line —— British line ●●● French line ▲▲▲

KILOMETRES
0 2 4 6 8 10

BELGIUM
Calais
Boulogne
●Lille
Area covered
by main map
Arras
Somme
St.
Quentin
Amiens

machine-gun positions in High Wood, but their forcing pace took the battalions across the crest into the eastern extension of the switch line. About 7 o'clock all assault battalions of XV Corps – were on their first objectives, the supports and reserve battalions being close behind. For fifteen or twenty minutes the captured enemy line was a confusion of different units crowding in, many without their commanding officers and company commanders who lay amongst the killed and wounded strewn above and below ground.

Enemy shelling intensified but the second waves advanced in high spirits to the point where their own barrage was boiling noisily before moving on. When it lifted, some were directly opposed by rifles and bombs; some found uncut wire, particularly on the New Zealand left; scattered fire came from Flers and a concentration of machine-guns opened from the east. In the centre, tanks caught up the infantry advance at 8 o'clock, as a mixed force, principally 15th Hampshire and 11th Royal West Kent, came up to the edge of Flers and recognised that this fortress had to he cleared.

They were in no proper formation and had few leaders.[43] Their pace slowed; a number actually halted on the open road. While one or two of the young second lieutenants of the Hampshires drew together to discuss what action they should take, a field gun, concealed in a ruin near the southern cross roads, opened fire at a range of less than 200 yards.

From the rear, tank number sixteen of D Squadron, commanded by Lieutenant Hastie, rumbled forward on its caterpillars, slewed round on to the line of the main street and advanced, 'fire spitting from its guns'. Three other tanks, D6, D9 and D17, were already scourging the eastern buildings, firing into dugouts and weapon emplacements, crushing barriers and obstructions under their tracks. The speed of Hastie's advance, the invulnerability of his crew to machine-gun fire and shrapnel splinters, the power of his weapons to retaliate at close range made an immediate impact on the uncoordinated infantry watching. Running forward on to the road spontaneously, they moved on, cheering, in the wake of Hastie's tank to search the defences. Flers had fallen. The watching aeroplanes of IV Brigade, RFC, took back the message to Horne's headquarters that the infantry had cleared through to the northern edge by 10.10 am.

---

[43] These two battalions had not finished carrying stores forward until late the previous night. Orders were given out after dark. Many of the junior officers and NCO's believed their task was limited to capturing Flers and consolidating it.

About mid-morning, reports from ground and air reaching Rawlinson's headquarters indicated the likelihood of a break-through round Flers. The army commander and his staff were becoming too experienced to accept these first tidings as evidence of substantive success, however; there was already a conflict between the news sent by the Guards Division headquarters and observations of contact aircraft watching the advance of their two brigades. It was as well they checked their enthusiasm.

XIV Corps had attacked at zero with three divisions in the line and 16 tanks. 56th (London) Division on the right were to mask Combles by completing the occupation of the enemy's exterior trenches west of the town; in effect, to accomplish what their battalions had already failed to do thrice before. On this occasion, helped by two of the three tanks allotted – the other did not cross the start line – they made fair progress before one ditched at the far end of Bouleaux Wood and the second was hit by a shell while firing into the Loop trench 300 yards from the western outskirts of Combles. Though the latter's crew kept the machine-guns in action for a time, the engine caught fire after an hour or so and they had to abandon the vehicle to join the infantry.

56th Division might have done more, even though the German artillery found their range at 7.10 am, but for the failure of 6th Division on their left, the centre of the corps attack. The 6th Division had been completely held up in their advance towards Morval. 400 yards in front of their line, the Quadrilateral fortress barred all progress, having protected its inmates satisfactorily against every salvo of the bombardment. Lying partially on a reverse slope, its machine-guns denied movement forward of the British trenches except for a brief length of trench along the road east of Ginchy. It was an ideal target for the three tanks of the division – had they been there to operate.

They were not. At 5 am only one had reached the start line, from which it advanced on the northern side of the railway track leading out of Guillemont. At 5.50 it reached the British forward positions where, confused by the bombardment and the broken ground, it opened a heavy fire on 9th Norfolks, waiting for zero. An officer of the battalion managed to reach the tank, contact the crew and point out its correct course. But within a minute or so of moving on, it was seen by the Norfolks to be heading north until it found Straight Trench, above the Quadrilateral, which it fired into for a little while. Before the infantry needed its close support, it had returned damaged from the bank. At zero four battalions made a brave attempt but failed, their plight made worse by the open lanes left in the creeping barrage for the tanks to pass through. Thus the garrison of the Quadrilateral was free, a little later, to fire southward into the 56th Division and northward against the Guards advancing from Ginchy. More dangerous to the Guards, Straight Trench, above the Quadrilateral, was ideally sited behind the crest east of Ginchy to enfilade an advance across it. This the Bavarian company in occupation began to do at 6.10 am.

The Guards had a long advance to accomplish: 3600 yards north-east from Ginchy to and through the village of Lesboeufs. The first objective was a system of well-bombarded trenches 800 yards ahead on either side of the road. Keeping up well behind their creeping barrage, three battalions of Coldstream, one of Grenadiers picked their routes forward across the crater field in which in increasing numbers they found small parties of Bavarians who had survived the British shellfire. There was little resistance from these enemy soldiers. The danger for the Guards battalions lay on the flanks.

On the right, machine-guns opened a hot fire from Straight Trench, unsubdued – unmenaced – by 6th Division. On the left, Pint Trench, adjoining Ale and Hop Alleys and Lager Lane, remained in enemy possession. As on the right, the enemy was placed so as to shoot directly down the Guards ranks. They shot well. None of the tanks detailed to destroy the flanking trenches were available to do so – seven of ten allotted had appeared at the start line, but after crossing it they lost all sense of direction – and so the infantry took the consequences. To escape the hot fire, the leading companies of the two Guards brigades doubled across the remainder of No Man's Land in a charge on the enemy trench ahead.

When they had searched the shallow dugouts and sent back the prisoners – men of an *ad hoc* force of 7 Bavarian Regiment – a check was made amongst the units. Three-quarters of the officers had been killed or wounded, two-thirds of the men.

The Scots and Irish Guards and another battalion of the Grenadiers in support all had elements forward and all were ready to go on. Unfortunately no one was exactly sure where they were. It had seemed a long advance; they had passed over some old, broken trenches and scattered wire and seemed to be quite close to Lesboeufs. Ginchy could not be seen. After some discussion by the senior officers remaining – three of the eight commanding officers – it was decided that they had reached the third objective. A pigeon messenger was sent back with this news.

After the despatch of the message, Lieutenant-Colonel John Campbell of 3rd Coldstream came to the conclusion that they were further from Lesboeufs than he had at first thought. The survivors of the two brigades were reorganised in the trenches and each brigade party continued forward. But it was difficult still to know exactly where the actual second and third objectives lay; repeated bombardments had defaced trenches and pasture alike and, in any case, 500 yards of the second objective was an imaginary line drawn on the map. There was little resistance from the Bavarian infantry as the brigade parties advanced in bounds but continuous shellfire reduced their numbers still more. Between 11 and noon the various segments became progressively separated as they sought to reach Lesboeufs on the slope below.

While XIV Corps headquarters sought to convince the commander of the Guards Division that his leading troops had been seen by air contact patrols some way in rear of their third objective. General Horne was receiving reports of a rather different sort. Flers was clearly occupied by troops of the centre Division, the 41st. The 14th Division on their right confirmed the committal of the reserve brigade to an advance east of the village of Gueudecourt. Air observers confirmed that they could see the enemy in the Gird trenches between Flers and Gueudecourt village, the final objective, but said they were few in number. At 11.20 Horne spoke to Major-General Lawford, commander of the 41st, on the telephone. There was nothing indecisive about him on this occasion: he accepted the dangers of exposing the flanks of an advance from Flers; General Lawford was told to push on with all speed with as many men as possible. A brigade of the corps reserve would come forward from behind Montauban as quickly as he could move it.

What he did not know was that control had temporarily been lost in Flers village, while those on the right were held generally in check by German machine-guns as yet unassailed by the Guards.

During the afternoon Brigadier-General Clemson came forward to coordinate the attacks immediately east of Flers, when he was able to move companies piecemeal into positions along the line of the Flers-Lesboeufs road. Behind Flers village, Major Gwyn Thomas, brigade major of 122 Brigade, collected a party of sappers under Lieutenant Carter and sent them round the eastern edge to collect all detachments and stragglers. He said that he would do the same on the west. When these officers met again, on the northern outskirts, they had about eighty men between them. They were just in time to prevent the last of the Hampshires and West Kents from withdrawing, believing that they were isolated on the battlefield. They had seen four tanks advance into Gueudecourt, where the enemy in the covering trenches fled. After fifteen or twenty minutes three of the four tanks were knocked out by shellfire and the fourth withdrew, damaged; since when they had seen neither infantry nor armour. With a good deal of energy, Thomas organised his force into detachments and advanced a further 300 yards to seize a pair of bombing bays – used previously by the Germans for grenade training – which they occupied until reinforced by the brigade machine-gun company and two rifle companies of 23rd Middlesex. These resourceful measures secured the line until dusk against parties of enemy attempting to infiltrate back into Flers.

While Major Thomas was securing the village, the New Zealanders were advancing still on the west, often with difficulty because their left flank became increasingly exposed as they pushed on. It should have been covered by the Londoners' advance at High Wood, but we have seen how this was delayed.

So the afternoon wore on. From 1.30 pm the German artillery blazed into full fire all along the front, effectively preventing sufficient organised numbers from continuing the advance to Gueudecourt or Lesboeufs. The New Zealanders joined with Thomas' party, the last operational tank taking station with them for the night. In front of Lesboeufs some sixty of the Guards reached the enemy's covering trench but could not hold it. Enemy reserves were hurrying forward from le Transloy on the right, from Bapaume to Martinpuich and Courcelette on the left.

They were too late at Flers. At Martinpuich the Scots were too strong. At Courcelette the Canadians had been too quick, having attacked the village by surprise in broad daylight. The counter-attacks were held but the enemy's cannonade continued remorselessly. 'If hell is as bad as what I have seen at Courcelette' a commanding officer wrote in his diary, 'I would not wish my worst enemy to go there.'

At 3 pm Rawlinson ordered the closure of operations for the day. They had failed to break through and must try again on the 16th. But he knew from reports that the majority of his army was scattered, and from experience that it would take time to gather their strength again for a coordinated attack. And they had no more time at their disposal. Despite the presence of the tanks and vigour of fresh divisions, the inability of the army, corps, divisional and brigade commanders to speak to and hear from their troops at speed had given the enemy respite to react with artillery fire and reinforcing infantry to maintain the defence.

It grew dark quickly; rain began to fall. After the long day, the balloonists came down, the RFC drew off to rest their crews and refit their machines. They had fought in aerial combat over Bapaume, bombed General von Below's headquarters at Bourlon, attacked German batteries and trenches with their machine-guns, and kept a constant patrol for the infantry and artillery. Their casualties had not been light.

The battle of the Somme was not over – it had two months to run, as it happened. But the last opportunity had passed. 'There had been three: at Montauban on 1 July; at High Wood on the 14th; at Flers on 15 September, when the tanks *en masse* might have broken through for the cavalry. Of the total armour assembled at Bray Loop, twenty vehicles at least were capable of action at zero and would conceivably have broken quickly the trench and Quadrilateral defences between Flers and Morval as readily as they broke the enemy in the villages themselves. By the evening of the 15th the tank force was destroyed or scattered, however. It would be some time before the same force could be concentrated again; and the weather would not wait.

On 16 September three of the five cavalry divisions were moved back behind Albert, an acceptance by Haig of the situation. The two that remained forward were the embodiment of his optimism.

PART V

Judgement

FINALE

If the battle of the Somme ceased to have a potential for success on 15th September, why did Haig continue the fight?

Immediately, of course, he did not know how far the day's operations had progressed beyond the first and a few of the second objectives. What he was certain of was that they had not made a breach. Between the 16th and the 22nd, using almost every infantry reserve in Fourth Army, the tanks remaining in action and eleven heavy batteries of the French, the British line was linked up between Martinpuich and Flers, and advanced to within 1000 yards of Gueudecourt, Lesboeufs and Morval which remained, like Combles, securely in German hands.

At the conclusion of this venture Rawlinson was aware'that strategic success had escaped them for the year. Persistently, the commander-in-chief considered that the enemy, evidently very tired, might suddenly break at some crucial point in the line. 'We must never be unprepared to exploit an opportunity of that sort,' he warned the army commanders. Gough echoed his chief. Gradually, however, in their councils, the reasons for sustaining operations became tactical rather than strategic.

With the winter ahead it was desirable to have the entire ridge in their possession to give depth against counter-attack in the spring, and to hide from the enemy's view units in reserve, battery lines and the forward administrative areas. For similar reasons it was important to capture the enemy points of observation above the Ancre, from which they looked down the river valley to Albert. From 25 to 28 September Fourth Army combined with the French Sixth finally to clear the Germans from the eastern end of the ridge, while the Reserve Army assaulted north of the Albert-Bapaume road. It was Haig's hope that the opening of the former attack on the 25th would attract the enemy from the latter, to be launched next day. But the nature of the ground should have told him that events were running the opposite way. Fourth Army's advance was against an enemy stubbornly withdrawing from slopes which favoured the assailants. Thiepval was another case. Its defences continued to command the approaches from west and south, and new positions extended the arc to the east. II Corps and the Canadians had a savage fight to break in to the ruins and the strong-points in the trenches in rear. They were struggling amongst the old, highly developed first line, and it was not until the 30th that the Schwaben and Stuff Redoubts were fully secured. All that was now required to complete the clearance of the ridge south of the Ancre was a limited sweep 500 yards to the north and the reduction by attrition of St Pierre Divion to the valley. In enfilade to artillery from positions east of Thiepval, Beaumont Hamel and the heights above would not have resisted an infantry assault.

Instead, we find Haig employing Fourth Army to push further to the east and north-east, while Gough made ready for a major attack north of the Ancre assisted by Allenby's flank corps. After a fortnight Rawlinson's weak battalions managed to advance an average of 200 yards, a figure which takes account of the capture of le Sars village on the Bapaume road, 800 yards ahead, and the long stretches of line where there was no advance at all.

Between 13 and 19 November the Reserve[1] Army advanced on either side of the Ancre, failing to reach Grandcourt on the south bank but capturing the Hawthorn and Redan Ridges to the north, Beaucourt down by the river and the complex of defences in and about Beaumont Hamel village. Despite I Gough's confidence XIII Corps could not dispossess the

---

[1] The title 'Reserve' was changed to 'Fifth' Army at the end of October.

enemy of his defences immediately to the north, where Puisieux remained safe behind the last of the cruel Somme fortresses, aptly described by Crutwell as 'the sinister ruins of Serre'.

Before Gough could attempt to surmount this check with a widespread operation, Kiggell brought a message from the commander-in-chief to say that he should stand down until his return from Chantilly. On 16th November this order was passed on until, in the sleet on the morning of the 19th, the last infantry attack came to a halt.

Two months had elapsed since the failure to break through at Flers. The weather had changed. Long days of rain saturated. the ground, filling the trenches and dug-outs once more with mud in a season when there was no hope of a summer to dry them out. Frosts hardened the mud in November but there were frequent thaws.

...Whoever it is we are relieving, they have already gone.

The trench is empty. In the watery moonlight it appears a very ghostly place. Corpses lie along the parados, rotting in the wet: every now and then a booted foot appears jutting over the trench. The mud makes it all but impassable, and now, sunk in it up to the knees, I have the momentary terror of never being able to pull myself out. Such horror gives, frenzied energy, and I tear my legs free and go on. Turning sharply round a bend I come across a fearsome sight. Deep water lies in a descending right angle of the trench, and at arm's length from me, a body has fallen face downward in the water, barring the way. Shall I push the body aside and wade...

Thank goodness I brought six pairs of socks.

Morning and evening we make the men take off their boots and rub their feet; but it isn't much good: they simply cannot keep them warm or dry under such conditions, and some of them are already badly frost bitten.

This is the very limit of endurance.

The limit of endurance. Why were they put to operations beyond the needs of tactical security? A combination of reasons supplies an answer.

First, since July Haig had taken a stand on a single major offensive on the Somme; the double blow had been abandoned. With good reason,[2] he had informed the British Government that the enemy was finding it

[2] See Fourth and Reserve Army intelligence summaries including interrogation reports for September, confirmed by *Der Weltkrieg 1914 bis 1918*, Vol. XI, pp. 9-79. These indicate periods of collapse.

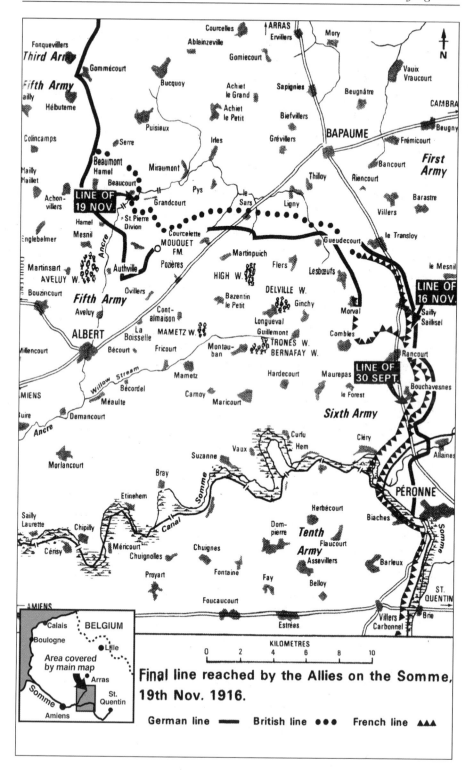

Final line reached by the Allies on the Somme, 19th Nov. 1916.

German line — British line ●●● French line ▲▲▲

extremely difficult to maintain a defence and with reports of enemy weaknesses accruing he had every encouragement to hold fast in the hope that one sector or another of Below's line would collapse suddenly. If we accept this, we must recognise that the commander-in-chief was unable or unwilling to see that his own men were also failing as the outflow of casualties placed a cumulative strain on the remaining infantry, for whom there were insufficient replacements. In these circumstances, though the enemy might collapse at one point, it was unlikely that either of the two British armies had units sufficiently vigorous to take advantage of it.

Second, Haig was under constant pressure from Joffre to sustain the offensive. Throughout August and September the French *géneralissime* urged on his ally. On 23 September, conscious that the failure to break out round Flers had cast down Fourth Army headquarters, Joffre proposed as a minimum objective a British advance to the line Achiet-le-Grand-Bapaume-Betincourt before the winter. He did not say what object this might serve, but the theme at GQG was always to wear down the enemy. In this respect, there was an identity of view between Haig and his colleague. Joffre had two arguments, moreover, of particular cogency: the one direct, the other indirect. If they halted for the winter, the Germans would have time and labour to build a new series of defences against the spring. In 1917 the Allies would have to begin all over again. Could they afford to do this? Indirectly, the French staff began to ask the British to take over more of the line. If they were not going to use their men to attack, they had numbers to spare for defence elsewhere. The French needed every man they could find as they were passing to the offensive at Verdun.

The Fourth Army attacks of 7-26 October followed these exchanges, giving Haig an opportunity to reply sharply to a letter of Joffre's, written on the 18th, demanding that he should '...*instamment de maintenir intégralement vos plans primitifs*...' They met on the 23rd at lunch to agree that there must be no weakening in the policy of aggression. Joffre gave Haig a signed photograph – '...*votre tout devoué J Joffre*'.

The spirit of cordiality diminished again in early November, when Haig wrote to say that, while accepting the front Vimy (Arras)-Bapaume for the 1917 offensive, and the need to continue the wearing down of the Germans throughout the winter:

...To enable me to undertake such extensive operations as early as the weather will permit next year, the training of my troops during the winter becomes a vital consideration, which affects the question of winter operations alluded to in the first paragraph of your letter...

...the supply of my troops, especially the Fourth Army, presents great difficulties in wet weather.

I beg that you will not deduce from this statement of my difficulties which I deem it advisable to make clear to you, that I have any intention of abandoning the winter offensive agreed on. But you will realise that such conditions impose limits on what I can do. They also affect the question alluded to in the last paragraph of your letter, as to modification of our respective fronts...[3]

To offset the effect of this, he followed with another letter on the 11th, offering to take over the French line to within 1000 yards of Bouchavesnes. Next day, Sunday 12 November:

...I rode to Toutencourt and saw Gough. He had been round all the divisions and most of the brigades detailed for the attack. Their commanders all now thought we had a fair chance[4] of success. He himself recommended that the attack should go on. I told him that a success at this rime was much wanted – firstly, on account of the (failing) situation in Roumania. It is important that we should prevent the enemy from withdrawing any divns. from France to that theatre.[5] Next, the feeling in Russia is not favourable either to the French or to ourselves. We are thought to be accomplishing little. The German party in Russia spreads these reports. Lastly, on account of the Chantilly Conference which meets on Wednesday. The British position will doubtless be much stronger (as memories are short) if I could appear there on the top of the capture of Beaumont Hamel for instance and 3000 German prisoners. It would show, too, that we had no intention of ceasing to press the enemy on the Somme. But the necessity for a success must not blind our eyes to the difficulties of ground and weather. Nothing is so

[3] Haig to Joffre, 6 November, 1916.
[4] This was not strictly correct. After several postponements battalion'and brigade commanders thought generally that the attack should either be on or off in the next period of fair weather, as it was unsettling to the soldiers to be kept in suspense.
[5] Two German divisions had already been sent from the Western front to Transylvania, in addition to those removed to the east against Russia.

costly as a failure!...

En route to Chantilly, Haig heard that they had taken Beaumont Hamel but, checked elsewhere, Gough planned to extend his operations. I hazard that the commander-in-chief was content to carry the Ancre heights as sufficient triumph to Chantilly while he ordered Fifth Army to stand down, in effect, for the winter.

CONSEQUENCES

'...The Chantilly Conference which meets on Wednesday...' had been called by Joffre to review their progress in 1916 and outline strategy for 1917. Russians, Rumanians, Serbs and Italians met with the French and British military chiefs, the former anxious to lodge bids for financial assistance and war-like stores, the latter to impose a strategy subordinated to the western front.

While this was in progress, the political representatives of the Allies were meeting in Paris, twenty-five miles distant, the principal decisions being taken in private meetings between the French and British prime ministers and selected colleagues from their Governments.

Asquith had brought only Lloyd George, the Secretary of State for War. Both men assured Haig at dinner on the 15th that the latest success on the Ancre heights enhanced their status in the negotiations. Asquith meant what he said. Lloyd George was outwardly on good terms with the commander-in-chief but had already resolved that he should not be permitted to mount an offensive similar to the Somme in 1917. The Secretary of State had many ideas of his own to test as alternatives – an attack through the Balkans or Turkey; an offensive by Russian armies supplied with all their needs by Britain and France. The political conference confirmed that the national Governments – and not the general staffs – must control strategic policy for the war and Lloyd George returned to London to advocate the reorganisation of their own Cabinet war committee so as to take full charge in this field. He suggested that he should take the chair.

A Government crisis now arose. There were many who disliked or mistrusted Asquith's apparent complacency in the direction of the war. The issue of the war committee, its membership, constitution and powers, became the focus of their antipathy. Though in no sense displaced in responsibility by Lloyd George's proposals, the Prime Minister eventually rejected them, fearing a move to oust him by his colleague. The key members of the Cabinet resigned and, after some political side-stepping, Lloyd George formed a Government of his own.

In a sense, this was a direct consequence of the Somme offensive. For the discontent with Asquith's administration arose amongst the wider circle of his critics from disappointment with the results of the summer campaign. The area of the advance appeared substantial in the maps published by the daily press but the toll of casualties could not be hidden; it was no less publicly displayed. The disparity between gains in territory and losses in men appalled a section of parliamentary opinion. Lord Lansdowne prepared a memorandum for Asquith and the Cabinet, while the Prime Minister was away, in which he argued that neither side could win the struggle. They would do better to make peace. Lloyd George was known to be utterly opposed to such an idea and his intransigence bound many influential men to his cause when Asquith's first coalition tottered. When the new ministry took office, therefore, none doubted its intention to continue to fight Germany until surrendered. The Government and its military commanders were at one on this first principle of war policy. It was the method of achieving victory that separated them thereafter. Robertson, the CIGS, and Haig, the commander-in-chief in France, were obdurate in their view that the battle would be won only in the west. Joffre stood with them, though he was removed from his post on 26 December,[6] discredited by political enemies and the failure of his offensive policies. But Briand, the prime minister who regretfully sacrificed him in order to remain in office, replaced him on the western front with a man no less dedicated to offence in that theatre, General Nivelle. He convinced Briand that he would win the war on the Aisne in the spring. The British might pursue a holding action above the Somme.

For a time Nivelle dazzled Lloyd George with his energy, incisiveness and clarity of exposition. Plans to re-equip Russia, the activities of the

---

[6] Joffre's dismissal did not arise from the failure of the Somme offensive, though his enemies referred to it in their criticism. He had been too long in office and had clashed with too many politicians. His retention became an issue in the French chamber at a time when Briand's government was once more under attack by Clemenceau and his supporters; and by the defeatist group under Caillaux. Briand's intention was to bring the old soldier to Paris as his adviser on war policy but Lyautey, newly appointed as war minister, would not accept the arrangement. Joffre was promoted marshal of France, an appointment in abeyance since 1870, and 'hoisted delicately' into complete retirement.

Allied expeditionary force in Macedonia, hopes for a defeat of the Turks in Palestine were overshadowed by a belief that the French were going to win a favourable decision on the Aisne. If he had had the power, the British Prime Minister would have placed the BEF directly under Nivelle's command; lacking it, Lloyd George attempted to have his way by underhand means, and this strengthened Haig's position. He retained his status as a colleague, as distinct from a subordinate in the Allied command on the western front. When Nivelle led his armies to disaster in April 1917, the relationship did not improve between Lloyd George and Haig. What lay between them always was casualties. The British Expeditionary Force was more than 100,000 men below its established strength and Haig asked not only for the posting of these numbers but an increase for the campaign he was preparing in Flanders.

The matter of the Somme casualties lay between Downing Street and Montreuil through the winter and spring until, in the summer of 1917, Lloyd George saw with anguish the prospect of another flood which he was powerless to prevent.

THE CASUALTIES

Of the many controversies accruing from the battle of the Somme, none has been more extensively argued than the matter of the casualties; in particular, the ratio between casualties on either side.

Haig has acted unwittingly as a catalyst in the argument. As time passed and he came to justify his policy, he did so less on the outcome of his original aim to break through than on the successes of his armies in weakening the enemy. While perceiving the change of emphasis, we surely understand that it was made as the result of a human and perhaps subconscious temptation to display one's workmanship in the best light. Whatever our judgement of him in this deception, two facts are incontrovertible: he did not succeed in breaking out; he weakened the German Army in the west in much the same way as the Russian Army weakened Hitler's at Stalingrad.[7]

The objection may be raised that Hitler's armies were attacking, the

---

[7] For example, Ludendorff, *op. cit*, p. 292, says '...The endurance of the troops had been weakened by long spells of defence under the powerful enemy artillery fire and their own losses. We were completely exhausted on the Western Front.' Hentig, *Psychologische Strategie des Grossen Krieges*, recounts experiences of fighting with the 3rd Guard Division: The Somme was the muddy grave of the German field anny.'

Russians defending, but this simply shows a difference in cause, not in effect. In the war of 1914-18 it may well prove that in prolonged battles the defence lost more ' heavily than the assault.

A great deal of the argument about the casualties has been accomplished by quotations of figures. I do not propose repeat these, two or three excellent sets being readily available for comparison.[8] Any study is worthless, however, if it fails to take into account the essential basis of the figures, that is the names of the dead and wounded.

The British Army employed – as it employs in improved form today – daily personal occurrence reports: reports sent in by each unit showing any change of status, physical or legal, to its officers and men. Every individual killed, missing or wounded was reported by *name, rank and number*. Moreover, every individual wounded, whether he remained at duty or not, was counted as a casualty in the final battle returns. Any individual missing when the roll was called each day in the trenches – whether an absentee without leave or genuinely lost temporarily – was shown as 'missing in battle' and counted as a casualty. Those that appeared later, when the unit was out of the trenches, were taken on effective strength once more but the correction of the battle figure was not made. The British figures therefore reflect the worst possible total.

The German figures must be studied in a different way. Firstly, they made returns thrice monthly, a system which took account of all 'missing' rejoining for duty. Second, they did not record as a casualty a lightly wounded man who remained in the corps medical holding units. As the capacity of these on any one day in the Somme area was approximately 2000, the numbers held over the period 1 July-19 November may be considerable.

Finally, as a measure of psychological warfare, the Germans took to falsifying their casualty figures, publishing after the war an enormous total of 'concealed' casualties relating to all the fronts. To assess exactly how many German soldiers were killed, wounded or prisoner as the direct result of the Somme battle would require a search of the casualty rolls maintained by name in the German archives.

They no longer exist, having been destroyed in the Second World War. But General Edmonds, the British official historian, gives us the pointer to

---

8 For example, *OH, 1916.* Vol. I, pp. 496-497, and W S Churchill, *op. cit..* Part I, Appendix I.

a reliable means of discovering the German casualties on the Somme. He advises a check amongst those regimental accounts '*Regt No...*' which contain the names of the fallen as an appendix. Such a check discloses, at first glance, an enormous discrepancy between the declared and the actual casualties, the balance of numbers lying heavily with the latter.

Whatever the exact final figure, the approximate total British/French[9] and German was about 600,000 *on either side*: 1,200,000 individuals.

Decades later, the sum of anguish which these figures represent horrifies us, as once it horrified Lloyd George. For what, we cry: Beaumont Hamel, Thiepval, Pozières, Trônes Wood, Delville Wood, Flers, Morval, the 'sinister ruins of Serre'? When we learn that the Germans pulled back secretly through the winter to a new line in rear, the protagonists of Haig claim, this abandonment by the enemy of his forward areas as a prize of the battle. The antagonists counter that proves the ground was not worth a battle at all. It is right that we should continue the argument, right that we should be moved to do so – by the knowledge of 1,200,000 killed, wounded and captive. It may be right to attack the military leaders, they held the responsibility: Joffre, Haig, Falkenhayn. But it is difficult to avoid the suspicion that they have become whipping posts or scapegoats. The Somme battle, as indeed the whole of the Great War, was ultimately the responsibility of the peoples of Europe and the United States, who permitted conditions to come to such a pass. As Cowper tells us:

> *...War's a game, which, were their subjects wise,*
> *Kings would not play at...*

(The Winter Walk at Noon)

---

[9] In the ratio approximately 3:1 of the Allied total in the battle.

Bibliography

Anon., *The War the Infantry Knew*, 1938

Army Quarterly, XXIV, *Verdun: Falkenhayn's Strategy*

Arthur, Sir G, *Haig*, 1928

Asquith, Earl of Oxford and, *Memories and Reflections*, 1933

Aston, Sir G, *Foch*, 1930

Atkinson, C T, *The 7th Division*, 1927; *Regimental History : of the Royal Hampshire Regiment*, 1952

Bacon, Adm. Sir R, *The Dover Patrol, 1915-17*, 1919

Bean, C E W, *Official History of Australia in the War of 1914-1918*, Vol, III, 1924

Beaverbrook, Lord, *Men and Power*, 1956 (re-issue)

Blake, R (*see Haig*)

Bonham Carter, V, *Soldier True* (Life of Sir Wm Robertson), 1963

Buchan, J, *The Battle of the Somme*, 1916

Chalmers, T, *History of the 16th Battalion. The Highland Light Infantry*, 1931

Charteris, Brig.-Gen. J, *At GHQ*, 1931

Churchill, W S, *The World Crisis*, 1927

Compton, T G, The Defence of Verdun (*RUSI Journal*, Vol. 66)

Crutwell, C R M F, *A History of the Great War, 1914-1918*, 1934

de la Gorce, P-M, *The French Army*, 1953

Duff Cooper, A, *Haig*, 1935

Edmonds, Brig.-Gen. Sir J, *British Official History 1914-1918*, 1922-8 (see also Miles)

État-Major de l'Armée, *Les armées françaises dans la grands guerre* (French Official History, Tome IV, Vols. II and III), 1929

Ewing, Maj. J, *The Royal Scots, 1914-1919*, 1925

Falkenhayn, Gen. E von, *General Headquarters, 1914-1916 and its Critical Decisions*, 1919

Foch, Marshal F, *Memoirs*, 1931

Fourth Army Headquarters, *The Fourth Army Papers*

Fox, Sir F, *The Royal Inniskilling Fusiliers in the First World War*, 1951

Fuller, Maj.-Gen. J F C, *Tanks in the Great War*, 1920

Gallwitz, Gen. M von, *Erleben im Westen, 1916-1918*, 1932

Gerster, M, *Die Schwaben an der Ancre*, 1920

Gibbs, P, *The Germans on the Somme*, 1917

Girard, G, *La bataille de la Somme*, 1937

Görlitz, W, *History of the German General Staff, 1657-1945*, 1953

Gough, Gen. Sir H, *The Fifth Army*, 1931

Guedalla, P, *The Two Marshals*, 1943

Haig, F-M Earl, *Despatches*, 1919; *The Private Papers of Douglas Haig* (ed. R Blake), 1952

Hankey, Lord, *The Supreme Command, 1914-1918*, 1961

Harington, Gen. Sir C, *Plumer of Messines*, 1935

Harvey, Col R N, Field Engineering (*RUSI Journal*, 14 Dec. 1921)

Headlam, Lt-Col C, *History of the Guards Division in the Great War*, 1924

Hindenburg, Marshal P von, *Out of my Life*, 1920

Hoffman, Maj.-Gen. M, *The War of Lost Opportunities*, 1924

Joffre, Marshal J J C, *Memoirs*, 1932

Jones, H A, *The War in the Air* (British Official History, Vol. II), 1922-8

Jünger, E, *The Storm of Steel*, 1929

Kabisch, E, *Somme, 1916*, 1937

Kincaid-Smith, Lt-Col M, *The 28th Division in Francs and Flanders*, 1919

Kuhl, Gen. H von, *Der Weltkrieg, 1914-1918*, 1929

Lawson, J A, *Memories of Delville Wood*, 1918

Liddell Hart, Capt. B H, *Foch, Man of Orleans*, 1931; *The Tanks: The History of the Royal Tank Regiment*, 1959

Lloyd George, D, *War Memoirs*, 1933

Ludendorff, Gen. E von, *My War Memoirs, 1914-1918*, 1919

Macdonagh, M, *The Irish on the Somme*, 1917

Magnus, L, *The West Riding Territorials in the Great War*, 1920

Magnus, P, Kitchener, *Portrait of an Imperialist*, 1958

Masefield, J, *The Old Front Line*, 1917; *The Battle of the Somme*, 1919

Maurice, Maj.-Gen. Sir F (ed.). *Life of Lord Rawlinson of Trent*, 1928

Maze, P, *A Frenchman in Khaki*, 1932

Miles, Capt. W, *Military Operations, France and Belgium*, 1916 (British Official History, Vols. I and II)

Möller, H., *Fritz von Below*, 1920

Moody, Col. R S H, *Historical Records of the Buffs, 1914-1919*, 1922

Nichols, Capt. G H F, *The 18th Division in the Great War*, 1922

Nicholson, Col. G W L, *Canadian Expeditionary Force, 1914-1919* (Canadian Official History), 1962

O'Neill, H C, *The Royal Fusiliers in the Great War*, 1922

Palat, Gen. B E, *La grande guerre sur le front occidental*, 1917-20

Pétain, Marshal P, *Verdun*, 1920

(Plowman, M) Mark VII, *A Subaltern on the Somme in 1916*, 1927

Poincaré, R, *Au service de la France: neuf années de souvenirs*, 1926-9

Priestley, Maj. R E, *The Signal Service in the European War, 1914-1918*, 1921

Reichsarchiv, *Schlachten des Weltkrieges: Somme-Nord*, 1927

Reichkriegsministerium, *Der Weltkrieg 1914 bis 1918: die militarischen Operationen zu Lande* (German Official History, Vols. X and XI), 1924-29

Ritter, G, *The Schlieffen Plan*, 1958

Robertson, F-M Sir Wm, *Soldiers and Statesmen, 1914-18*, 1926

Rupprecht, Kronprinz, *Mein Kriegstagebuch*, 1929

Sassoon, S, *Memoirs of an Infantry Officer*, 1930

Shakespear, Lt-Col. R, *The 34th Division, 1914-1919*, 1920.

Simpson, Maj.-Gen. C R (ed.), *The History of The Lincolnshire Regiment, 1914-1918*, 1931

Spears, Maj.-Gen. E L, *Liaison, 1914*, 1930; *Prelude to Victory*, 1939

Wendt, H, *Verdun, 1916*, 1931

Wilhelm, Kronprinz, *My War Experiences*, 1922

Wyrall, E, *History of the Somerset Light Infantry, 1914-1919*, 1927

Zwehl, Gen. A von, *Maubeuge, Aisne, Verdun*, 1921

Acknowledgements

Acknowledgement is due to the publishers for permission to quote from the following books: to George Allen & Unwin Ltd for *The Supreme Command* by Lord Hankey; to Geoffrey Bles Ltd for *The Memoirs of Marshal Joffre* by Marshal J J C Joffre, translated by Colonel T Bentley Mott; to Jonathan Cape Ltd for *Prelude to Victory* by Major-General E L Spears; to Eyre & Spottiswoode Ltd for *The Private Papers of Douglas Haig*, edited by R Blake; and to Hutchinson and Co Ltd for *General Headquarters, 1914-1916* by General E von Falkenhayn, and for *My War Memoirs* by General E von Ludendorff. Acknowledgement is also due to Christy & Moore Ltd for permission to quote from *A Frenchman in Khaki* by Paul Maze.

The Author and Publishers also wish to thank the following for permission to reproduce illustrations which appear in this book: the Radio Times Hulton Picture Library for; Ullstein Bilderdienst, Berlin; and the Imperial War Museum.

Index

content to bring campaign to a close, 217; relationship with CIG's, 176-177, 178-179

Haldane, 24, 67

Ham (town), 57, 63

Hamel, 48

Hamilton, Gen. Sir Lan, 23

Hankey, Col Sir M, 186, 194, 196

Hannescampes, 56

Hardécourt, 170, 172, 173, 180

Hastie, Lieut, 206

Hawthorn Redoubt, 86, 97, 101, 104

Hawkins, Captain, 130

Headlam,Brig-Gen C, 131

Hébuterne, 56, 48

Heidentopf, The, 95, 100, 106, 107

Heligoland Redoubt, 124, 127

Hem (village), 63, 142, 172, 173

Henderson, A, 78

Herbécourt, 139

Herr, Gen, 34, 35, 37, 38

Hiatt, Captain, 118

High Wood, 52, 163, 164, 165, 166, 167, 168, 169, 171, 172, 179, 189, 191, 200, 202, 210, 211

Hindenburg, and Tannenberg, 12; advances into Poland, 12; struggle for reinforcements in east, 12; undertakes winter battle of Masuria, 13; appointed Chief of the General Stag, 173; visits the western front, 174-176; defence concept, 176

Hop Alley, 198, 208

Horne, Gen, 56, 127, 130, 148, 150, 151, 154, 164, 166, 167, 172, 190, 198, 206, 209

Hudson, Maj-Gen, 119

Hunter-Weston, Gen, 49, 50, 88, 94, 97, 106, 143

Ilse, Gen, 177

Irles, 134

Joffre, character and background, 14, 141; redeploys forces, 1914, 11, 14-16; attack and failure, 15-16, 20; policy of attrition, 21; review at end of 1915, 22-23; selects offensive area for 1916, 25; and Verdun, 34-35, 135; and Somme battle policy, 41-46, 56-60, 62-63, 64, 80-81, 151; presses Haig to continue offensive through winter, 217; prepares strategy for 1917,217; removed from his post, 219

Johnson, Pte, 124

Kern Redoubt, 93

Kiggell, 81, 149, 195, 214

Kitchener, Gen M P, 23, 24, 67, 68, 69, 158, 186

Knobelsdorf, Gen Schmidt von, 31, 32, 39, 169

Kuhl, Gen. H von, 175

Lager Lane, 208

Laidlaw, Col D, 111

Lambton, Maj-Gen, 107

de Langle, de Cary, 16, 17

Lansdowne, Lord, 218

Lassigny, 25, 45

Lawford, Maj-Gen, 209

Leipzig Redoubt, 109, 110, 111, 112, 119, 125, 154

Lens, 78

FORMATIONS AND UNITS

(to which specific reference has been made)